Of Juliette's Blood

A Novel of Love and the Law

Phil Snyder

ISBN: 978-1-7373244-0-9

Library of Congress Control Number: 2021910810

First Edition, First Printing

Designing and typesetting by Phil Snyder

Manufactured in the United States of America

Acknowledgments

The author wishes to acknowledge his family, friends, lovers, teachers, professors, colleagues, clients, cohorts and many other souls who, throughout the years of his life, have provided a spark to light his Fire Within.

Contents

Reunion

He had not seen her for almost sixteen years, not since that hot afternoon in late July when he casually told her he thought he should date other girls. After he called and said he wanted to come over, she checked her hair in the mirror, gave it a quick brushing, put a sprits or two of perfume in the right places, and slipped into the yellow and green flowered sun dress he liked so much. She answered the doorbell, shouting to her mother and sister "I've got it," and then stepped outside to sit with him on the front porch swing.

He had never been one to back down from an unpleasant encounter or needlessly beat around the bush. When he broke the bad news, he saw the twinkle disappear from her deep green eyes. He watched those lips – the ones he had grown up learning to kiss – turn down as her mouth began to form a shape of disappointment. But when he saw her chin start to tremble, he turned tail and ran. He could not stay around to watch her cry. He was too much of an emotional coward.

He had just turned seventeen three months before and was still very wet behind the ears when it came to forming – and ending – relationships with the opposite sex. They had dated for years, beginning with the crush he got on her way back in the eighth grade. He first noticed her when they sat right across from each other in French class, and he pursued her with all the gusto his budding pubescence could muster and master.

About six weeks into the semester, when their French teacher began to instruct them in the use of verbs, he paid particular attention to the proper conjugation of *aimer*, meaning "to love." Over the course of the next three afternoons, even though he lived about ten blocks southwest of the school, he clandestinely tracked her and her best friend, who also happened to be her next-door neighbor, as they followed their eight-block course north toward home. On the fourth afternoon of stalking, he rushed ahead of the two girls, armed only with his boyish bravado and the piece of chalk he had purloined from the blackboard tray in his sixth period class. Finding a conspicuous place on her route, where the root of a massive maple had cracked the sidewalk, lifting the chunk of concrete half a foot and tipping its face slightly toward oncoming pedestrians, he hurriedly scratched the words *"J'aime tu, Juliet"* in huge letters on the sidewalk near a street corner. As he stood there admiring his calligraphic handiwork, his valor soared. But when he espied the two girls turning the corner half a block away, he took off like a scared rabbit.

It was more than two weeks later that his French teacher got to the chapter on reflexive verbs and their pronouns. He was mortified to discover that his magnificent attempt at engendering true love through public sidewalk art contained a serious grammatical error. It should have read *"Je t'aime, Juliet."* No matter. The object of his affection had not studied that chapter yet, either. Besides, she probably would have fallen for him anyway. After all, the gesture was the key, not the grammar.

Once the bonds of puppy love had formed, he wrote her lengthy notes, which he furtively passed to her in class. He carried her books between classes. He walked her home from school. When their middle school sponsored social functions, they danced almost every dance together. On Saturday afternoons, they met at the local movie theater for the matinee, holding hands under cover of darkness as they shared a box of popcorn. Funny that he never could remember much of anything about a single movie they had seen together but had no problems relating to his buddies every detail of the ones he had seen with his little brother.

When ninth grade began, they were both permitted to go on more formal dates. Of course, their parents had to drive them everywhere, but, at that age, he conceded, *you have to put up with all sorts of embarrassing stuff*. Then suddenly, not quite two months into the school year, sometime around Columbus Day, she inexplicably broke it off. He was crestfallen. She would not talk to him at school; she would not take his phone calls; she would not even read his notes. And when he tried to plead his case with her best friends and find out what had brought about her abrupt change, they had no idea what was going on within her fourteen-year-old psyche. He lived through the next several months feeling as though he had been blinded in one eye. Nothing seemed complete.

Of Juliette's Blood

He never quite knew what compelled him to do it. They had not so much as spoken to each other for four months, in spite of the fact that they shared three classes together, even sitting right next to each other in English. But on the day before Valentine's Day, he mailed her a card. Nothing special, nothing fancy. But with his meager allowance, it cost him a pretty penny.

The next evening, as he and his family were getting ready to go out for dinner, she called to thank him for the gesture. Parched for her tender love, he gulped down the sound of her voice until the incessant whining of his younger brother and a stern warning from his hungry father made further conversation impossible. For the next two and a half years, he and Juliette were again a steady item.

During the period of the Great Silence, as they would later jokingly called it, she underwent many subtle transformations, becoming more woman than girl. Among other things, as teenage girls are wont to do she changed the spelling of her first name, adding a superfluous "te" on the end. Roman always thought it was because of the teasing they took for the similarity of their names to the fabled young lovers of Shakespeare's greatest romantic tragedy, standard reading fare for eighth grade literature. However silly it seemed to him, that small alteration gave her a quick, albeit irrelevant, comeback to the wisecracks. "I don't even spell my name that way!"

As puberty struck with wild abandon the summer after his sixteenth birthday, Roman shot up a full four inches in height in as many months. Now when they danced, finally his eyes glanced slightly down at hers, even when she wore those one-and-a-half inch party pumps. For all the kidding she endured about her name, it paled in comparison with the sometimes brutal ribbing he got from his male classmates. Odd that he had never been self-conscious about his lack of height before he started hanging around with girls.

After that brief July afternoon on her porch the summer before their senior year, they had not spoken to each other at all. Fortunately, in a high school with more than 1,200 students, they did not have to run into each other every day. In fact, they had no classes together that year. Although they occasionally saw each other in the halls from a distance, they both went out of their way to avoid the discomfort of a face-to-face confrontation. When fateful circumstance brought them within arm's length, they would manage to pass without so much as a word, their eyes focusing on the tops of their shoes or the cracks in the sidewalk instead. Not that they did not want to be friends. But after sharing their early adolescence as a couple – after her first "real kiss" from a boy, their first "French kiss," the heavy breathing and "almost petting," after all the car dates with their parents driving, the double-dating with older schoolmates, the solo dating when Roman got his driver's license, after all the post-date parking on the isolated overlooks, when the windows literally dripped with condensed respiratory steam, and after that May evening when they almost went "all the way" – they did not know how to be "just friends."

Now, here he was at his fifteenth year class reunion – maybe ten pounds heavier than his high school weight but twice as handsome. Gone was the formerly-fashionable haircut of the disco age. His wavy brown hair was neatly styled with a '90s look – somewhere between Robert Redford and Ted Koppel. Gone, too, were the one hundred percent polyester shirts and double-knit suits, replaced, at least in that evening's wardrobe, by a light blue pima cotton shirt, a tan summer-weight worsted wool suit, and a navy blue and gold striped tie. Even without the pair of platform shoes he had worn to most of the dances during his senior year, he was still just under six feet tall in his Johnston & Murphy loafers.

It was a Saturday evening in early July, and he and over 200 other members of the Denver South High School graduating class of 1977, along with an equal number of their spouses or significant others, had gathered in one of the ballrooms of the Denver Hilton South to see what additional changes everyone had undergone during the five years since the tenth-year class reunion. As might have been expected, the usual group of girls – now women – from their senior class were frantically putting the final touches on the weekend's festivities, diligently trying to improve on the prior gathering. And, of course, they were hoping that some of the new leads they had gotten on missing members of the Class of '77 would pan out. But, no matter. The best gossip of high school reunions often turned out to be not a matter of who showed up but who did not.

The chance that Juliette might make it to the tenth reunion had crossed Roman's mind on more than one occasion before that early July weekend five years before. He had scoured the area apprehensively all afternoon during the barbeque at the high school practice field, but she never showed. Even though he was not able to make it to the party that evening, he later heard from one of his close friends that she had not made an appearance then either. *Silly of me to even think about that*, he reflected after that weekend was over as he hung his memories of her back into one of the many closets in his mind.

Nearly five years later, almost to the day, and this time Roman Marchetti had not even thought about Juliette Abbott once since he first got word of plans for the upcoming gala. Maybe it was his fragile psyche, still trying to heal the wounds from his failed first marriage, that lowered the mental curtain. Or maybe another part of him did not want his intellect contriving fantasies that would have only cheapened the moment that was to come.

He was standing toward the back end of the ballroom, near the cash bar, talking about personal computers with Glenn Matson, one of his closest buddies during his junior and senior years, when he felt compelled to turn his head and look toward the doorway. Maybe it was a subtle movement of Glenn's eyes or a slight jut of his chin, or maybe it was *kismet*.

She was wearing a teal blue sleeveless evening dress, not too flashy, but not too casual either. Her straight, light brown hair gracefully draped down over her shoulders. She had just picked up her name tag and raffle ticket from the greeting table at the door. Her eyes nonchalantly scanned the crowd from left to right for a second or two before she spotted him looking directly at her. She felt the intensity of his gaze as though he was standing right next to her. For a moment, her heart thumped high up in her throat. She took a deep breath to clear away the flash of anxiety but hesitated, unsure whether she should wave to him or not. *What if he's looking at someone else over this way?* she rationalized. Uncertain and a bit wary, she decided to circulate to her left, finding the familiar face of a classmate here and there and staring with that particular kind of discomfort and occasional embarrassment that only come at such reunions when even name tags do not help with the burden of recognizing an old acquaintance.

As he watched her merge into the sea of bodies, he wondered why the memories of her had not even crossed his mind during the weeks leading up to this reunion like they had five years ago. After all, he had considered whether other old friends, both male and female, might show up at the gathering. It was as though a cloak had been wrapped around his memory, obscuring the view of such recollections until something inexplicable moved him to glance across the room at the very moment she made her entrance. Lost in his mental wanderings, he heard Glenn's voice dragging him back to reality.

"Earth to Roman. Are you still with us?" He looked back to see his friend's head cocked quizzically.

"I've seen somebody I've got to say hello to. Let's pick this up later, okay?" Roman said as he patted Glenn on the shoulder and began to circle to his left. But crossing the crowded ballroom with a singular purpose turned out to be about as difficult as traversing a minefield at a dead run. Every other face was the cover of a book of memories, ready to be opened.

Finally, an excruciating thirty minutes later, each of them had made it far enough through the throngs of thirty-three-year-olds to come face to face. Over the din of nearby and distant conversations, they exchanged the pleasantries befitting the awkwardness of the moment. "Hi!" "How are you?" "What have you been doing with yourself?" "Where are you living now?" She politely offered her hand. He opted for the less formal hands on the shoulders and kiss on the cheek. All these things had to be said and done before they could broach the subject of the feelings that had overwhelmed them when their eyes made contact.

Between sips of her white wine and brief interruptions from other classmates passing by, Juliette informed him that she was now a senior research botanist at the University of Texas in Austin, studying the medicinal value of plants, especially species native to North America. Roman owned a computer supply business in Castle Rock, Colorado, less than an hour's drive from Denver down I-25. They learned that each of them had been married once, but, given the moment, their conversation was understandably sparse on the details. Neither had had children. At least that much was understood. Both sets of parents were doing well. Her folks had left the Denver area for the warmer climes of Arizona in 1982. Her older brother and younger sister were still in the area – Martin in Evergreen and Audrey in Boulder. Roman's parents were still living in the same house he grew up in and his younger brother was also in Denver.

Roman fidgeted with the rim of his bottle of beer, looking down at the brown glass circle each time Juliette's eyes met his. Their verbal skills were taxed to the limit as they danced and dodged around the heart of the matter. A part of their past still left each of them too uncomfortable in the other's presence to put into words what the sparks and flashes from their eyes were trying to convey.

As the crowd of bodies packed in tighter, he found himself continually readjusting his position, each time edging a little closer to her. And then he caught the first trace of her perfume. White Shoulders. Of the dozens of girls and women he had dated since Juliette, no one else had worn that fragrance. When he recognized it on one of the women he met in a business situation, it always reminded him of his first real love. Now, his nostrils inhaled each subtle whiff with the relish of a thirsty traveler at a remote watering hole.

Their conversation was abruptly interrupted by several loud *thumps* and a short wail of screeching feedback as the emcee tested and then brutalized the stage microphone. "Is this on?" he asked. "Hello?" *Thump*! "Can everyone hear me?" *Thump*, *thump*! As irritating a moment as it was, it was right effective in getting the attention of the 400 or so revelers.

At the suggestion of the emcee, the crowd cleared the dance floor. Roman and Juliette sat down with several other classmates and their spouses at a nearby table, where they found themselves repeating the same recitation of biographical facts of self and family as familiar face after face appeared at the table. When the live band finally got around to playing a decent slow tune, Juliette seized the opportunity to break from the factual feeding frenzy and get a few moments alone with him.

"Dance?" she succinctly asked.

"My pleasure," he replied, pushing back from the table and extending his hand.

Holding her in his arms for that first turn around the floor was almost more than he could bear. He felt the warmth of her silky cheek against his as he drank the scent pulsing from her neck in gulps instead of occasional whiffs. His arm slid around her waist; his hand flat against the small of her back. He felt so comfortable, so natural. His mind faded back to the first time they danced at the middle school cafeteria. It was eighth grade. It was the Halloween Hop. *What a name!* he chuckled.

She had to know. "What's so funny?"

He pulled back a bit and looked at her, shaking his head as if to say that it was nothing, really.

"Well?" she inquired, almost insisting on an explanation.

He pulled her back toward him and put his cheek up against hers. He spoke softly into her ear. "I was thinking of that first time we danced. Remember?" He paused for a response – two seconds, four, six. He could tell she was drawing a blank.

"At the middle school cafeteria back in eighth grade. It was the Friday night before Halloween. And they called it the Halloween Hop. Remember?"

He could feel her shaking her head no.

"All the tables had been folded up and stacked at the back of the room, but they'd left a quarter of the chairs out and lined them up against the walls. There were all these orange and black crepe paper streamers looped crisscross along the ceiling. And dozens of orange and black balloons filled with helium were bouncing around up there too. Every once in a while, a balloon they'd filled up first a day or two before would float down to the floor and one of the guys would relish the opportunity to pop it. Each time one exploded, all the girls screamed. And that became the highlight of the party. Some boy popped a balloon and the girls let out these shrill squeals – probably more from delight than fright. And it went on until the principal showed up about half an hour before it was supposed to be over and everyone – including the chaperoning teachers – straightened up."

He could feel her snickering with a recollection of her own. "Oh, yeah," she said. "But what I remember most was how all the boys gathered on one side and the girls on the other. It was like the Civil War, with the blue-coated Northerners on one side and the gray-coated rebels on the other. And every once in a while, one of the boys would break ranks and suffer the indignity of his buddies' teasing and come across the demilitarized zone to ask one of us to dance." She paused for a second and then pulled back to look at him. "And if I remember correctly, you were one of the first ones to make across the floor, weren't you?"

"I really don't remember that," Roman replied. His face expressed genuine wonder. "Was I really?"

"Yep," she answered conclusively. "You came right up to me with your face shining like a red beet and with all your so-called friends catcalling from the other side." She hesitated as memories and impressions slowly resurfaced. "I remember thinking that night, 'That boy's sure got courage.' I guess that's what always impressed me about you. You had that ability to make up your mind and then go for it – no matter what people said."

They finished their dance without further conversation, just feeling each other with senses beyond the normal five. As the night progressed, they mixed with other classmates but always managed to find their way back to each other for the majority of the slow songs, when the music was soft and quiet reminiscence was possible. But mostly they talked about their awkward years in eighth and ninth grade. The door was closed, at least temporarily, to their high school days.

After an hour of dancing and mingling, the emcee again attacked the sound system to announce that the buffet was ready to serve. Slowly the party-goers made their way through the line, heaping their plates with pasta salad, cut vegetables and dips, baked cod, and thin slices of prime rib. Through the dinner, drinks, and more dancing, they exchanged updates on classmates, both those in attendance and those in absentia. Who had married whom? Who had gotten divorced? Who had kids; who did not? Who was a roaring financial success; who was flat broke; who was in jail?

A few of their high school teachers, most of whom had now retired or were getting close to it, showed up too. There was James Beamon, the English teacher, who had finally come out after all those years. From the darkness of the closet to the bright light of the public soapbox, he openly talked to anyone who would listen about the evils of the recent Colorado initiative which permitted local jurisdictions to discriminate against homosexuals in employment practices. "The scourge of the state," he pontificated as he handed out cards for an organization which was challenging the law in court. "We're gonna take this thing all the way to the U.S. Supreme Court if we have to," he proclaimed.

Clear on the far end of the room was Jane Southern, who taught civics and American history. A pixie of a woman, not even standing five feet tall in the highest of high heels, she had more wrinkles on her face, Roman thought back then, than any person he had ever seen. Probably had something to do with those three packs of cigarettes she smoked every day, a good share of which were consumed in the quiet sanctity of the teachers' lounge. If any one person could have been a model for the Dick Tracy villain Pruneface, it would have been Miss Southern. Now, fifteen years later, at age seventy-seven, she was as spry and spunky as ever. And still just as wrinkled.

Two tables away was Charlotte Lehman, the algebra teacher, still in her same position, preparing the brightest for college-level math. Only two more years until retirement – and that well-deserved pension. At the same table was Raul Castro, the band teacher, who had gone over to a rival high school five years before and had just retired at the end of the preceding school year. Making more money, he claimed, giving private lessons during all that free time he now had than he ever made on a teacher's salary.

Finally, standing near the main entrance was Allen Howton, the geometry teacher, who had decided that teaching was not his forte and had gone into administration a couple of years after the class of '77 graduated. He had spent three years as an assistant principal at one of the middle schools, then bounced around three different high schools in the area as second assistant principal, then first assistant. Two years ago, he returned to Denver South as the head man. But his aspirations were not fulfilled. He was hoping for an appointment to the superintendent's office downtown in a year or two. He still had a good ten years left until retirement and he wanted to get his pay scale as high as possible before that pension income got fixed.

The night was not all good news and fond memories, however. Stories circulated about some of their missing classmates. What about Peter Herman, who went off to potential fame at Yale? Talk was he got heavily into the drug scene and began trafficking. For the past ten years or so, the rumors went, the authorities had been staking out his parents' home, waiting for him to show. Sources who claimed to be in the know said he was living somewhere in Europe. More than that they would not say.

But most tragic of all was the fate of Damon Rodgers. Born with a birth defect that retarded the development of his legs, he wore braces and used crutches through most of his school years. Unable to cope with the burden, his mother took alcohol as her form of crutch, alternating between living in the bottle for a year or two and then staying on the wagon as Damon grew up. Due to his father's steady influence and in spite of his disability, Damon excelled at his studies throughout his school years, beating out Missy Parmeter for the honor of being the valedictorian of the class of '77.

But his years at Cal Tech were troubled. In and out twice, he finally graduated with a degree in computer science in 1983 and returned to the Denver area. At the root of it all, so went the speculation, was his lack of success at forming meaningful relationships with women. Finally, when his most recent engagement fell apart in the late summer of 1990, he drove over to Sam Baker's house about three or four o'clock one morning, let himself into the backyard through the side gate, knelt down in the middle of the flourishing vegetable garden, put the muzzle of the revolver in his mouth, and pulled the trigger. Strange how the mouth and brain matter seemed to act like a silencer.

No one reported hearing the shot, so muffled it was that the noise did not even alert one of the neighborhood watch dogs.

Sam was left to discover their classmate's body a couple of hours later as he sipped his first cup of coffee and flipped through the morning paper at the breakfast nook in the kitchen. Even though Sam and Damon had both attended the ten-year reunion, Sam could not bring himself to make it to the next one. In fact, he had taken a job in Omaha six months after Damon's suicide, suffered a loss on the sale of his house, and moved his family east. No one in their class had seen or heard from him since.

Before the partygoers knew it, the sand in the hourglass of recollections had run out. The band packed up their instruments. The caterers cleaned up the buffet table. The bartenders corked and capped all bottles with significant residue. And the emcee abused the microphone one last time, bidding *adieu* to those revelers who had made it to the midnight hour.

Juliette gathered her things, said her goodbyes to the two couples still remaining at their table, and turned toward Roman. Her eyes shimmered in the soft candlelight. She was at a loss for the right words to say. Something like "It's been great!" would have been too trite, too superficial. But she dared not open up her heart to him – not yet, not here, not without really getting to know him all over again. Roman handled the awkwardness of the moment deftly

"It's time for me too," he said, rising and extending his hand across the table to their remaining companions. Turning back to Juliette, he added, "It's late. I'll walk you to your car." Dealing with the distractions from old acquaintances, they finally stepped out into the crisp night air. Juliette broke the moment of silence as they approached her car.

"It's been just great to see you again," she said.

"That goes for me too," Roman replied. "We oughta get together again sometime. If you make it back up to Colorado anytime soon, look me up." He reached into his back trouser pocket and pulled out his wallet. Fumbling through the compartments as they walked, he found one of his business cards. "Here. Let me put my home number on the back of this." They paused a few yards from her car as Roman pulled a pen from his inside jacket pocket and wrote on the back of the card.

As he handed it to her, their eyes met. No crowds to bump them. No long-lost acquaintances to interrupt their conversation. No buffoonery from a clumsy emcee. Nothing to keep them apart but their own self-inflicted wounds of the heart. Their feelings were like wild, unbroken horses, full of vigor and strength but without the reins of guidance. So a moment so full of the promise of magic found only a promise for the future.

"Really, call me if you come back," he entreated. "I'd like to see you again." Then he bent forward and kissed her lightly on the lips.

Surprised by his advance, it took all the composure and self-restraint she had to keep from throwing her arms around his neck and returning the kiss with passion. But the instant of opportunity came and went before she could react. She could only drop her head in the shy manner of a teenager and reply to his invitation. "Sure." She paused to clear her throat. Then she glanced up at him and smiled. "I'd like that too." Pulling the rental car key from her evening bag, she slipped it into the door lock. Roman reached across and pulled the handle, opening the door, and Juliette slid into the driver's seat.

"'Night," he said as he swung the door closed. With a pane of glass between them, her verbal reply was muted. She raised her hand and gave a quick wave, then started the car and drove slowly away. Roman stood there silently as he watched her car disappear from the brightly lit parking lot into the darkness of the street. *I should have said more*, he thought, *but what?*

He had not felt this way in a long time. He had been alone for the past year, but not lonely. Now, he felt as though an elastic band was attached to his heart. With each breath, something tugged the band gently, stimulating memories of a host of deep-seated feelings too profound to describe with mere words and manifesting to his inner sight a glimpse of that empty space within he so needed to fill.

The Waystation

A week after the reunion, Roman received a postcard. The picture on the front was the University of Texas tower at night bathed in orange light. "Sure enjoyed the evening with everyone," it read on the back. "By the way," she added, "the invitation is reciprocal. If you're ever in Austin, I'd love to see you again. The hills here aren't as big, but they grow on you. Jules." He had not heard the pet name he used only in affectionate circumstances in years. He certainly thought it might be too forward of him to refer to her that way now, what with her being a professional woman and all, and since they had not even spoken for sixteen years before the night of the reunion party. *Interesting,* he thought, *that she chose to sign off that way. What does it mean?*

He tussled with the idea of writing her a long letter and pouring his feelings out onto white linen stationery but elected instead to take it in small steps, answering one postcard with another. Finding a suitable scenic card of the Garden of the Gods just outside of Colorado Springs, he penned a quick response. "May take you up on that Austin visit. Dell is sponsoring a big computer seminar there in for November. Now I have an excuse to go." He wrestled with the way to sign off. *Should I write "Love, Roman" or is that too fast, too soon?* He finally settled for just his name and made a special trip to the post office on Sunday to mail it.

A week passed – then another. Every day when he came home from work, he flipped expectantly through his mail, hoping to see something from Juliette. But there was nothing, not even another card. He tried hard not to make anything of it, but his emotions kept playing games with his mind. Then, on an evening in late July, as he was reviewing the bookkeeper's report on his company's accounts receivable, his home phone rang.

"Hey, Roman," the familiar female voice said. He did not have to hear the next phrase. He knew who it was. "It's Juliette. How are you? Did I call at a bad time?"

"No. I'm fine," he responded with a sudden zip in his voice. "Sure, it's a good time. I was just in the middle of a bunch of financial statements and needed an excuse for a distraction. How've you been?" With the cordless phone pressed fast against his ear, he pushed away from his desk and wandered out of the converted bedroom to relax on his couch. They exchanged societal pleasantries for a few minutes before she changed course and revealed the purpose of her call.

"Listen, what you said after the reunion – about getting together if I came back to the area, was that serious?"

"Of course!" he insisted as his pulse accelerated another notch. "Why? What's up?"

"Well," she began, "I've been finishing up my current project and I'm looking around for ideas for another proposal. What I'm thinking about writing up is a field study of medicinal plants in the Rocky Mountains. So I've been looking at coming back to Denver for a day or two and then heading out for points north and south for a week to see if I can get enough preliminary data for a study plan."

"Sounds great," he said. "Have you got any particular places in mind? Something special you're looking for?"

"I'd like to get down as far south as the Taos area and maybe over to the San Juans and then up to the region around Rocky Mountain National Park."

"Sounds like a pretty big trip. Sure you wanna do all that driving? Must be close to 2,000 miles."

"Unfortunately," she quipped, "they don't rent a driver with the car."

"I've got a proposal of my own, if you're interested," he volunteered. "I usually take some vacation time before the summer's over and I haven't gotten in any yet this season. For the past four years, I've gone backpacking up into the high country. And I've gotten to know a few spots here and there. How about if I take a week off and share the driving duties with you? That way, we could spend some real time together – you know, more than just an hour or two at a reunion. That is, as long as I wouldn't be interfering with your work?"

"Oh, no!" she insisted. "It's not going to be anything that intensive. Just a cursory field study – reconnoitering various areas so I can come up with concrete ideas for a new proposal."

"You sure you can take seven days in the wilderness with me?" he joked.

"Are you really serious about this?" she asked.

"Sure. Why not?"

"No reason. Just wanted to make sure. Giving you a last chance to back out."

"Not me, darlin'." He hadn't called her that in a long time, but it rolled so comfortably off his tongue that he didn't have time to take it back. Juliette noticed it, thought about what it meant for an instant, and then put it in her mind's storehouse for later dissection.

"Okay! Let's do it!" she bubbled. "Sounds like a hoot!"

The rest of the phone conversation was spent checking their calendars, talking about airline fares, and discussing in a preliminary way what clothing and camping equipment she might need to bring or buy. When Roman hung up, the plan was for Juliette to fly into Denver on September 1, the Tuesday before Labor Day. They would spend a night or two in Castle Rock and then head south toward Taos. Further plans would be formulated day to day.

Letters and phone calls continued over the next five weeks – lots of it chitchat, but also serious questions about hiking boots, sleeping bags and pads, and the all-important backpack. Had it not been for that, Roman thought, he would have died a slow death from the agony of expectation he suffered through, waiting for those endless days and weeks to pass.

She flew into Stapleton Airport, arriving right on schedule in midafternoon. As she was renting her car, she realized she would probably get to Castle Rock before Roman had closed his office for the day. She thought about piddling around in Denver to kill an hour or two, maybe checking out the antique shops on lower Broadway, or driving around the old neighborhoods from her high school days. But as she swung over to I-225 and down I-25, she bypassed each and every exit, frozen with indecision. Something in her was more than a little anxious about the next week or so. *Maybe he's left work early today,* she thought, *and then I'd be killing time I could be spending with him.* Besides, she had to admit, this trip was about a lot more than Rocky Mountain flora.

Of Juliette's Blood

Beating the commuter traffic out of the metro area, she hit the city limits of Castle Rock about half past four. Roman had sent her a handmade map of the easiest route to his house, so she had no trouble finding the exits, intersections, and landmarks, pulling into his driveway about a quarter of five. Since his office was a scant five minutes off the freeway, she had initially contemplated dropping by there first in case he had not left yet. But she quickly scratched the idea when she realized how uncomfortable he might feel greeting her in front of his employees. Besides, Roman had left an extra house key for her under the welcome mat and encouraged her to let herself in and get comfortable if he got stuck at work and was not able to get there before she arrived.

As she walked up the cobblestone pathway to his front door, her curiosity was aroused by the several stones that appeared to have been colored with yellow chalk. Reaching to ring the doorbell, she saw an envelope with her name on it taped to the door handle. She opened it and pulled out three pages. The first one read in bold colored letters: "Welcome to the Land of Oz – Castle Rock Way Station." She smiled, partly bewildered and partly enchanted. *The Wizard of Oz* had always been one of her favorite movies.

For the first time in years, she thought about the rainbow pin – sterling silver inlaid with five colors of enamel – that he had given her back in the tenth grade. It was the Easter season and she had invited Roman over to watch the annual television broadcast of the movie with her family. They sat out in the back yard after the show was over and she talked about all the wonderful allegories written into the story. A week later, Roman gave her the pin. "'Cause you're the rainbow in my life," he had said as she pulled the top off the box. Turning to the second page, she read:

> Once there was a fair young maiden named Dorothy, who often went by the alias of Juliette. She dreamed of faraway lands, intriguing people, and beauties of nature which would take her breath away. One morning, after she awoke from a peaceful slumber, she went to search for her faithful companion, Toto. But, alas, Toto was nowhere to be found. She called to him: "Toto! Toto!" She whistled, but he did not respond. Frantically she shouted at the top of her lungs, but her screams echoed against the side of the house and the nearby hills and then trailed off, absorbed into the vast silence.

Brokenhearted, she fell to the ground, for she knew some terrible misfortune had befallen her constant companion. She thought back to a time not so long ago when the evil witch had kidnaped Toto. "That's it!" she exclaimed, knowing exactly where to search. But as quickly as the idea came to her, it left. The mean old witch was no more, Dorothy realized, knowing the evil woman had been served her own deserving fate on a platter during their last encounter.

As she sat there dispirited, she heard a whisper in her ear. She thought she had imagined it all, but then she heard it again. The sound came from the left, some distance away, but growing closer. Suddenly it was directly at her left ear; then it passed through her and back out her right ear, trailing off into the distance again. It was saying something about where Toto was, but she could not make it all out. So she sat as still as a marble statue, being ever so quiet, knowing that if it had come by before, it would come round again.

She focused her perceptual senses on her left, until it felt like that entire side of her body was a part of her auditory system. She heard the rustle of leaves as the wind blew them about. Each gentle wave of sound seemed to be rubbing against her arm and the side of her face. She was startled by the chirp of a cricket only a few feet away, and the surface of her skin began to tingle. And then she heard the sound she was waiting for, again coming from the distant hills on the left, like some intelligent energy circling in an orbit that passed directly through her. But it all went by too fast and then it was gone.

It must come back again, she prayed, so she waited. She felt the tension of the moment in the fibers of her muscles, in the speed of her heartbeat, and in the arrhythmia of her breathing, and she recalled the words of a great wise man she had once known who taught her about how emotions affect the body and interfere with the ability to perceive the surrounding world. So she began to relax her body. Once more she heard the leaves rustle, but as she calmed her emotions and stilled her mind the sounds became like a gentle caress on her cheek. She heard the cricket's chirp too, but it was no longer shrill and startling. Instead, she felt the left side of her body absorb the sound; she felt it reverberate within her and then pass out on the other side.

And then she heard that sound coming from far away. Directing her senses and freeing herself from the bonds of her emotions, she heard the message, fully and clearly. "Toto has gone back to Oz," the voice said. And she knew it was true, and she knew why. It was something the aged wizard had told her many years ago. Something so simple that it had seemed then like the babbling of a fool. She was young and the ramblings of old people had no value to someone her age.

So that's it, she realized. *The wizard was right!* Somehow, she believed, Toto knew it too. Yet he had stayed with her all these years, just waiting for the day when he would leave to discover the mystery of the old man's wisdom for himself. "Well, that's it," she exclaimed, "I must go back to Oz!" And she gathered her belongings, carefully packed them into her knapsack, and headed down the walkway to the street. *Now, where to start,* she wondered. She looked up the street to the east and she looked down the street to the west. *I don't have a clue how to get back there. I know it's not on any of the maps. I doubt Toto left a trail of bread crumbs.* And she plopped down right there on the sidewalk, not even knowing whether to turn left or right.

And suddenly she remembered something else the old wizard had mumbled. Something foolish then, but now it seemed like an answer from heaven. "There are no right or wrong turns on the path of life. Each and every fork in the road still leads to the same place – to your destiny." So up she sprang like a jack-in-the-box, looked right, looked left, and then headed to the west to find the land of Oz.

INSTRUCTIONS ON PLAYING THE GAME **FIND THE LAND OF OZ**:

1. LISTEN
2. LOOK
3. FEEL
4. FORGET EVERYTHING
5. REMEMBER EVERYTHING
6. GRASP EVERYTHING
7. LET GO OF EVERYTHING

WARNINGS:

PLAYING THIS GAME CAN BE ADDICTIVE, THOUGH NEVER FATAL. HOWEVER, DEATH ALWAYS EVENTUALLY COMES TO THOSE WHO NEVER PLAY. NEVER BE IN A HURRY TO PLAY. THE GAME CAN ONLY BE PLAYED AT ONE PACE. FINDING YOUR OWN PACE IS THE FIRST PART OF THE GAME. DO NOT EXPECT TO REACH THE LAND OF OZ IMMEDIATELY. SAVORING THE SEARCH IS THE SECOND PART OF THE GAME.
GOOD LUCK, DOROTHY!

As Juliette finished the story, feelings of anticipation mixed with elation. Intrigued by the charm and mystery of the allegorical fable, she wondered about its source. *Did Roman write this? Did he write it just for me?* Thrilled by the romantic thought, she instinctively took a deep breath. *Easy, girl!* she cautioned. Folding up the pages and carefully inserting them back into their envelope, she rang the doorbell once and waited a few seconds. Then she lifted up the mat to find the hidden key. She unlocked the door, decided to get a bag or two from the car first, and then stepped inside.

His house was nothing fancy – three bedrooms, two baths, about 1800 square feet in one of the newer middle-class subdivisions in the burgeoning suburban community south of Denver. The front room was light and airy, with skylights in the vaulted ceiling and large south-facing windows to catch the warmth of the sun on those cold winter days. As she surveyed the room, her eyes were drawn to a luxurious-looking red velour sofa. Flanking each arm and in front were tables with tops of highly polished blue pearl granite. A large burgundy leather rocker-recliner sat off to the side, facing a large golden oak entertainment center, with stereo, television, and VCR. The room felt so comfortable, Juliette set her bags to one side and eased down onto the couch to reread the story.

After two more readings, she went over to her carry-on bag and pulled out the novel she had been reading on the plane. As she finished the chapter she had just started when the plane touched down, she heard a car pull into the driveway. A few moments later, she caught a glimpse of a large figure as it whisked past the front picture window, which was obscured by thin white curtains. She popped off the sofa and pulled open the door just as he reached for the outside handle. Roman's face beamed with delight when he saw her.

"Howzit goin', Cowboy?" she said, imitating the syrupy Texas drawl she had still not quite perfected.

"Jes' fine, little lady," he replied, mimicking her accent as he held out his arms. She took his hands in hers, feeling awkward with the moment. Not to be denied any longer, he gently pulled her toward him until their arms wrapped around each other. The hug was long and silent as they said what they had to say with their breathing and their biochemistry. His nostrils flared as he indulged in that familiar fragrance. After a minute, he pulled his head back. She did likewise as social convention elbowed its way back to the forefront.

Roman broke the silence. "It's really good to see you again."

She gave him three pats on the side of the arm. "Good to be here." As she cleared her throat, she felt a wave of emotion rise up through her until it forced an expression. She slipped a hand behind his neck, stroked it softly once, and then leaned forward and kissed him.

He had not felt such warmth from a pair of lips in years – soft and moist, with just a hint of lipstick. They lingered on his for a few seconds until she slowly pulled back. Her eyes had a dreamlike appearance – as though he was looking at them through a sheer piece of soft, white silk. He was about to say how beautiful she looked when she began to feel uncomfortable about how impulsively she had kissed him – and hardly a minute or two since he had walked in the door. She cleared her throat again, stepped on the brake pedal of her affections, and less than artfully changed the subject.

"This is a nice place you've got here," she said as she swept one arm around the room. "At least, what I've seen so far looks really nice."

As much as he wanted to pull her body back up against his, he resisted. *Plenty of time – no hurry – don't wanna push things*, he thought. So he picked up the cue and gave her the history of the house and its furnishings as he showed her from room to room. After sharing a glass of Johann Riesling, they got the rest of her luggage out of the rental car, and she unpacked in the guest room while Roman called his favorite seafood restaurant for a reservation.

Over a leisurely dinner of grilled salmon and shrimp scampi, sauteed vegetables, and homemade breads, they revived their reunion conversation about their old high school classmates, then skipped on to their college days and their current jobs. As they left the restaurant to stroll around the few blocks which constituted downtown Castle Rock, their hands simultaneously reached out, drawn together by some unseen force. The touch was so casual, so comfortable, so like those many years ago when they were full of innocence but their feelings were raw and unrefined. Now, the feel of palm against palm was not a sudden electric shock but more a strong current of soothing warmth. Awkward as they were still feeling about how much they expressed and how soon they expressed it, holding hands just seemed so right.

Returning to Roman's house, they settled down onto his big red couch with a couple of glasses of port. Willie Nelson's gravelly voice softly crooned the pining tunes of lonely cowboys in the background. Away from the dinner crowds and the always-there-at-the-wrong-moment-waiters, their conversation turned to the more personal side of their lives.

Juliette had gotten a scholarship to the University of Kansas and graduated in 1981 with a bachelor of science in biology. Then she went on to get her Ph.D. in botany at the University of Texas in 1985. During the summer between receiving her M.S. and starting the doctorate program, she met and married another grad student – Jake Cummings. Their marriage was good for the first three years, but he had problems with his dissertation, could not keep himself together emotionally, and failed to land the kind of job he wanted. He started drinking heavily. During the fourth year of the marriage, he hit her a couple of times. She threatened to walk out if he refused to get help for his drinking, so he joined AA and stayed sober for about a year.

But something was eating at him and his poor job performance kept him from getting the usual pay raises. After an ugly incident at work, Jake's boss threatened him with immediate termination, but he was able to put enough effort into his work to hold on to the job. Unfortunately, he started drinking again with a couple of his other disgruntled buddies shortly afterward – a fact he was able to hide from Juliette for months. Finally, during the sixth year of their marriage, he lost it and came home drunk. He blamed all his troubles on her and beat her up. She called the cops, had him arrested, got a divorce lawyer, and never looked back.

Roman had gone to the University of Colorado in Boulder after high school, graduating in 1982 with a degree in electrical engineering. He had really gotten into computers during his college years, so he went to work for IBM's new personal computer division that summer. In mid-1984, he was enticed away by a frat buddy who talked him into working with him at Apple on the newly-released Macintosh line. After another two years there, Roman decided he wanted to be his own boss, so he came back to Colorado and opened his own business. He believed in the future growth of the personal computer market and wanted to utilize the state-of-the-art skills and knowledge he had picked up with the big companies to his best advantage.

He met his first wife, Sarah, at one of the banks to which he sold CPUs and components. They dated for six months and then married in 1988. She was only twenty-one, eight years younger than he, and not really ready to settle down. In hindsight, he now realized they should have talked about family before they got married. But both of them just assumed that things would work out. He wanted kids. She wanted to wait. A year and a half into the marriage, Sarah finally agreed to start working toward building a family. But secretly, she was still taking her birth control pills.

Roman studied all the family planning literature from Planned Parenthood, the library, the health food store, and any other credible source he could find. He suggested and Sarah appeared to willingly comply with many of the various methods to increase their chances of conception. After about ten months with no success, he convinced her to go to a fertility specialist. He paused in his narrative.

Juliette tried to read his face. Was this getting too personal? Was he becoming uncomfortable talking about this? Then she saw his expression change from one of solemnity to humor. He smiled broadly as he put his chin to his chest and shook his head slowly. His face looked slightly flushed.

"Well," she demanded, "what's so funny, Bub?"

He shook his head a little more vigorously as the smile turned into a chuckle.

"Now, that's not fair," she complained. "If it's all that funny, you should let me in on it."

Roman looked up at her and started to speak, but all that came out was another spurt or two of laughter. Juliette waited patiently, arms crossed to signal her determination.

"Okay," he said as he breathed deeply a couple of times to regain his composure. "I'll tell you. But this is between us, okay?" She nodded assent.

"Well," he began, "this was the first appointment we'd had at the fertility clinic. And I didn't really know my way around the place all that much. But we spent the first hour going through this very detailed questionnaire, some twenty pages or so. And, of course, it asked lots of personal questions about our sex lives – things like what techniques we'd tried to increase our chances of conceiving, our sexual histories before marriage, whether we'd ever been tested for fertility before, and all that.

"So after we give the forms to the nurse, she shows us back to the examining rooms. And we go in the first one and another nurse comes in and draws some blood from both of us. Then the first nurse comes in and takes Sarah down the hall to another examining room. And so I'm sitting there for a few minutes alone and then the second nurse, the one who took the blood, comes back in and hands me a specimen cup. And she leads me down the hall, around a couple of corners and points to the bathroom on the left. Then she points back up the hall and says to bring it back to the front.

"So I get the specimen and all and come back out of the bathroom. Somehow I managed to find my way back up to the front, so I handed the cup to the nurse and she says 'You can go join your wife if you want.' So I nodded, turned and got my bearings, and headed for the room I'd seen Juliette go into a few minutes before."

Roman's face became even more flushed. He continued: "So I get to the door and slowly push it open. Though I'd only seen the doctor once, I recognized his round bald head from the back. He was sitting at the end of an examining table on a stool and she was lying down on it, wearing just one of those hospital gowns, her feet up in the stirrups. He was a pretty broad shouldered guy so two bare knees sticking up framing his ears was about all of her I could see. I was about to call her name when the doctor leaned over to the right to pick up something from a tray. And suddenly it hit me. *My Sarah isn't a redhead!*"

Juliette burst out laughing with a force that not even Roman would have expected. He smiled sheepishly each time she gathered her composure sufficiently to glance up at him. But a second later she was rolling back on the sofa and grabbing her sides to lessen the pain from the laughter. By the time she surfaced for about the fifth or sixth time, she was at least coherent enough to string a few phrases together between soft bursts of muffled chuckles.

"Oh, Roman," she said as she reached out and stroked his cheek affectionately. "That's one of the things I've always loved about you. You have this great ability to tell these outrageously funny stories, and they always have you turning up to be the butt of the joke, so to speak." She realized too late that she had let the "love" word slip out. But maybe, she thought, it was appropriate given the context in which it was said. *Maybe he didn't even notice.*

But she was wrong. His radar screen flashed brightly at the suggestiveness of her language. Reaching up to his face, he took her hand and brought it slowly to his lips. One kiss, then a second, on the back of her hand. Then he gently turned it over, tenderly massaged each finger and the palm, and then kissed it. As he looked up at her face and their eyes met, words were not necessary for complete communication of their thoughts. In a split second, they were in each other's arms, their emotions hungrily feeding for the sensuality that could only be transmitted through their lips.

The grip of their passionate mood was broken by the ring of the telephone. Within a few seconds, he was back on the sofa. "Wrong number," he explained.

"So what happened to your marriage?" Juliette inquired as she sipped the last of her port.

"Well, the clinic did all the lab tests. And after the doctor got the results, he confronted Sarah and told her he knew she was taking birth control pills," Roman continued. "He told her she had to confess the whole thing to me – that it wasn't fair to put him in a kind of an ethical dilemma about whether her medical test results were privileged information he couldn't disclose even to me. But, the doctor pointed out, he had a duty to me too, because I was equally his patient and had a right to know I wasn't the reason Sarah wasn't getting pregnant. The doctor told her I had the right to know I was wasting my money on fertility counseling.

"So Sarah agreed to tell me and, at our next appointment, the doctor introduced us to one of his medical staff experienced in counseling. And she did. And I was just stunned – just sat there feeling like the world's biggest fool. So the counselor recommended that we go to a family therapist to try to work this thing out, but Sarah refused to go.

"One night, maybe a couple of weeks later, I came home to find that she'd gone – packed all her clothes while I was at work and moved out. Left a note saying she had to work it out in her own mind and asking me not to try to pressure her. Said she needed the time and the space. Two months later, I got served with a summons and divorce petition. So I settled up with her lawyer quickly and cashed her out on her part of the marital property. We got the matter resolved within about six weeks and the divorce became final in April of last year. So that's the story of my first attempt at marriage – or at least my side of it." He rose from the couch, picked up the two wine glasses, and disappeared into the kitchen for a small refill.

As the evening and their mutual desire for further conversation wound down, Roman and Juliette drew closer physically to each other, cuddling in the warm glow of candlelight as their emotions were swayed by the sultry songs of Whitney Houston. The words were sparse, the kisses many. Roman sensed that he was being swept away by the current of a raging river and holding on to Juliette was like grabbing a large rock in midstream and clinging to it for dear life. She likened her embrace of him to finding the lost teddy bear she'd had when she was only six. After a series of long passionate kisses, the music stopped. Roman glanced at the clock next to the stereo. Half past eleven. He gazed back down at her and peered intently into her eyes, looking for a hint of an answer to the awkward question he was about to ask.

"For your sake, as well as mine, I'd better ask now, before . . ." His voice tapered off as he fumbled for the most tactful way to phrase his thoughts. She looked at him quizzically, with a hint of hope in her eyes. He looked back at her and smiled. Then, almost clinically the words came out, with just a touch of innocence. "Would you feel more comfortable sleeping in the guest room tonight or with me?"

"With you," came her hushed response.

Rocky Mountain High

The next ten days were saturated with exploration of some of the most magnificent beauties of nature. And there was much time for them come to understand who and what they each had become in their years apart. A day hike on one of the many trails in the Pike's Peak National Forest gave Juliette time to become acclimated to the altitude. But her five-foot, six-inch frame was in great physical shape at 110 pounds, so the adjustment was rapid. As the afternoon drew to a close, they drove to highest lookout on the famous peak and watched the build up of clouds hanging low in the western sky burn with brilliant golds, fiery oranges, and varied tones of red as the sun disappeared below the ridge.

Thursday morning at daybreak, they loaded Roman's 4Runner with a week's worth of gear and headed south toward Taos, arriving shortly after the noon hour. Since Juliette had never been to the tourist monstrosity that had developed out of the quiet Native American pueblo, they lingered over a southwestern lunch and wandered around the many arts and crafts shops until mid-afternoon. With a load of pottery and silver trinkets in tow, they backtracked up north and located a rustic campground near Questa, at the foot of Wheeler Peak, the highest point in the state. After pitching the dome tent and unloading enough of their gear and food for the first overnight, they found a nearby foot trail and hiked for two hours, with Juliette busily making field notes as she inspected the flora of the region.

Returning to their campsite, they snacked on oranges while Roman heated up the by-now-defrosted salmon he had grilled and then frozen the week before. The evening's meal was topped off with a bottle of white wine, chilled to perfection in the huge cooler. They danced around the campfire a Mary Chapin Carpenter cassette for an hour, until the chilly night air got the best of them, then crawled into the tent and made the best double-bag bed out of their two-single-bag situation.

Rising the next morning to a persistent woodpecker's steady tapping on the trunk of a nearby dead pine and the incessant screech of a group of jays, Roman suggested a trip across the Rio Grande over to the Jemez mountain range around Los Alamos. After lunch at a restaurant near the entrance to the world-famous laboratory, they stopped at Bandolier National Monument for a hike on the park trails. Over the next three hours, Juliette would notice a particular plant every three or four minutes and stop to inspect it, adding to her growing collection of notes. Even though the sudden stops interrupted his usual hiking pace, Roman never voiced any complaint, being happy to have the time and opportunity to gaze at her.

Back in the vehicle, they wandered the roads which snaked through the gently sloping mountains around Redondo Peak, now merely a semblance of the Valles caldera, what was once thought to have been a 14,000-foot mountain that had erupted a little more than a million years ago in one of the world's largest volcanic explosions, according to geologists. Winding north and west on the highway and then back east down a National Forest dirt and gravel road, Roman remained mysterious about their destination. Juliette had proposed checking into a hotel every other night or so to wash off the trail dust, but Roman had persuaded her to give it one more night before they succumbed, temporarily, to the creature comforts of civilization.

Five miles off the paved highway, the dirt road sloped down steeply into a large flat parking area. Roman came to a stop at the north end. "We're here," he announced as he hopped out, shouldered his backpack, grabbed the tent, and forded the fifteen-foot-wide stream across the felled log bridge over to a grassy meadow. Not having the same level of experience roughing it as her camping mate, Juliette followed with her share of the gear, gliding ever so deliberately across the log bridge. About a hundred yards up a trail, they turned the bend and found a wide level spot next to two huge rocks. The sharp turn in the trail obscured their view of the meadow and parking area. Whatever campers had been in the area during the previous week had packed up and gone. They would be alone that Friday night – at least until the Labor Day crowd began arriving the next day.

They set up camp, gathered an ample supply of firewood, and started a roaring fire in a stacked-rock pit at the foot of the boulders. An early supper having satisfied the gnawing hunger, Roman recommended a short hike up the east slope of the canyon to a place where the view of the sun setting behind the western canyon wall made the trek well worth the effort. When she agreed, he slipped into the tent and stuffed some things into his backpack. Within minutes they were heading back down the meadow trail.

After a challenging twenty-minute climb up a steep mountain path, they came to the end of a forested area. Juliette stopped right behind him, hands on her hips and gasping for breath. She could hear his deep, labored wheezing too. Finally, her oxygen balance restored, she looked up. Roman swept his arm in a manner befitting the gallant knights of old toward an open area strewn with piles of rock cascading down the steep mountain slope. "Your bath awaits, M'Lady."

Juliette was mystified by the clouds of steam she saw rising from the rocks. As she stepped closer, she noticed that some of the rocks had been arranged in semicircular shapes to form barriers. And uphill from each barrier were various sizes of pools of water, wisps of vapor rising intermittently from each. She looked at him dumbfounded, then scanned the area.

A large concrete bunker had been built over what she presumed to be the source of the spring. From its front, hundreds of gallons of 106-degree water poured out of three six-inch pipes. The top pool looked to be about fifteen feet across and seven wide, with a depth of three feet at its deepest point. The bottom was covered with small grain gravel. Her sense of smell did not detect any odor of the sulphur prevalent at many other geothermal sites. Juliette stepped down from the edge of the bunker and leaned forward to stick her hand under one of the streams of clear hot water. *It's so soft,* she thought, *it feels like liquid velvet*. The water looked so inviting, it was all she could do to keep from jumping right in, clothes and all.

The hot springs were deserted as the orange glow of the descending sun set the clouds ablaze. Roman pulled two bottles of water out of his backpack, along with a couple of towels, their two pairs of rubber sandals, and a blue compacted foam pad. With the water all to themselves, they disrobed, slipped on the sandals, and soaked for an hour. Lying back on the foam pad, suspended effortlessly in the warmth of the water, Juliette watched the sky turn from deep blue to violet to inky black. One by one, she saw millions of stars pop out from nowhere.

As they washed away the worries of the world, they spoke of the many marvels of nature they had seen before on other vacations. When mutual neck massages generated more intimate contact, the top pool became too warm. So they carefully slipped down a couple of levels to a smaller pool which was three or four degrees cooler. There they kissed and gently caressed each other until their passion demanded fulfillment. Awkward as it was physically, they finally found a position comfortable enough not to distract them from their goal. Straddling Roman as he laid back on the pad against the rocks, Juliette rocked back and forth to an internal rhythm. Her pelvis and legs submerged in the warm waters, the building heat in the lower part of her torso was exotically balanced by a cool mountain breeze blowing ever so gently against her back. When she finally came to orgasm, it was harder and deeper than anything she had ever experienced. The millions of stars in the sky paled in comparison to the billions of stars that exploded inside her head.

Even though the ground under their tent was hard and bumpy, they both fell into a deep, sound sleep on their thick Thermarest pads. After a hasty breakfast, they hiked back to the pools for a quick early morning bath. Then they trekked up the canyon, following the crystal water upstream until the high canyon walls gave way to an open valley. Roman prepared something to eat while Juliette added to her field notes.

After breaking camp about midmorning, they headed west through the Jemez, stopping for lunch at a superb Mexican-American restaurant in the small New Mexico town of Cuba before driving north up to the southwest Colorado town of Durango. Roman had reserved a room for Saturday night at the town's landmark hotel, The Strater, where they enjoyed its antique Old West charm. The evening was topped off by a fabulous dinner of grilled mahi-mahi at one of the local restaurants and a casual stroll up and down Main Street, enjoying some of the folksy appeal of a town rich in the traditions of mining, railroads, and cowboys.

Early Sunday morning, they drove north over Coal Bank Pass, pulling into a Forest Service parking area near Andrews Lake. From there, they backpacked three miles south along the trail to Crater Lake on the north side of 13,000-foot Twilight Peak, where they met two other couples who had packed into the same area. Around a large communal campfire, they shared stories about other camping and hiking locations with their newfound friends.

In the morning, they hiked out and drove north to the rustic high mountain mining town of Silverton, where they shopped for an hour and watched the first morning sightseeing train come in from Durango. After a scenic jaunt over Red Mountain Pass and down the

Million Dollar Highway to Ouray, they stopped for lunch before heading west to Telluride. They checked into a reasonably-priced condo that Roman had reserved, rode the gondola from the town to the luxurious ski village and back down, and shopped around town with the million other Labor Day tourists until their feet ached. Forgoing the night life, they crawled into their king-size bed and promptly fell asleep.

Wednesday took them northeast to lunch in Montrose and then north to Grand Mesa, where they found a campground and took another long late afternoon hike. Rising early the next morning, Roman packed up the 4Runner while Juliette surveyed another trail and prepared her last notes. After a three-hour drive over to Aspen for lunch, sightseeing, and gawking at the rich and famous, they caught I-70 for the long drive back to the eastern slope.

As they approached metropolitan Denver, Roman left the interstate a few miles west of the city limits just as the late summer skies were beginning to darken. "New shortcut to Castle Rock?" she asked.

"Nope," he replied with a sly grin on his face. "Just a little whipped cream to top the week off."

"What devious plan are you hatching now?" she inquired warily, with a touch of weariness in her voice.

Roman gestured toward the glove compartment. "In there," he explained, "a small light blue envelope. Get it."

Fumbling around through the warranty papers and vehicle operator's manual, she finally found the object of her search. Offering it to Roman, he shook his head. "Open it," he directed.

"Ooh," she squealed as she pulled out two slips of paper. "Tickets to Red Rocks – the Moody Blues!" She lunged over to kiss him but, forgetting that she was strapped into the seat, was so severely restrained by her shoulder belt that it almost knocked the wind out of her.

Never one to pass up an opportunity for a playful jibe, Roman quipped, "I just leave you breathless, don't I?"

The concert in the magnificent outdoor amphitheater, carved into the jutting rock of the red sandstone foothills, was, in many respects, the pinnacle of their week-long odyssey. As Justin Hayward's baritone voice reverberated off the stone backdrop, Roman held his childhood sweetheart tightly. Lyrics from the group's 1986 rock ballad about long-lost love, *Your Wildest Dreams*, seemed as though they had been written and sung just for the two reborn lovers.

Once beneath the stars the universe was ours.
Love was all we knew, and all I knew was you.
I wonder where you are. I wonder if you think about it
Once upon a time in your wildest dreams.

When the group broke into their sequel hit from 1988, *I Know You're Out There Somewhere*, the lovers' spirits soared like two hawks riding effortlessly on the vortex of musical currents. Again Hayward's lyrics pierced the night air.

The secret of your beauty and the mystery of your soul
I've been searching for in everyone I meet.
And the times I've been mistaken it's impossible to say,
And the grass is growing underneath our feet.
I know you're out there somewhere, somewhere, somewhere
I know you're out there somewhere, and somehow I'll return again to you.

Exhausted from the long day and longer night but exhilarated by the inspiration of the night of mystical music, they finally returned to Roman's house near midnight and collapsed into bed, leaving the unloading of their gear until morning.

Their last day together was filled with repeated episodes of spontaneous embracing, each followed by an intense wave of melancholy. As Juliette packed her bags, Roman busied himself with all the chores around a house that had been unattended to for over a week. But every ten or fifteen minutes, they would find themselves drifting back into each other's space and a word or a touch would lead to a heartfelt hug and a meaningful kiss. Roman cooked a fabulous Chinese stir-fry for dinner and even had a couple of fortune cookies for the end of the meal, which he had coaxed from the owner of one of his favorite restaurants the week before Juliette came. His fortune was stock Oriental wisdom: "The journey of a thousand miles begins with but a single step."

But Juliette's strip of paper bore a message with a deeper meaning: "Answer just what your heart prompts you." She stared at the slip for a moment as if an angel had whispered directly in her ear. Then she looked up at him with tears in her eyes, stood up, walked around to him, put her arms around his neck, and gave him a big squeeze. Then she swung around to look him in the eye penetratingly, gave him a deep passionate kiss, put her forehead against his, and let the words come out as easily as a breath. "I love you." She opened her eyes seeking reaction from him. "I always have, I guess," she continued. She leaned over and whispered in his ear. "I always will."

"I've never stopped loving you either," he replied. "I realized that when you left the reunion party. I'd never felt such emptiness before."

They spent the rest of the evening in bed, talking through their feelings. After a solemn breakfast the next morning, he helped her load her luggage into the rental car. As she pulled out of the driveway, he busied himself with lawn and gardening chores. But never in his life had he felt so hollow. It was as though someone had shoved a vacuum hose down into his lungs. Every minute or two, he'd find himself taking a really deep breath as he tried to still the waves of emotion running crashing down onto his usually stable peace of mind.

Tooling up the interstate in her rental car, Juliette found herself fighting the urge at each freeway exit to U-turn right back to his house. She knew she had left a couple of hours earlier than necessary, thinking she might stop at a favorite clothing store in Denver she had frequented when she attended conferences in the city. By the time she hit I-225, the urge to go back to Castle Rock had subsided, but she could not keep from calling him from the airport as she waited for her flight to leave.

They spoke frequently and at great length during the evenings over the next week. Late one afternoon, Roman found a surprise telephone message on his spike when he came back to the office. He quickly returned the call to Juliette, who was gurgling with excitement.

"Guess what?" she chortled. Without giving him any time to respond, she answered her own question. "I've gotten approval on my grant proposal, so I'm coming back to Colorado to do some last-minute field work and a bit of research at the local libraries."

"When? How soon?" was his only response.

"Pretty soon. Looks like the last day or two of September and a few days in October. I've got a couple of meetings to schedule with some fellow researchers, but I can take care of those Wednesday and Thursday. Then I'd have a three-day weekend before I've got to be back at work. Do you think we could swing another camping trip before the weather gets too cold?"

"Absolutely," he replied. "And I've got just the place in mind."

"Oh, yeah? Where this time?"

"Oh, you're gonna have to just wait till you get here. Just consider it another surprise."

"Well, if it's half as good as the other surprises you've cooked up, it'll be fine with me."

In the Rainbow

Juliette arrived back in Colorado just as the fall colors transformed the mountainous landscape into an earthbound rainbow. The leaves on the white-trunked quaking aspens had reached their deepest gold. Surrounding the groves of spindly giants, the different contrasting shades of the aspens' stately evergreen companions – pines, spruces, and firs – made the yellow leaves shine even more brightly. At the lower elevations, the radiant rust reds of the stands of scrub oak whirled about, mixing with the deep greens of the cedars and pinon pines as if painted on the countryside by the broad strokes of an artist's brush. Even the heavens contributed to the grandeur, capping the craggy peaks above tree line with an early dusting of snow, more luminous set against a cloudless, royal blue sky.

Her business appointments in Denver occupied all of her daytime hours during the first two days, but her nights were spent with Roman, who made the short jaunt up to the city for dinner on Wednesday, stayed over at her hotel, and drove her back to Castle Rock early Thursday evening after his final call of the day on a customer near the Denver Tech Center. While he fixed dinner, she popped down to the video store to rent one of her favorites, *Moonstruck*.

After the movie, they cleared the dining table and pulled out a topographical atlas of the state. Roman showed her the general area in the south central mountains that they had not gotten to see in early September. Even though she and her family had lived in Colorado for ten years before she went off to college, she acknowledged that she was not that familiar with the western branch of the Rockies called the San Juans. Since her mother and father were not the outdoors type, her family's summer excursions to the mountains had been limited to Pike's Peak and its environs, the Rocky Mountain National Park, and the area around Evergreen. Of course, she had skied the Summit County resorts during the winter months, but, with the exception of her trek along the far western slope four weeks ago, everything west of the San Luis Valley was considered new territory.

They rose at a reasonable hour on Friday morning, loaded the 4Runner, and drove south on the interstate to Colorado Springs, then west on U.S. 24 over Ute and Wilkerson passes, down U.S. 285 through the stark expanse of the San Luis Valley, then west on U.S. 160. By the time they arrived in the mushrooming little tourist Mecca known as South Fork, they were famished. After a quick lunch at one of the local dives, they snaked their way to the top of Wolf Creek Pass, then slowly began the winding descent toward Pagosa Springs. Eight miles down from the summit, just past the turnout for Treasure Falls, Roman turned right onto the Forest Service road for the West Fork Campground. About five miles up the dusty road, they came to the trail head.

After Roman parked the vehicle off the roadway, they dropped the tailgate and put the finishing touches on their backpacks. Setting his at the edge, Roman pulled a detailed map of the Weminuche Wilderness out of a side pocket and spread it out.

"We're right here," he indicated, pointing to boxed "TH" symbol, "and we're heading up this trail." His finger traced a meandering dashed line heading generally north-northwest along the west fork of the San Juan River. "It's about four miles and pretty much uphill, but . . ." he added as a measure of reassurance, "it's not too bad overall. Three or four pretty steep climbs, but we're not too heavily loaded for just a couple of nights. Probably take us about two, two and a half hours." He folded the map and stuffed back into the pack.

"Don't worry about me, Bub," Juliette chided him playfully as she turned and hoisted her pack onto the first shoulder. "I held my own last time. Remember?"

"Hey," he quickly retorted in self-defense, hunching down and slipping his arms through both straps. "I was just trying to describe it for you so you wouldn't be asking every ten minutes, 'Are we there yet?'"

When he parroted her with a whine, she dropped the pack from her shoulder, plopping it on the ground, and went straight for Roman's midsection. Looking down as he struggled to adjust the clip on his waist belt, he was caught by surprise. Her two hands grabbed his stomach like claws and gave a hard squeeze. He jerked back so instinctively he did not have time to see what was behind him. His left heel came down on top of a rock and he lost his balance, tumbling backward right onto his pack. But Juliette's clinch was iron tight and the force of his fall dragged her right down on top of him.

After the moment of shock passed, he put his arms around her and hugged her warmly. She started giggling. "Tough man," she said in a gravelly voice, then changing to her Betty Boop imitation, she added, "but kind of soft in the middle, huh?" He just smiled and looked into her eyes. Then he moved his arms up her back and, placing his hands on the back of her neck, brought her face down to his. A warm kiss or two later, she pushed herself up and brushed off her knees. He reached up with both hands.

"How 'bout a lift?" he requested.

She giggled again. "You look like a turtle that's been turned over on its back and can't get up."

"Very funny," he replied, as he motioned with his fingers for her to grasp his hands. After one more gurgle of laughter, she reached down, clasped his hands, and leaned back to lever him up.

Gear fully strapped to their backs, they set out along the winding trail on the west side of the canyon. After about two miles, they descended a switchback trail to the West Fork's edge, coming upon a pair of large, sturdy bridges recently built by the Forest Service. Crossing the first, they rested in the shade of an evergreen grove near the banks of the rushing river. Half an hour later, they were again huffing and puffing through the steep climb back up to the main trail as it ran high above the river on the east side.

A little over an hour later, they reached a large clearing in the forest overlooking the river about sixty feet below. Evidence of the summer's visitors could be seen everywhere, mostly remains of campfires, circles of rocks and white ash, with large logs pulled near to serve as seating. They selected a flat, grassy area with a bit of scrap firewood left over, set up the dome tent, and stashed the rest of their gear inside. Then they both headed out in different directions to scrounge for any leftover wood that could serve as fuel. After about an hour, they had assembled a sizable stack, enough to feed a fire for two nights.

Basic chores accomplished, Roman dug into his pack and pulled out a sack of dried figs and cashews and invited his companion to join him on the large log next to the fire pit. As they both relaxed from the strenuous trek, he offered the next idea. "How about we wash up down by the river?" Juliette took a look at her arms and legs, smudged with mud and debris from the forest booty she had collected. "But I don't suppose you could make it a steaming hot bath again like that place in the Jemez," she replied with a touch of sarcasm.

Roman's face broke into a mischievous grin. "Is there a hot spring around here?" she asked incredulously. She surmised the answer from his impish expression. "Really? Where?"

"Grab your towel and I'll show you."

In a matter of seconds, she had rifled through not only her own backpack but his as well, producing their two towels. "I'm ready," she announced.

Walking along the trail at the edge of a steep cliff, Roman pointed down to a barricade of rocks surrounding a still pool near the edge of the riverbed. They made their way ever so cautiously down one of the many precarious foot trails until they came to the edge of the pool. It was about five feet wide and ten feet long, a little over two feet deep, with a small grain gravel bottom. Roman pointed at the sharply sloping rock face that rose thirty feet above them. About two-thirds of the way up, Juliette could see a large hole in the rock, from which gushed a rivulet of clear water.

"They call this place Rainbow Hot Springs," Roman explained as Juliette noticed the peculiar coloration on the rock below the source. "I don't know if that's the reason, but the different colors of the algae – those bright greens, yellows, and oranges – kinda look like a rainbow to me."

"So is that why they call this the Rainbow Trail?" she asked. "I saw a couple of signs along the way and I was going to ask you why it was called that."

"I think so," he replied. "At least, that's my understanding. They call it the Rainbow Trail because it leads to Rainbow Hot Springs. Or maybe it's the other way around. Maybe they named the trail first and then named the springs after the trail." He shrugged. "But one thing I'm sure of . . ." He paused, a most serious expression on his face.

She took the bait. "What's that?"

"I'll be in that water before you!" And he began to strip off his clothes as though they were full of ants.

"That's not fair," she cried as she peeled off her sweatshirt and dropped her shorts. "You can't start the race and run it too!"

"This isn't about fair," he retorted. "It's about hot water!" And with that comment, he pulled off his last sock and slipped over a large boulder into the inviting pool.

Within a matter of seconds, she was by his side, soaking away her aches and pains and rinsing off the trail dust and forest muck. As the early afternoon sun dropped behind the high canyon wall, they explored the pool area. Roman got warm enough to brave a quick dip into the ice-cold river water running only a few feet from the hot pool. Juliette found a shallow pool big enough for only one or two persons about eight feet up the rock face. When she got a little chilled due to its lack of depth, she rejoined him in the bottom pool.

As the sky turned darker, they huddled a little closer together, sharing their body heat. When their hunger turned more toward thoughts of food for their stomachs than for romantic souls, they toweled off and dressed by the light of the moon, then found an easier way back up to the campsite with the help of their flashlight. Some kind of freeze-dried mushroom and pasta dish swelled up with sufficient volume to fill the cooking pot and then expanded equally well in their bellies. As they sat around the flickering fire, snuggling together to ward off the Autumn evening chill, Juliette remembered the fanciful fable Roman had taped to the door the day she first arrived at his house.

"Is this Oz?" she asked.

"What?" He paused. Then it came back to him. "Oh, yeah. That. No, my dear, we're not quite there yet. But this is one of those places you have to go to before you can get to Oz."

She backed away to get a good look at his face in the glow of the last flaming logs. "So have you got something more cookin' in there, Bub? Something better?"

"We'll just have to see about that," he replied, pulling her close back to him.

"It's going to be awfully hard to top this," she said. "Rainbow Hot Springs. Hmm." She exhaled with a deep sense of satisfaction. "Are we going to stay here tomorrow too, or is there another spot for tomorrow night?"

"No, we're going to stay here till Sunday morning and then head back. You've got that late-night flight back to Austin, so we'll have to get away early, but we should make it all right."

"Umm," she said as she cuddled even closer and nestled her head between his chin and shoulder. "Goooood. This is good."

They began Saturday with a quick soak in the bottom pool and then set out on a short hike on up the trail about a mile. True to her professional training, she could not help but make notes on a few of the plants still identifiable in the high country at that time of year. When they returned to camp, they noticed that three other tents had sprung up in the area like brightly-colored mushrooms after a sudden rainstorm. As the afternoon wore on and their bodies wore down, they took the now-familiar trail down to the main pool, which they found occupied by four naked strangers.

Nudity has a way of making friends out of total strangers real fast, Roman thought, as he engaged in conversations with the group. The older couple, probably in their sixties, had hiked up from the same trail head. Residents of Durango, they came to Rainbow several times each year, often hiking all the way up the Rainbow Trail to where it connected to the Continental Divide Trail near Piedras Pass. The younger two girls, both in their twenties, had come down the Beaver Creek Trail after spending the night up near Sawtooth Mountain. Having backpacked around the area for the past four days, they were looking forward to meeting their ride at the trail head late Sunday afternoon. Roman listened with great interest to their descriptions of the superb vistas from the Continental Divide and made mental notes of the campsites his bathing companions had located. When Juliette's skin began to take on the appearance of one of the many dried fruits she had been eating on the trail, she took her leave from the group and slowly found her way back up the trail. Roman soon followed.

After another inflated one-pot supper of pasta and assorted bits of vegetables with a heavy onion flavoring, they loaded several of the larger pieces of firewood into the pit and nuzzled by the roaring fire.

"Hope I'm that energetic when I'm in my sixties," Juliette remarked, reflecting on the elderly couple in the pool, "hiking all over these mountains."

"Me too." Roman chimed in. "Wonder what their secret is?"

"You mean you couldn't tell?" she asked incredulously

"Tell what?"

"What keeps them going . . . keeps them young."

He looked at her to see if she was pulling his leg. Satisfied that she was not, he followed up. "Okay, what? What are you talking about?"

"Well, remember . . . Mary said they'd been married a little over thirty years. Or at least she said they'd spent their thirtieth anniversary up here at Rainbow two summers ago."

"I guess I didn't hear that. Maybe I was talking to Fred or something. Or whatever. But so what? What's your point?"

"The point is, they've been married all those years and they're still so in love."

"Well, I don't have any reason to doubt that, but I don't quite understand how you get from here to there. What does the fact that they love each other enough to stay married for more than thirty years have to do with them trekking these high mountain trails when most people their age are content to sit at home and watch golf or soap operas?"

"So you didn't see them?"

"See them what? What are you talking about?" His voice showed the slightest sign of irritation.

"What they were doing in the pool," she explained.

He pulled back to look at her again. With an air of the voyeur, he asked the expected question. "You mean . . . ? No . . . Really?" Although there was no one within a hundred feet of their campfire, he asked in a hushed voice, "What were they doing?"

Even in the dim light of the fire, he could see Juliette blush just slightly. "Well, when we first got there, he had his arm around her shoulders. And later, he put it more down around her waist. But then I noticed that she kind of tilted her hips a little and his hand disappeared under her bottom. And I could tell that he was playing with her . . . you know."

"How do you know that?"

"From the expression on her face. It's just . . . a woman knows how a woman looks when she's . . . well, you know . . . feeling that way."

"Well, I'll be . . ."

"And that wasn't all." She paused for dramatic effect. Roman was all ears. "When it got a little dark, I saw her slip her hand under his leg and play around with him a little bit."

"Really?" Roman was not completely sure that he was not the one who was really being diddled with, at least mentally. "Did he have that look on his face too?" he asked with a touch of sarcasm.

"I didn't need to see the look on his face," she said curtly. "A man's expression is told by the size of his erection."

"You mean . . ."

She didn't let him finish the question. "A good six inches, unless the hot water has some strange magnifying properties I don't know about."

"Well, those old devils," he said, convinced now that she would not carry a fantasy this far.

"So, back to my original point," she reminded him. "I think if you're that much in love and if you can keep your sexual interest in each other going even into your old age, maybe the physical fitness thing will just follow along. What do you think?"

"Maybe you're right," he agreed. "It sure seems to be working for them."

As the fire burned down, Roman rose from his place next to Juliette and placed several more large pieces over the coals. With a minute or two of fanning the pit with the lid to the cooking pot, he had the fire roaring again. He slipped over to the tent and rummaged around in one of the side pockets of his backpack while Juliette warmed the palms of her hands by the flames. Returning to his place on the log, he took her left hand and kissed its warm palm. Looking into her eyes, he chose his words with great care.

"It's taken me nearly twenty years to realize that I've been in love with you since the day we sat next to each other in eighth grade. I like to think of myself as a clearheaded kind of guy, but when I look back all those years, I can't believe I could've been so dense. I think back on it now and I try and try to remember what was going through my head and I've come to one great realization. And that is: I have absolutely no idea why I ever broke up with you." He slipped his fingers into the pocket of his shorts and pulled out his senior class ring. He had not worn it since his freshman year in college. It just sat in his jewelry box, tarnishing.

"After all we went through together in middle school and on into high school, this may seem a little silly now, but this is something you should've had from me during our senior year. So, as outdated as it may seem, I want you to have it now." He gently placed the ring in her open palm and carefully closed her fingers around it.

With a tear trickling down her cheek, she nodded and put her lips to his. As she examined the ring, Roman slid off the log and dropped to one knee. She looked at him quizzically as his fingers dug into the breast pocket of his shirt and pulled out a small black box. He looked up into her eyes, flickering from the firelight.

"Maybe at least with this, my timing won't be so rotten," he prefaced. Opening the box to reveal a diamond solitaire, he asked, "Juliette. Will you marry me?"

A flow of tears left numerous tracks down her cheeks as she nodded her head. Gaining her composure, she looked from the ring to Roman's face. "Yes. Yes. Of course I will."

"Then let me do this," Roman said as he took the ring from the box and slid it onto her finger. "We've got to do this right," he explained, "what with all that stuff Cher said in the movie the other night."

"Of course," she agreed, "we don't want to hex ourselves."

They sat by the campfire in quietude, feeling an internal warmth which rivaled that of the embers and flames. He broke the silence. "I've been giving it a lot of thought over the last couple of weeks, and I've talked to an agent about listing my business and getting into something similar down in Texas. You know, Austin is developing into quite a center for the computer industry. Someday it might rival Silicon Valley."

She lifted her head from his shoulder and turned to face him. "I've got a confession to make," she announced as she sheepishly dipped her head.

"Oh?"

"Well . . . I've been talking to some people . . . about coming back to Colorado." He could not tell if she was pausing to build up the dramatic effect or simply searching for the right words. "In fact . . . the people in Denver I was with a few days ago have been trying to get me to come up and work for them. Sooooo . . . I've been sort of interviewing for a job they have in mind while we worked on the project too. And, I've sort of already got an unspoken offer . . . if I'm interested."

"So, you'd move back here? Great! All right! Okay!" The usually eloquent Roman was suddenly struck with simple synonym disease.

"Besides, if you hadn't asked me to marry you tonight, tradition and hocus-pocus and *Moonstruck* hexes be damned, I probably would've brought up the 'M' word tomorrow."

Tears of Joy, Tears of Pain

They married on a crisp Saturday afternoon in late October – one of those perfect Indian summer days that bless Colorado in abundance between short-lived early fall snowstorms. Even though everything had to be arranged on rather short notice, few settings could have been more romantic. An old CU fraternity brother of Roman, who was also a longtime customer, had offered the use of his ranch just a few miles west of Castle Rock off Colorado Highway 67. Hesitant at first to have the wedding any place other than their home-to-be, when the groom informed his bride that his friend's address was on Rainbow Creek Road, the deal was sealed.

Auspiciously, the weather bestowed its blessing on the union and the backyard service did not have to be moved indoors to the spacious living room, which had been set up for the reception. As a concession to speed, they had declined to go for the big production. Only about fifty guests had been invited, mostly the family members and closest friends.

Since Roman's computer business was right at the high point of the selling season and Juliette had promised her new employer she would start within a week after relocating, the newlyweds had also decided to forgo a honeymoon. However, they promised each other that they would make time for it the next summer. Besides, they rationalized, they had enjoyed what could have amounted to two honeymoons over the past few months. Tentative plans were made to take another week late the next summer after Juliette had worked the six months required to earn a chunk of vacation time.

As winter set in, they found their days immersed in their work, Juliette adjusting to a for-profit, non-educational work environment for the first time in her career and Roman just trying to keep up with the thriving pace of the personal computing market. However, the nights were still filled with discovering and fulfilling the special desires each had held in reserve for the other since their adolescent days. Almost every weekend was devoted to skiing, hopping from resort to resort more like tourists than long-time residents. By the time the new year rolled around, Juliette had almost returned to peak form, even challenging a black diamond slope when the mood struck.

Shortly after their engagement, Roman had canceled his preliminary plans to go to the November seminar in Austin, electing instead to go to a large trade show in Atlanta the next March – then another in Dallas in late June. Juliette, too, was somewhat on the go after the worst of the winter weather ebbed. Early April saw her flying down to Albuquerque for a one-day seminar. In early June she was off to Phoenix for a two-day affair. Then in late August she flew to a prestigious three-day conference in Chicago, partly to schmooze on behalf of her new employer and partly to present a short paper that, her employer hoped, would serve as the springboard for a comprehensive book on the medicinal plants of the Rocky Mountains.

Since Juliette was scheduled to catch a nonstop flight out of O'Hare late Saturday afternoon, Roman drove up to Stapleton Airport to pick her up and take her to dinner downtown at one of their favorite Larimer Street bistros. Even though she had only been gone since Thursday morning, she greeted him with an atypically expressive hug and kiss as she came out from the jetway. As they walked through the terminal to the baggage claim, Juliette wrapped both of her arms around one of his and squeezed affectionately. Roman could not help but notice the furtive glint in her eyes and the duplicitous grin affixed to her face like a mask.

"So, you seem to be in a particularly good mood," he commented, hoping to draw her out. "How'd everything go at the conference?"

"Oh, fine," she replied demurely, glancing at him and then looking away, as though her mind was elsewhere.

"Was your paper well received?"

"Huh?"

"Your paper – the paper you delivered at the conference," he repeated, "how'd that go?"

"Oh, I'm sorry. It went just fine. Just fine." Again she seemed to drift off into her own space. Roman's inquiry was postponed by their arrival at the baggage claim.

As they stood there waiting for the conveyor belt to start up, he watched her mien intently. *No change*, he thought. She seemed to be enjoying a moment of personal reverie. Slightly piqued that there was something she was reluctant to share with him, he persisted. "Well?"

"Well, what?" she retorted. But her smile exposed her charade of baffled naivete.

"Well! I can't help but notice you're in a particularly good mood about something and I just wanna know what it is."

"Oh, it's nothing," she insisted, waving her hand at him and trying to look quite somber. But again an emerging simper betrayed her.

Roman's readied rebuttal was interrupted by the loud buzzer and sudden clang of the baggage system. "Oh, there it is. It's the green foldover," she said, pointing to the third bag emerging from the chute. Not to be put off, Roman persisted with his line of inquiry as they stepped out of the terminal into the dry heat of the late August afternoon and headed toward the parking lot. "Let's get to the car," she responded as shuttles, buses, and other vehicles whizzed all around them. "It's too noisy out here. I'll tell you all about Chicago once we get there."

Reaching their space, Roman opened the trunk and handed her the keys. "Go ahead and unlock the doors," he directed, "while I take care of this."

As he tossed the bag in and shut the trunk lid, he saw Juliette still standing by the rear wheel. Gone was that suppressed half-smile, replaced instead by a grin that ran from ear to ear.

"Okay, Jules," he demanded, employing her pet name with a tone he used only when he wanted her to know he was serious. "What gives? You've been looking like the cat that swallowed the canary ever since you got off the plane. So don't tell me 'Oh, nothing' again. What's got you so . . ." he insisted, waving his hands in the air in small upward spirals, "whatever you are?"

Her smile broadened even more. She took a couple of steps closer to him and rested the outside edges of her wrists on his shoulders. With her long fingers she stroked the back of his neck. She had just opened her mouth to speak when a spotlight went on in his head. He started to smile too.

Interrupting her, he asked expectantly, "Are you pregnant?"

She beamed and then nodded bashfully. He hugged her tightly, then kissed her passionately. As he drew back from the kiss, he clinched her tightly around the waist, arched his back, raising her feet up off the ground, and whirled her round and round, whooping. An older couple two cars away stared at their goings-on. A little embarrassed by the boisterousness of his reaction, Juliette tried to get him to quiet down.

"Roman," she whispered in his ear, "you're making a scene. Come on, put me down."

As the spinning came to a stop and he set her feet back on the ground, he noticed the older couple out of the corner of his eye. "We're pregnant!" he shouted to them. The white-haired woman just smiled and gave a slight nod in acknowledgment, but the old gentleman with the cane gave Roman forceful "thumbs-up" sign.

He turned to Juliette. "When? I mean, are you sure? How do you know?"

"I did a test when I was in Chicago. One of those over-the-counter things. And when it came out positive, I couldn't believe it, so I went back to the drugstore the next night and bought another brand and tried it. And it came out positive, too."

"Well, how far along are you? Do you know that? I mean, can those home test kits tell you that?"

"No, they don't do that. I've got to go to an OB/Gyn to find that out. And that reminds me, I haven't had any need to go to a doctor since I've moved up here. I had my usual checkup right before I left Austin. So we're going to have to look around and find someone. But to answer your first question, I think I'm about six or seven weeks along, but I'm not really sure. I was expecting my period to start around the twenty-fifth, but it didn't. And while I was wiling away the hours in my hotel room that first night away from you, flipping through a magazine, I saw an ad for that test kit and remembered that I had sort of missed my period about the end of July, too.

"I didn't think much of it then, what with all the changes, moving up to the mountains, you know, the altitude and all, marrying you, living in a new home, starting a new job with a new boss and new coworkers, and making new friends. And then there's been a lot of pressure for the last five or six weeks getting everything ready to present my paper in Chicago. I've missed months before when I was under stress and all, so I didn't think much of it. But this image popped into my mind when I saw that ad, so I asked the concierge where the nearest drugstore was and took a cab over there and bought one and rushed back to the hotel all giggly. I'm sure the driver thought I'd run in for a six-pack of condoms or something. So if my July period should've started about the twentieth or so, then I would have been fertile about the first week of July. That'd make me a little over six weeks now – maybe seven."

"But have you been experiencing any morning sickness?"

"Nope. None of that. But not every woman gets morning sickness. At least that's what it says in the pregnancy book I bought when I went back to the drugstore the second time. Or it might come on later during the pregnancy. But, whatever, I'll find a doctor and get this confirmed again. I guess it's possible that two different tests could be wrong."

"No, they're not wrong," Roman asserted. "The way you look . . ." he paused, searching for the right words. "I've heard people talk about that special glow a woman gets when she's pregnant and I've never really understood what they were talking about. But looking at you, I know now what it means." He broke into a grin broader than hers. "We're gonna have a baby!" he squealed as he broke free from her embrace and did a jig, complete with two 360-degree spins, right there in the parking lot.

Roman was on the phone all day Sunday, calling several of his closest friends who had families to find out who they had used in Castle Rock for an obstetrician. Juliette talked at some length to two of the wives, discussing their prenatal and childbirth experiences and covering subjects ranging from doctors to midwives and from hospitals to natural childbirth classes. When Juliette went into work on Monday, she pulled out of her file cabinet all the health plan literature she had been given during her first week on the job – pamphlets she had hardly even glanced through at the time. After digesting the written information and talking to the office manager, who had used the coverage when she gave birth to her now two-year-old, she called the health management organization's administrative offices. Somewhat to her surprise, the insurance company was able to provide her with only one name from its approved list of OB/Gyns in the south Denver metro area. His office was in Littleton, not Castle Rock, and he only had hospital privileges at Swedish Medical Center in Englewood. That evening, Juliette discussed with her husband the lack of local doctors available through her employer's HMO.

"Then why don't you let me see what I can find out through my company's health plan?" Roman offered. "We've never looked into covering you under my plan since you had one available at work, but I doubt that it'd cost me much more to add you to my coverage. And you might get another kind of perk if you drop out of your company's health plan."

"No," she countered. "I asked Jane, our office manager, about that already. Seems she thought of the same thing a couple of years back.

She and her husband live out in Aurora and she wanted an OB/Gyn out there and was hoping to be able to go to Aurora Presbyterian for the birth since it was only a few blocks from her home, but she had to go to Doctor Sanders too. And it worked out well for her."

"Did she end up going to Swedish for the birth?"

"Yeah. She's an avid mountain biker, so she was in pretty good physical shape through her pregnancy. Not that she still went mountain biking during the pregnancy, of course. But she decided to try to work up to the delivery, although she switched to half-time about two weeks before her due date. So when the real labor pains started a couple of days early, the doctor's office told her to go on over to Swedish to get it checked out. She was at our office in the Tech Center and Sally, my secretary, took her right up I-25 to 285 and it was a straight shot over to Englewood. Got there with plenty of time to spare. Of course, she was several hours into labor before the hospital staff even called Doctor Sanders. So she said it all worked out better for her than the Aurora hospital would've."

"You planning to work up until you're due too?"

"I've been thinking about it," she replied, "but I haven't talked it over with anybody yet. Jane and Sally are the only ones I've told I'm pregnant." She laughed sarcastically. "Of course, with those two, it's probably all over the office by now."

"So, who's this Doctor Sanderson?"

"Sanders," she corrected him. "Paul Sanders. Don't know much of anything about him except what Jane told me. She liked him okay, even though she prefers her gynecologist in Aurora for regular things. But Sanders is the only obstetrician the health plan approves on the south side. There are a couple closer to downtown near Mercy and University hospitals, and there's one out on the west side in Wheat Ridge, who uses Lutheran, and another up in Thornton near St. Anthony's, but the company just hasn't caught up with the growth spurt down here in Douglas County, so Sanders is the only one down this way. At least for now."

"Well," he conceded, "I guess that wouldn't be so bad. You said his office is in Littleton?"

"Yeah. On Santa Fe."

"Okay. That's just a straight shot up 85 from our house – probably only about fifteen miles. And then Swedish is just another four miles. I guess I could handle that when I'm in a state of panic."

"Look, Bub," she jested as she poked him in the ribs, "you're not going to have the luxury of panicking when I go into labor. I'll have a monopoly on the panic. You're going to remain your usual cool and collected self. You can freak out all you want to once the baby is born – but not before. Understand?"

"Yes, ma'am," he answered, backpedaling out of range of her sometimes lethal right index finger. "Whatever you say."

"Okay. That's better."

"So what do you want me to do about calling the health plan my company uses?"

"Nothing right now," she replied, contemplating a plan. "Let's do this. I'll set up an appointment with Doctor Sanders tomorrow. Then I'll go in for the confirmatory test and the prenatal thing and see if I like him and his staff. If I don't, then we'll think about alternatives." With that, their conversation turned to whether they should cancel their tentative plans for that overdue honeymoon coming up in late September.

Juliette was able to get a first appointment for the end of the next week. Roman took off a couple of hours in midafternoon and went with her to Sanders' office. As expected, the office-administered blood test confirmed her pregnancy. After the nurse-midwife completed the intake interview, she gave the couple several brochures on prenatal care, vitamins, do's and don'ts, sex during pregnancy, and natural childbirth classes. Toward the end of the visit, another nurse showed the couple into Dr. Sanders' private office.

About five minutes later, a tall, athletically-built man in his mid-forties whisked in the door. With his boyish good looks and a full head of dark hair, Juliette thought him more a candidate for a guest spot on *ER* than an actual practicing obstetrician. After offering his congratulations, Sanders engaged them in chitchat on a variety of subjects – most of which were covered in the office literature they had been perusing. When a nurse knocked on the door and handed him the next chart, he apologized for being so busy that he could not spend more time with them and excused himself. The nurse-midwife took the parents-to-be back to the front examining room, where she outlined a general appointment schedule, set the next appointment, and handed Juliette a recommended list of vitamins and other supplements. As Roman drove Juliette back to her office, they agreed that Sanders' office had appeared to meet their expectations and that the personnel seemed to be pleasant enough – even, Juliette added, "the now-you-see-me-now-you-don't obstetrician."

A little over two weeks after her first appointment, Juliette's good fortune in avoiding morning sickness ran out. "I don't know why they call it morning sickness," she complained one evening after another spate of nausea had passed. Then a few nights later, Juliette was roused from a deep sleep by slight pelvic cramping. Even though she took an Ibuprofen tablet, she remained restless through the rest of the night, finally dozing off for the last time just an hour before Roman got up for an early Friday staff meeting. Aware of her tossing and turning, he was careful not to disturb her slumber as he slipped out of bed, showered, dressed, and drove away. When Juliette finally rolled out of bed an hour later, she noticed slight spotting on the sheets. Disrobing for her shower, she found traces of blood on the backside of her nightgown. After telephoning her office to say she was running a bit late, she called Sanders' office about the bleeding and managed to squeeze in a quick appointment for ten o'clock.

At the medical office, the nurse took a blood sample and sent it over to the lab for analysis of Juliette's human chorionic gonadotropin level. Sanders reviewed her chart and reassured her that light spotting was not necessarily an indication of trouble with the pregnancy. While it was not normal, he said, it was not that unusual. However, he instructed her to telephone his office or answering service immediately if she began to have any additional cramping with a loss of blood or if the bleeding became heavy enough to require changing sanitary pads as frequently as once per hour. And if she was still spotting, even just lightly, on Monday morning, she was to call.

To Juliette's great relief, the bleeding stopped about midday Saturday. But the next Monday, just after lunch, she began feeling even more severe cramps below her abdomen on the right. In the ladies' room, she found that her pad was saturated. From her office, she called the doctor. A nurse instructed her to come over immediately. After reviewing the new HCG levels from the lab and performing a transvaginal ultrasound examination, Sanders delivered the bad news. "Juliette, I'm afraid you have an ectopic pregnancy," he said as he put his hand on her shoulder to comfort her.

"What?" she asked apprehensively. "What kind of pregnancy?"

"Ectopic," he repeated. "What it means is that the fertilized egg was not able to pass through the fallopian tube and down to the uterus as it should, and it's lodged in the tube and growing there."

"That doesn't sound good." She looked him in the eye, hesitant to ask the expected next question. "It's pretty bad, isn't it?"

"It's not a good situation, no," he replied. "In fact, it could be very dangerous. In many cases this kind of situation isn't caught it time and the embryo keeps growing in a space that's not big enough for it. And that can cause the fallopian tube to rupture. In less developed countries or in areas where women do not have an opportunity for good prenatal care, it's one of the leading causes of death related to pregnancy. So you're a lucky lady. I think we've caught this one, but we don't have any time to waste." Seeing her fighting to hold back the tears, he reached for the box of tissues on the table beside him and offered her one.

"I'm going to lose the baby, aren't I?"

"Yes, Juliette. The embryo never had a chance. If it can't make it down to the uterus and attach to the uterine wall . . ." He broke off his explanation as she lost her composure, pressing her tear-streaked face against his white coat. Holding her with his right arm, he reached for the intercom buzzer with his left. Ten seconds later, the midwife entered the room.

"Call Swedish and get me an OR as soon as possible. And see if Trisha Hill is on duty today. Last time I had an ectopic, she assisted me. If not, find out which surgical residents are there and let me know. And call Juliette's husband. He'll want to be there," he added, turning to his patient. "Won't he?" She nodded in agreement.

A Loss of Heart

Forty-five minutes later, Sanders strode into the surgery prep room, dressed in a pair of newly-starched green scrubs. "We've given you a very mild sedative just to calm you down a little," he said to Juliette, "to take the edge off. I know you didn't want us to take you into the operating room until your husband arrived, but we shouldn't wait too much longer. Hopefully, he'll be here in just a minute or two."

"Thanks," replied a subdued Juliette, dabbing at the corners of her eyes with a well-worn piece of tissue.

"My office had a difficult time locating him," the doctor explained. "I guess he'd just left for a luncheon appointment when we called. But if he doesn't get here in a couple of minutes, we'll have to go ahead." He put his hand on her shoulder. "Okay?"

In between wipes of her cheeks and her nose, she managed to glance up and give him the best smile she could muster – under the circumstances.

"Good. Good," Sanders repeated. "While we're waiting, I want to explain a little bit more to you about ectopic pregnancies and how they happen. I've been looking over your chart and the history questionnaire you filled out and I realize you've only been my patient for a few days and we haven't had much time to get to know you, but I wanted to get a little more detail if I can about your reproductive history." He paused to make sure he had her full attention. "You indicated that you've never had an IUD. Is that right?"

"Yes," she answered. "Never had one."

"And you said here you've never had any sexually transmitted diseases. Right?"

"No. Never."

"Can you think of anything about your sexual or reproductive history that you haven't told us about?"

"Well, the forms you gave me didn't have much room for detailed explanations and there are some things I just don't talk about much, not because I'm trying to hide my medical history, but because they were things I've had a difficult time putting behind me. And I don't like to dig them up. It's a painful part of my life to relive, you know?"

"I understand what you're saying, Juliette, but-"

She cut him off. "No. No. You don't have to explain. I'm not trying to hide it. I understand you may need to know because it may have something to do with my situation. So, it's okay. It's okay." She hesitated and then took a deep breath. "During my first marriage, several years ago, my ex got a little too physical with me." She paused again. "No, that's not right. It's just a bad habit I have of mincing my words when it comes to talking about him, kind of like I'm apologizing or something. I don't know." She looked Sanders directly in the eye. "To tell it like it was, he beat the crap out of me.

"The first time was about six years ago. The second one was a couple of years later. He'd hit me once or twice before the first real beating, but he'd get so down on himself when he saw my black eye or split lip that he'd cry and cry and beg me to forgive him. You know, really repentant. Classic pattern of the batterer. But I didn't know that then.

"So the first time he really beat me up, he avoided hitting my face – probably because he didn't want to have to look at the evidence of his handiwork. So that time, he pushed me down and kicked me in the stomach. I remember spitting up blood and having to go into the ER. Of course, I lied to them and said I'd fallen down the stairs." She snickered at the obvious flaw in her deception. "We didn't even have any stairs in our house. It was a one story.

"Anyway, the second time was worse. I had to have a friend take me to the ER again. And I had some vaginal bleeding for a couple of days afterward. Luckily, my friend called a woman's shelter and they came over to the hospital and counseled me on the spot, so I didn't go back to him this time. I went to a lawyer instead."

She looked up at the doctor, who had been busily making notes, awaiting his response. Then another piece of her history came to mind. "Oh, something else. Shortly after the first beating, I had a series of pelvic infections, like about every other month or so. They lasted for about three years, off and on. Guess the antibiotics the doctors gave me finally worked. But I haven't had any problems like that for years now. Not even menstrual cramps – at least until the last week. I don't know if that's significant, but I thought I'd mention it."

Just as Sanders finished writing, his attention turned to a knock at the door. Two orderlies and the prep room nurse wheeled the gurney into position beside the bed and loaded the patient onto it. As the orderlies left the room, another nurse brought Roman to the door. Sanders recommended that his patient and her husband be allowed a few moments alone and left the room with the nurses, closing the door behind them.

"We're losing the baby," Juliette said as Roman held her tight and stroked the back of her head.

"I know," he replied. "Sanders' nurse explained things to me on the car phone while I was driving in." He kissed the side of her neck, working his way to her cheek, then to her lips. "But you're gonna be okay. They've caught it in time and you're gonna be okay." She could manage no more than an affirmative nod. "We'll have the opportunity for other babies, Jules. This one just wasn't meant to be. Just not yet. But soon, honey. Real soon."

As they rocked in a tight embrace, Juliette felt a sudden stabbing pain on the right that not even the sedative could dull. When she let out a piercing shriek, he released her and pulled back, fearing that his vigorous embrace had precipitated her anguish. "Roman," she cried, falling backward on the bed, both hands tight against her stomach. "Get the doctor! Quick!"

Just steps down the hall, Sanders heard her wail. Hurrying back to his patient's side, he quickly assessed Juliette's situation. "Get her to the OR, stat!" he barked to one of the nurses. Roman jumped to the side as the nurses and an orderly rushed into position. "It's gonna be okay," he promised as he grasped her hand. Leaning over to give her one last quick kiss, he loosened his grip as the attendants rushed the gurney out into the hall. "She'll be okay, won't she, Doctor?" he implored.

"We were hoping to get in there before the tube ruptured," the surgeon replied. "Let's hope we're still in time." Sanders hurried down the hall to get ahead of the gurney, leaving Roman to a nurse, who directed him to the waiting room.

A little over an hour later, Sanders found Juliette's husband pacing nervously in the lounge. The surgery had gone well under the circumstances, he explained. Roman's wife was out of danger. They had stopped the hemorrhaging and successfully removed all of the embryonic tissue. Going in, the doctor thought he might be able to save the tube, but it had already ruptured by the time they got her open. After initially assessing the damage, he was hoping there would still be enough good tube remaining to make a repair, but he wanted to have the tissue samples examined by the lab before he attempted that.

"Due to your wife's history of extensive battery in and about the pelvic area," Sanders went on, "I suspect that the lab will find evidence of numerous occlusions within the right fallopian tube."

"Wait a minute," Roman stammered. "What battery? What are you talking about?"

"I assume your wife has discussed the problems in her first marriage with you?"

"Yeah. Well, I guess so. She told me the jerk hit her a couple of times," Roman responded, his face tensing with alarm, "but I get the impression there are some things I don't know. Is that right?"

"I don't know what she's told you and what she hasn't," Sanders answered, lowering his voice slightly, "but there are things you should know if you're going to counsel her about her situation. We may have some decisions to make in the next hour or so that'll have a significant effect on both of you – and your marriage."

"You're really starting to scare me, Doctor."

"I don't mean to alarm you, Mister Marchetti," the surgeon said in his most reassuring tone. "She's past the real danger point. We got to the hemorrhage before the bleeding could endanger her life. But . . ." He was interrupted by the surgical nurse, relaying the news that Juliette was coming out from under the anesthetic.

Turning back to Roman, Sanders motioned for him to follow. "Let's continue this with your wife."

Juliette was still somewhat groggy when her doctor and her husband arrived in the recovery room. Before Sanders could even speak, one of the orderlies knocked on the door and held a piece of paper up to the window. A nurse fetched the lab report and brought it over to the surgeon, who studied it while Roman stroked his wife's face.

"How're you feeling?" Sanders asked his patient.

"Okay, I guess," she mumbled, dragging her words.

"Juliette," the surgeon instructed, "you've got to try really hard to understand what I'm going to tell you. I know your mind is still a little fuzzy from the anesthetic, so I'll go slowly. And if there's something you're not following, you let me know and I'll explain it again. Now since your husband is here, if you don't think your mind is clear enough to understand what's going on and make decisions for yourself, you can let him make those decisions for you. Do you understand that?"

Juliette looked from the doctor to her husband and gave Roman's hand a reassuring squeeze. "Yes, I do."

Sanders repeated what he had told Roman in the waiting room and then explained the significance of the laboratory findings to them. "The lab has examined those portions of your right tube I sent over, and they're of the opinion that what remains of the tube is so severely occluded as to make any future chance of a normal pregnancy impossible. It's very likely that scar tissue formed both within and around the tube as a result of the two severe incidents when your ex-husband kicked you repeatedly in the pelvic area." Roman tried to mask his shock as he heard the words. *Oh, my poor darling*, he thought. *Why didn't you tell me about all that?*

Sanders continued. "Damage internal to the tube also could've come from any of the various pelvic infections you suffered after the beatings." *Beatings?* Roman wondered. *More than one? Oh, my God.* It was so like Juliette to not want to burden anyone else with her emotional baggage, he concluded. He held her hand tighter and gently stroked her forearm.

"While I had you open," the doctor explained, "I took a good look at the left side too. Unfortunately, what I saw doesn't bode well for your desire to have a family. Significant scar tissue was visible on the peritoneal tissue surrounding the fallopian tubes, not only on the right, where the ectopic was, but also on the left.

"Now, we don't know what the interior of the remaining tube is like without performing a hysterosalpingogram. That's a procedure where we inject some dye into the fallopian tube and track its movement with x-rays. But at this point, with what I see outside the left tube and comparing it to the right side, I think it's highly probable that the left tube is as occluded as the right. If the results of the HSG show what I fear, it'll mean that any further pregnancy via your left tube would be just as likely to be ectopic as well." Juliette cringed at the news, squeezing Roman's hand reflexively.

Sanders went on with his explanation. "Now, we've also got the question of the right tube to deal with. There's just enough tissue left to try to suture the ends together so that a pregnancy by way of the right side could be accomplished. However, I believe that tests will show that what remains of the right tube is just as occluded with adhesions as the tissue samples we sent to the lab. That means that any future pregnancy on the right side would be equally likely to be ectopic. And we know what a danger an ectopic pregnancy can be to a woman's life.

"So, what I'm going to recommend if the HSG results come back unfavorable is that you consider having a tubal ligation on the left while we've got you here now. That way, you wouldn't have to come back in a few weeks or months and go through this thing all over again. And, of course, I wouldn't make any attempt to restore the right side." The doctor could tell from Roman's expression that he had the husband's complete attention. And in spite of the medications, Juliette seemed to be absorbing every detail.

"Now this procedure will not totally foreclose the possibility of a future pregnancy," Sanders added. "You just won't be able to conceive without medical assistance. And what that means is that you won't be able to conceive by the usual means of sexual intercourse alone – where the sperm travels up the fallopian tube to meet the egg coming down from the ovary and then the fertilized egg travels back down the tube to the uterus. However, many women in similar situations have been able to bear children through the use of modern fertility methods. I'd be happy to recommend an excellent fertility clinic that specializes in in vitro fertilization and implantation. And there's nothing I've seen so far that would indicate you wouldn't be capable of having a perfectly normal pregnancy, or several of them for that matter, by such means."

Sanders rose from the bedside stool and took Juliette's other hand. "Do you have any questions?" The Marchettis both shook their heads. "Then you two talk it over for a few minutes while I check on a few things. If you want to do this now, we can have it wrapped up within the hour. If you want to wait, we'll have to decide whether you want me to try to suture the right tube or tie it off or leave it for another day. Okay?"

The silence of the recovery room enwrapped the two lovers like a shroud. Having hardly had time to mourn their loss of the promise of a first child, they were burdened with the task of making a major decision about their reproductive futures in the span of a just few minutes. Rising from his bedside chair to comfort his wife with a supportive embrace, Roman spoke first.

"What the doctor said, you know, about us not having to make a decision right now about the tubal ligation – maybe that's what we should tell him. That we're not ready to contemplate all these things. I mean, we've hardly had time to think about any of this."

"But I want to give you a baby," she entreated. "I don't know if I'm ready to have my tubes tied. It's just not something I've given a lot of thought, you know?"

"Remember what he said there at the end. Even if you can't get pregnant in the usual way, you can still get pregnant with medical assistance – in vitro or whatever. It's not like we can't afford that. But if you do get pregnant again through the remaining tube and it's ectopic, we might not be as lucky next time. I mean, he said that women can die from this. And even if the doctors catch it early enough again, maybe there could be damage to you internally that could complicate a future in vitro pregnancy." Trying to allay her fears and dispel the melancholy engendered by their predicament, he offered a moment of comfort. "I know it's your body and you have to be the one who makes the decision, but I'll be just as happy with a test tube baby as I will be with a fallopian tube baby."

"But we don't have to decide now, right?"

"No, we don't," he agreed. "But what's going to change? So we go home and you recuperate and we talk about our future and children and all, you're still going to decide that getting pregnant with medical assistance is safer than trying to get pregnant again through normal sex. The doctor says the right tube was clogged with scar tissue and that's why the embryo got trapped in the tube. And he says this test may show that the left tube is damaged the same way. So if by some slim chance sperm make it up the left tube and fertilize an egg, it'll get stuck coming back down the tube just like this one did. What's important here is your life. We've got a lot of other options for having children, but there's only one you."

He put his hand under her chin and peered deeply into her eyes. "I just can't take a chance on losing you like this again. I was terrified when I got the call from the doctor's office. I've just lived through the worst two hours of my life. If the doctor concludes that natural conception is too risky, then we should let him do what he thinks is best. Putting it off won't make the decision any different. And you'll have to come back for another operation in a couple of months and go through it all over again."

"You're right," she admitted. "If I weren't so doped up, I'd see everything as clearly as you and Sanders do. It's just that I'm not able to focus too clearly right now. There are lots of emotional things going on inside of me and I just don't have my usual clarity. But I hear what you say and I understand it all and I know it's right. So forgive me if I don't make sense at times but . . ."

Roman put his finger to her lips. "Shhh. It's okay. I understand." He caressed her cheek and leaned forward to kiss her lightly.

"Why don't you see if you can find the doctor?" she suggested.

Roman was two steps from the door when Sanders came back in, surgical consent forms in hand. After he described the procedures and informed both the patient and her husband of the risks, Juliette signed the paperwork. As the nurse restarted the anesthetic drip and summoned the orderly to wheel the gurney back to the OR, Roman took Sanders aside.

"I just wanted you to know," he said, "that having children is really important to both Juliette and me. But we've just found each other again after seventeen years and I just can't lose her. We understand what you said about alternatives to normal conception. If we still want to have children after the memories of this scare are behind us, the in vitro procedure sounds promising. Or we could adopt. Or maybe children just aren't in the cards for us. But however that part of it turns out, we want you to do whatever you think is best. If that test shows the remaining tube is blocked too, just do what you have to do so this won't happen again. I just can't lose this woman, Doctor. I just can't!"

Sanders burst through the double-hinged doors of the scrub room with the gusto of a boxer entering the ring. Trisha Hill, the surgical resident who had assisted him during the first part of the operation, was busily scrubbing at the wash basin. A petite brunette with a slim build, she was just completing her first year of residency at Swedish. Eager, bright, and energetic, she was a sure bet for a lucrative position in a private practice when her training was completed. Sanders joined her at the faucets.

"Is everything set up for the HSG?" he queried.

"Yes, Doctor," Hill replied.

"What about the tubal ligation? Have you gotten the spring clips ready to go?"

"Yes, sir," she answered. "Everything's in place." She switched her scrub brush over to the other hand. "May I ask why you're inserting clips instead of doing modified Pomeroy?"

"Sure you may ask," Sanders replied, assuming the air of teacher as he soaped and scrubbed. "Clips add the element of reversibility that snipping and tying off the tube don't have. This isn't a matronly woman who's already given birth to her fair share and wants to make sure she can never get pregnant again. This is a relatively young woman – early thirties or so – with no previous childbirths or even pregnancies. And she and her husband both want to be able to have a family.

"There have been a number of advances in microsurgical fertility techniques over the last few years that suggest to me that we may soon have reliable ways to clear even fallopian tubes as badly damaged as hers are of adhesions and obstructions. If these developments are refined while this patient is still fertile, she may have good odds of a normal pregnancy through that remaining tube."

"I went over to the lab and took a look at those specimens," Hill pointed out, "and I seriously doubt that any procedure will be able to clear the damage to the remaining tube if it's as bad as right tube was. But, I guess, if reversibility is that important to the patient and her husband, then clips are the way to go." Finishing her scrub, she turned to signal the nurse to help her into her operating gown. "If it's clips they want, it's clips they get."

"Well," Sanders admitted, "they didn't specify clips. That's my decision."

"Don't you have to discuss those things with the patient?" she asked as she waited, arms outstretched, for the nurse to bring in the surgical garb.

"Oh, no. That's the surgeon's decision – an exercise of judgmental discretion. The standard of care doesn't require me to discuss every little detail with patient."

"Well, you learn something new every day," Hill declared.

"They'll thank me down the road a bit," added Sanders as he turned from the scrub basin and waited for his gown.

An hour later, Sanders hurried down to the waiting room to find the patient's husband. "Everything went well," he said as he somberly detailed the results. "Unfortunately, the HSG showed extensive blockage in the left tube, and there just wasn't enough on the right to make a good connection. So we went ahead with the procedures we discussed with you earlier." He reached across and gave Roman a couple of pats on the shoulder, with a slight smile on his lips. "Your wife held up very well through the procedure. A real trooper. She should be coming out from under in about five more minutes."

"Thank God," said Roman as he reached out to grasp Sanders' hand with both of his. "Thank you. Thank you . . . for everything." He choked on the last words as emotion got the better of him.

"It's okay, son," the doctor said. "It's just what we do."

A New Approach

For the six months following her surgery, Juliette, still mending from the minilaparotomy, was more than a little gun-shy about another pregnancy – by whatever means. And Roman was certainly not in a frame of mind to push her. But as the colors of new spring growth came again to the mountains, reminding her of their magical trip along the Rainbow Trail, her desire to share a family with the man she so wholeheartedly loved rose to the surface. One evening after work, she surprised him with a handful of literature she had procured from a fertility clinic just a few blocks from her office in the Tech Center. Two weeks later, they had their first appointment at Mountain Fertility Specialists to discuss reproductive options, including in vitro fertilization.

A man of small physical stature, barely five foot six, but a giant in the field of reproductive medicine, Dr. Pirkit Radhavishnu was Indian by birth but American by training. Educated at the University of North Carolina and Duke Medical School, he had been one of the pioneers in the refinement of techniques of in vitro fertilization and other alternative means of conception since the early 1970s. Now graying, in his late fifties, his years of living the American way of life had done little to dampen his thick accent.

"Our clinic's success rate with IVF over the last year and a half is approaching twenty-five percent in actual births," the doctor explained after he had reviewed the results of all the preliminary tests his staff had performed on the couple, "largely because we have been refining our techniques, especially the chemical makeup of the medium in which we culture the fertilized embryo. That, and some other techniques we've helped pioneer, gives us a success rate a little bit above the national average. Now, don't misunderstand me. We're not to be tooting our own horn, so to speak," he added. Roman and Juliette glanced at each other, obviously sharing their humor at the doctor's choice of idiomatic phrases. "Overall, the success rate of in vitro is not as high as we think it someday can be. But when you see that only fifty-five percent of pregnancies begun through sexual intercourse result in a live birth, then the success rates of all the various assisted reproduction techniques are not really so bad."

When the results of Juliette's extensive physical work-up at the clinic and of Roman's sperm motility analysis pronounced the couple good candidates for IVF, in early July of 1994, the fertility specialists began treating her with a program of hormonal stimulation – Lupron, Pergonal, and HCG – to increase her production of ova. After nine daily ovarian sonograms and estrogen-level checks, the clinic staff was ready to retrieve the eggs. While Juliette had experienced some slight physical discomfort from the swelling of her reproductive organs due to the hyperstimulation, the couple's greatest source of discomfort was the burden of having to abstain from sexual activity for the last four days so Roman could provide sufficient ejaculate to fertilize the number of eggs the doctor hoped to harvest.

Juliette and Roman drove to the clinic early Monday morning, full of hope but cognizant of the depth of their previous disappointment. After Juliette was lightly sedated and comfortably positioned supine on the examining table, Radhavishnu began the delicate retrieval process. Directing a transvaginal needle toward the ovaries with the guidance of an ultrasound monitor, he pierced the vaginal wall and ovary and aspirated a total of fifteen eggs from their follicular sacs.

"This is very good," he told the couple as he completed the procedure. "Fifteen eggs is very good for a woman in her thirties . . . very good indeed." A little over an hour after the sedative wore off, Roman was able to take his wife home.

Late Wednesday morning, the Marchettis returned to the MFS offices. The in vitro procedure seemed simple enough to the unwary layperson. Each of the eggs retrieved on Monday had been fertilized in its own petri dish with approximately a million of the sperm Roman had brought that morning, placed in a carbon dioxide incubator for about fifteen hours, then examined with a microscope to verify conception and graded for viability. Radhavishnu had selected four for implantation and the remainder had been preserved in liquid nitrogen by a special freezing technique for possible future use.

As Juliette lay back on the examination table, her feet up in the stirrups, Roman held her hand tightly, stroking her brow or cheek when she felt a twinge of pain. Employing a catheter, Dr. Radhavishnu removed each embryo from its dish, placed the instrument into Juliette's vaginal canal, guided it carefully through the cervix, and delicately deposited the fertilized eggs as close as possible to the back of the uterine wall. Then ever so slowly, so as not to disturb the embryos' positions, he withdrew the implement. Within ten minutes, the entire procedure was complete. As Juliette rested on the table for a predetermined amount of time, the doctor wrote out a prescription for progesterone suppositories and instructed her on their use. Then he helped her rise and discharged her, directing her to return in ten days for a blood pregnancy test to see if her body had begun to react to the attachment of one of the embryos to the uterine wall.

The ten-day waiting period dragged on like twenty or thirty for Juliette. Usually calm and organized in her business affairs, she was given to shorts bursts of pacing about in her office as she watched the red-encircled date on her calendar draw closer. At home during the evenings and on the weekends, Roman noticed her flitting about the house, creating busy work and dusting everything in sight – sometimes twice in the same day.

Juliette was radiantly apprehensive the morning she left for the clinic, forcing down a breakfast substantial enough to conform to prenatal expectations. But when the blood test failed to indicate any hormonal change associated with pregnancy, her visage showed the strain of her disappointment. Yet Dr. Radhavishnu remained confident that his patient was a good candidate for the procedure.

Putting his arm around her shoulder as she sat on the edge of an examining table, he did his best to comfort her. "There are lots of mysteries about the human body that we don't quite understand," he reassured her in that thick Indian accent. "And the miracle of bringing forth a new life is certainly one of them. But you mustn't be discouraged by this failure. Most candidates for in vitro implantation fail on their first try. Many fail on their second as well." Releasing her shoulder, he stepped around in front of her and put his hand gently under her chin, raising her head just slightly. "There are so many things about these little eggs that we don't understand, but we keep trying and, more often than not, with the help of nature, we finally get it right." His beaming smile was infectious.

Before Juliette left the office, the nurse scheduled a second implantation for early September. The couple spent the intervening two months trying not to dwell on their first failure. Juliette, especially, became more and more upbeat as the next appointment approached.

As a trained scientist, she had learned to accept small failures in technique or theory throughout her career. For her own peace of mind, she now sought sanctuary within the same principles for dealing with matters of a deeply personal nature.

When the designated day came, the couple felt themselves better prepared psychologically for the next challenge. Having meticulously restored the cryopreserved embryos from the first egg harvest, Radhavishnu completed the second implantation with mechanical precision. Again, Roman was at his wife's side through the procedure, the discomfort of which Juliette seemed to take more in stride. But the blood test results ten days later were a little bit harder to take – for both of them.

"Don't give up," the doctor comforted her as he again broke the bad news back in an examining room. "We still have two good embryos in the freezer. Let's use those next time and do another egg retrieval first. And remember what I told you. A lot of women don't take the implantation until the third or fourth time. We'll adjust your progesterone levels again. Maybe that will help get your uterus more receptive." Juliette nodded in agreement, but Radhavishnu could discern that her zeal was beginning to wane.

The second egg retrieval was identical to the first procedure, a nine-day regimen of hormonal stimulation and aspiration in late November followed by another implantation the first week of December. But again Juliette's blood test failed to reveal a pregnancy. Her hopes for an early Christmas present for her husband were shattered.

"I know you're heartbroken over this," the doctor counseled her in his private office, "but I think we should give it one more try. I explained to you when we started this procedure that four implantations was my recommended maximum. Some fertility clinics may do as many as six before they get an implantation to take. But I don't recommend more than four. So let's use the best of your last embryos and give it one more try. Okay?" But he could tell from the lack of luster in her eyes that her hope was all but gone.

By the time early February rolled around, Roman had managed to lift Juliette's spirits and expectations. In spite of her personal discouragement over another negative test result, her husband had made their second Christmas together a real family affair, with the elder Marchettis making the short drive down from Littleton, the elder Abbotts flying in from their Arizona retirement community, and brothers and sisters in the Colorado area joining the throng. When the last of the relatives had departed, he had whisked her away for a New Year's holiday at Breckenridge. Even the pressure from Juliette's work had eased as her team wrapped up another major project the second week of January.

The couple's fourth in vitro procedure went as smoothly as the others, with Juliette trying to keep her attitude completely positive. Eleven days later, early on a Monday morning, she returned to the clinic for another blood test. Waiting in the reception area for the results, she unconsciously tapped her foot in a nervous staccato as she flipped from magazine to magazine, eventually finding reading matter acceptable to her current temperament. Not even halfway through the article in the *Newsweek* science section, Radhavishnu popped through the door, his smile beaming so wide Juliette could have counted every one of his brilliant white teeth.

"It looks like we've made a baby!" he exclaimed, waving a fax of the test report in the air. Mary Ann, his head nurse, was standing at his right shoulder. Juliette exploded out of her chair and the magazine went flying. After warm embraces and congratulatory words from the entire staff, she asked if she could use the office phone. The doctor escorted her back to his private office and shut the door behind him as he left.

"We're pregnant!" she squealed to her husband.

"For sure?" Roman cautiously inquired.

"The doctor said the blood test was positive. So I've got those chemicals in my body that only a pregnant woman has." Toning down her enthusiasm, she offered a conservative thought. "Of course, I guess he's going to want to confirm it with more tests later on, but he said the embryo has affixed itself to my uterine wall. Now we just do all the right things for the next eight or nine months and keep our fingers crossed."

"How 'bout a special dinner tonight?" Roman suggested. "Maybe Chinese, or whatever kind of cuisine is best for pregnant women. Your choice."

"I'll think about it and call you later today from my office. My mind is a little too scrambled to think about a dinner menu right now."

"That's fine. Or if you just wanna come home and I'll cook a special dinner here, that'd be okay too. Just let me know. Call me later." He paused. "Oh, and Jules? I love you . . . with all my heart."

Of Juliette's Blood

By the time she arrived at her office, the florist in the building around the corner had already delivered a dozen long-stemmed red and yellow roses. Sally, her secretary, looked at her expectantly. After a simple nod of affirmation from Juliette, both broke into girlish giggles. When Juliette finally had a moment of privacy in her office, she pulled the envelope from among the flowers and took out the card. "To Juliette. My dearest Love, whose courage and passion light all the rainbows of my days. Roman."

It was a crisp mid-April day. Eight inches of spring snow had fallen late in the afternoon the day before, playing havoc with the traffic in the booming mountain metropolitan center. But the clouds had blown through with the night, leaving a clear, deep blue sky hovering over the checkerboard of black roads and white lots that Juliette could see from her high-rise office window.

By Radhavishnu's count, she was now entering her tenth week of pregnancy. A five-week period of morning sickness had come and gone. After receiving repeated reassurances from her doctor, she and her husband were again able to enjoy something of a normal sex life, though the frequency had been cut in half. And she was receiving a measure of praise and recognition – from both inside her workplace and in the botanical research community as a whole – for her latest writing. Her life could not have been better.

The first pains, slight, yet persistent, struck during the last ten minutes of a Friday morning staff meeting. Concerned but committed to remaining calm, she disappeared into the ladies' room to check for any warning signs as soon as the conference concluded. As she peeled down her panties, her heart raced at the sight of two small spots of fresh blood on the crotch. Redressing with due haste, she returned to her office and telephoned the clinic.

Sally, sensing her boss' sudden distress, came to the doorway as Juliette hung up the phone. In her late twenties, with bright red hair and a face full of freckles, her looks and bubbly personality conjured up an image in Juliette's mind of a child star who had grown too big to play the lead role in *Annie* anymore. Although married for eight years and a mother of two, Sally still had a childish quirkiness about her that charmed her boss.

"Juliette," she inquired, "is everything all right?"

"I don't know," came the reply, as Juliette searched for her purse and car keys. Finding them, she looked at the worried face of her assistant. "I had a twinge of pain this morning. And there were a couple of drops of blood. It's probably nothing, but the doctor said to come right in." She tried to maintain her professional composure, but the strain forced a spurt of anxious emotion as she stepped toward the door. "This is too much like the first time when I lost the baby." Her face reflected her deepest fear. "I'm so afraid I might miscarry."

Sally reached out and offered a comforting embrace. "Did you call your husband?"

"Yeah," she replied as she fought to regain her composure. "Yeah, I did. He was down in Colorado Springs, but he's heading right up. He'll meet me there."

"You want me to drive you over?"

"No, that's okay."

Sally persisted. "Please. I'd feel better if you didn't have to worry about managing this traffic too. It's pretty bad out there."

Taking a deep breath brought on a rational moment. "Okay. Yeah. I'd appreciate that. Here," she added, handing her secretary the keys.

Within the hour, Juliette was wearing the familiar gown and sitting nervously on the edge of the examining table as Sally held her hand and offered words of support. Radhavishnu did his best to reassure her while he conducted an examination. But less than a minute after he disappeared down the hall, Juliette felt a sharp, stabbing pain below her abdomen. A few moments later, a second pang almost doubled her over. Sally had to grab her by the shoulders to keep her from falling headfirst off the table.

As the pain subsided, Juliette's face took on a look of panic. "Get the doctor back," she pleaded to Sally. "Blood. It feels like blood running between my legs."

Sally shot out of the room and into the hallway, calling for the doctor, the nurse or someone. From opposite ends of the hall, both Radhavishnu and Mary Ann raced to the examining room. With Juliette reclined on the table, the doctor and nurse captured what they could of the bloody discharge. "Rush this downstairs to the lab, stat," he ordered. "I'll get her cleaned up." Mary Ann disappeared down the hall at a quick trot.

After giving Juliette a light sedative and performing another pelvic exam, the doctor told his patient to change back into her street clothes. "We should have the preliminary results back by the time you're dressed," he added. "You can wait in here."

The lab report came back within fifteen minutes. The expression the doctor bore on his face as he walked back into the examining room just about broke Juliette's heart. "I'm sorry," he said, offering both hands as a gesture of consolation. "The lab report indicates that you've miscarried." Juliette fell into her doctor's open arms, staining his white coat with tears and mascara. Sally turned toward the window, her hands clasped together against her cheeks, emotion choking her breathing, and wept silently.

"I know it's of little comfort, now," the doctor tried to encourage her, "but miscarriages happen all the time. It's not anything you did or didn't do. It's just part of the process." As the doctor finished his sentence, Roman rushed into the examining room. Already having been told the bad news by the nurse, he took his wife in his arms and held her tight. The doctor signaled to Sally and they left the couple to grieve in private.

A True Friend

The last two months of that spring seemed to drag on at a snail's pace. Although Juliette was able to immerse herself in her work after taking a week of sick leave, the sight of small children or expectant mothers at the grocery store regenerated her melancholy. Try as he might to lift her spirits again and strengthen their personal bonds, Roman knew that she took the miscarriage as the final chapter in the story of her reproductive failures. And Juliette had never failed at anything. Never!

As the first signs of summer warmth graced the long afternoons of mid-June, Roman contacted an attorney up in Denver who had come highly recommended for her success in representing childless couples wishing to adopt. Although Juliette resisted the suggestion, Roman gave her a week's advance notice, hoping that the notion would sink in. During supper on the evening before the appointment, Roman broached the subject for one last time.

"We've got that meeting with the adoption lawyer tomorrow downtown," he reminded her.

"Roman . . ." she stated as though about to voice an objection.

He interrupted her. "If you can't make it, don't worry about it. It's just a preliminary meeting – fact finding and all that. We're not going to do anything but talk about the process and things like the costs and our chances. Nothing formal. No applications or anything like that. So if you can't make it, that's okay. I'll bring some literature home and you can read it – if you want."

"I just don't know if I'm ready to think about that right now," she explained. She could see the disappointment in his eyes, try as he might to mask it. "I'm sorry." She shrugged her shoulders and let out a deep sigh. "I'm just . . . " She did not know how to explain herself to him.

Roman reached across the dining table and took her hand. "Hey, I love you. If you feel happy, I love you. If you feel sad, I love you. For better, for worse, for richer or poorer, in sickness and in health and all that. Nothing's gonna change between us. Nothing's gonna change how I feel. If you aren't ready to talk about these other options, that's okay. You don't have to go . . . if you're not ready. It's okay." She nodded.

He arrived at the downtown office on Arapaho a few minutes late. Fortunately, Cynthia Belatron had been delayed by a hearing at the courthouse, getting back to her office just two minutes after Roman started leafing through a recent copy of *People*. A pleasant-looking matron in her mid-fifties, her once-girlish figure ravaged by the unrestrainable spread of middle-age, with short, speckled brownish-gray hair, she was smartly attired in a navy blue suit and flowered silk blouse. She quickly shed her jacket as she ushered Roman into her office.

"Gets a little warm when the sun is shining like it is today," she explained as she fanned the underside of her neck with the back of her hand, "especially when you're hurrying to get back on time to impress a new client." Roman liked her self-effacing sense of humor. After inviting him to sit down, she queried, "Your wife couldn't make it, or is she running a bit late too?"

"I don't think she's going to be able to make it," he confessed, avoiding the personal details until he warmed up to the stranger before him.

"Okay, then. We should get started." She took her seat behind the desk and pulled a fresh yellow legal pad out from one of the lower drawers. After taking some preliminary information, such as names, home and work addresses and phone numbers, and the like, she pushed the pad to the side and leaned back in her swivel chair, intertwining her fingers and resting her hands on her stomach. "This is the part where I go into my spiel," she explained as though offering words of caution. But before Belatron could begin, a secretary knocked and stuck her head in.

"Missus Marchetti is here," she announced.

"Good. Show her in," came the quick reply.

Juliette walked in with a forced air of professional composure, apologized for her tardiness, greeted the attorney as Roman made the introductions, and took a seat next to her husband, who moved his chair close to hers and took her hand. She gave him a reassuring squeeze as if to say, "I'm all right; I'll get through this."

"You haven't missed anything of significance," the lawyer offered. "I was just getting ready to explain the basic facts of life – as it were – about adoption – the law, the process, the problems and the joys." Again she assumed the position she had taken before the interruption – then talked for twenty minutes straight, detailing everything a hopeful couple could possibly want to know, all but the name of their first child. "Any questions?" she asked when she finally hit the end of her oration. Both the Marchettis shook their heads.

"Good. You two talk it over. Take some time to sort out your feelings about adoption. As I've said, the process can be painfully slow and sometimes the decisions can be difficult ones. My secretary will give you some literature to read over, just to refresh your memory on what we've talked about today. And she'll give you an extensive application form that you'll have to fill out and submit to the authorities. And she'll give you a copy of my fee agreement. If you wish to retain me, complete everything and then set another appointment. When you bring in the paperwork and the retainer fee, I'll get things in the works." She glanced at the two somber faces before her.

"You know, adoption can be a wonderful opportunity for people who haven't had the usual success with having a family. But the time lag can be exasperating . . . and frustrating . . . and intimidating. If you're willing to put up with the waiting, for what could be months or even years before a suitable child is found, then it's worth it."

Juliette broke her silence. "Do you have any children?"

"Three," was the reply. Belatron paused. "Aren't you going to ask the next question?"

"Do you read minds too?" Juliette asked.

"Sometimes," joked the lawyer, "when it's obvious." Juliette glanced over at Roman, who seemed genuinely puzzled by the apparent telepathic exchange between the two women.

"Are any of them adopted?" Juliette inquired.

"Two."

Juliette nodded, as if she had known somehow what the answer would be. Belatron continued. "I had some serious difficulties with my first childbirth. Oh, my son was okay, but I got messed up physically. And after that, I couldn't give birth anymore. But my husband and I wanted a second child, so we took the adoption road. And after a year of waiting, we found a beautiful two-year-old girl. That's where we were going to stop, but a few years ago, after my children were pretty well grown, two of our closest friends died in a traffic accident. But their baby son survived. And we were his godparents and there weren't any close relatives who wanted to take on the responsibility, so we adopted him. He's eight now and quite a young boy." She turned a picture on her desk around and the couple leaned forward, their curiosity aroused by the child's face. "Down's Syndrome," Belatron offered in explanation.

Their initial consultation concluded, Juliette and her husband walked out to the parking garage in silence. But back home over dinner that evening, Juliette finally dispelled the emotional fog that had enveloped her for months.

"What'd you think of her?" Juliette asked as she took another bite of broccoli.

It took Roman a minute to get his bearings. "You mean the attorney?"

"Yeah. What'd you think?"

"She certainly seems to know her stuff," he offered.

"And she lives it too," Juliette added. Roman nodded in assent.

"So do you think we should try to adopt?" she continued.

"Let's give it some time, like she said. Think about it for a week or two. Read through the literature and all. If you want to work on the application, we could do that in the next week or so. And if we're still going that direction when we finish with the forms, we'll give her a call. Okay?"

"Okay," agreed Juliette as she finished her trout and began to clear the table.

A week later, the Marchettis retained the services of Cynthia Belatron to represent them through the adoption process. But, as the attorney had cautioned, the demand for healthy Caucasian babies was high and the supply low. After almost four months had passed without even a glint of progress, Belatron asked them to come to the office to discuss their status. After rehashing her efforts of the past several months, the lawyer broached a new subject.

"Have you ever considered surrogacy?"

The clients turned to each other, seeking to refresh their memories, and then looked back at the attorney. Roman spoke up. "No. We haven't. But isn't that kind of complicated? I mean, haven't there been problems with the surrogate mother running off with the child?"

"Those incidents are few and far between," Cindy explained. "Most of them happened years ago, when the law concerning surrogacy was unresolved. And the courts were relying on legal principles and precedents that hadn't kept up with modern medical technology. Remember, when they wrote most of those laws decades or centuries ago, no one but maybe Jules Verne – or I guess Aldous Huxley would be more accurate – had conceived of the idea that a woman's egg, fertilized with her husband's sperm, could be successfully implanted into another woman's body. So while the courts were screwing around trying to make a silk purse out of a sow's ear, people were getting hurt – and surrogacy was getting a bad rap."

Belatron eased back in her chair and assumed her lecture position. Her clients recognized the posture and settled back for a concise lecture on the state of the law. "Now I can't say that the law in this state has necessarily kept up with the times. Our legislature is woefully inadequate in dealing with these kinds of issues. Unless it involves taxes or finance or a powerful legislator has a particular interest in the legal problems surrounding surrogacy, say a wife or daughter who is personally involved, things just don't get done. But I've read up a bit on the way these matters have been handled in states similar to Colorado – meaning states that are at least a little forward thinking and don't outlaw surrogacy outright as a form of baby selling – and I've talked to a couple of practitioners in the area who have managed to get a thing or two through the legal system. To put it simply, I think we've got a good chance, especially if the surrogate carries a baby that is genetically yours. From what you've told me, the fertility doctor you went to seemed pleased with the quality of the embryos he was getting."

Roman spoke up for them. "Yeah. We didn't have any problem getting them to grow in the dish. It's just . . ." He hesitated, fearing that the subject matter would make Juliette uncomfortable. Sensing it, she squeezed his hand to signify her strength.

"You see," the lawyer continued, "the problems that have gotten all the bad press and notoriety have come about in cases where the prospective mother is infertile due to an inability to produce a viable egg. So a surrogate is artificially inseminated by the sperm donated by the prospective father. Unfortunately, a few of the surrogates, at least the ones that captured the national attention, formed deep bonds during the pregnancy to a child who is genetically half theirs.

"Now I don't want you to get the idea that this will be a legal cakewalk. Far from it. The law in this state is too unclear. It just doesn't anticipate this situation, at least in black and white. But I've sketched out a legal strategy I hope will be a simple resolution. And if it doesn't work, we take the long route there. Whatever path we end up taking, we'll get there. If we can get the right woman for a surrogate and your fertility doctor can get her pregnant with your fertilized egg, you'll become the child's legal parents."

Over the week, the couple openly discussed the new idea. Juliette even called Dr. Radhavishnu and sounded him out. Yes, his clinic still had a few of her fertilized eggs in storage, as well as a sufficient quantity of Roman's sperm. Sure, another set of embryos could be implanted into the proper candidate. But he strongly suggested they find a woman of sufficient emotional maturity and childbirth experience. "If it's her first pregnancy," he explained, echoing Belatron's counsel, "there's a much greater danger that she will form a deep emotional attachment to the child. So be careful. Be sure you've got the right person."

After returning home from a Friday-night movie, Juliette brought up her telephone conversation with the Indian fertility specialist. Roman listened attentively as he watched his wife's enthusiasm and strength build. "So, what do you think? Should we give this option a try too? I mean, we can still have Cindy keep the adoption search going, but we'd just be walking down another path at the same time." She waited for his response.

"Jules," he replied, taking her hand and gently stroking the back of it, "I'm always ready to try anything. It's your decision. If you think you're strong enough to deal with the possibility of failure again – and Radhavishnu said there'd be that chance – I'll support you. Whatever you decide, I'll be there."

She leaned over and kissed him lightly. "I think I'm ready to handle it. I understand about the failure rate and all that, but I think it'll be different if I have to deal with that again – since it won't be my body that's being affected by the pregnancy. I'm strong enough to deal with what we're going to have to go through to find a suitable surrogate. Cindy's already cautioned us about that. And I really believe I'm ready to deal with the other problems that could come up if we actually find someone and implant my . . . I mean our . . . baby in her." She studied her husband's face and reflected on her luck to be sharing her life with such a man. "So, I'll call Cindy on Monday, okay?" He assented.

On the first Tuesday in November, Juliette dropped by Belatron's office and tendered a deposit to the lawyer's trust fund account.

Transposing the pertinent data from her clients' adoption application to a new surrogacy file, the attorney sent out letters to her various contacts and sat back to wait for results.

It was the middle of November. Juliette and Sally sat in their favorite booth in their office building's basement delicatessen, finishing their sandwiches and Snapples. "How's the adoption thing going?" the secretary inquired, hoping her boss did not take it as prying. They had become fast friends since the second implantation failure.

"Not much of anything going on there," Juliette replied. She glanced around as though making sure no one was eavesdropping and in a low voice added, "But I think we're going in another direction, now."

Sally's curiosity was aroused. "Are you going to go back to the fertility clinic again?"

Juliette shook her head. "No. No. Not that. I couldn't go through that again . . . I mean the miscarriage. I don't think I could handle another one." She glanced around again as though she were going to tell a juicy secret. "We're looking into surrogacy. Or at least our attorney is looking into it."

"Really?"

"Yeah. The fertility clinic still has some of my viable eggs in storage – as well as Roman's semen. So our lawyer is looking around for the right woman to be a surrogate."

"Let me get this straight. They'd implant your fertilized egg – yours and Roman's – into another woman and she'd get pregnant and give birth to a child that was actually yours and his?"

"Well, that's the plan," Juliette conceded, "but it's not as simple it seems to be. What I mean is finding the right woman to be the surrogate is the hard part. Our attorney has been making her contacts and getting some files of prospects for us and we've been reviewing the applicants, I guess you'd call them, but I don't know. A couple of them have physical or psychological problems – bad home environment and so forth. Makes you worry they might run off with our child or something. And one or two seem to be desperate for money, and that's a danger sign."

"Well, what are you going to do?" Sally pressed.

"Just keep looking, I guess. The right woman will come along. I can just feel it."

A little more than two weeks later, Sally knocked on Juliette's half-open office door, entering upon her boss' invitation. Closing the door behind her, she announced that she needed to talk about something. The seriousness of the secretary's mood caused Juliette a moment of concern.

"Don't you dare give me notice," Juliette warned, fearing that her trusted subordinate had found a better job.

Sally looked stunned, then figured out what Juliette was talking about. "Oh, no, no. I'm not leaving. No. I'm sorry. That's not what I meant."

"Whew!" Juliette said as she breathed a sigh of relief. Looking up at her secretary and friend with an air of expectation, she added, "Okay. What's up?"

Sally hesitated, as if groping for the right thing to say. Finally, the words just burst out. "I was trying to think how to put this so it sounds as important as it is, but I'm not that poetic or anything and everything I think of saying sounds corny, so I'll just say it. I want to be your surrogate!"

Juliette was truly stunned into silence. The two women just sat there looking at each other, waiting for the thoughts behind the words to sink in. Finally, Juliette's expression of astonishment transformed to one of curious amusement. "Oh, Sally, that's a lovely thought, but . . ."

"I'm serious," Sally interrupted, sensing that her boss had not absorbed the import of her offer.

Juliette's expression changed again, this time to sober inquiry. "You're serious?"

"I've talked it over with Bill, my husband, and it's okay with him."

"But why?"

"Lots of reasons. First, I really love being pregnant. Bill and I don't want to have any more children ourselves. The two we've got are enough for us. We'd never planned to have more than that anyway. And I really enjoy working and earning a paycheck and I don't think we could afford for me to take all the time off like I did after the first two were born. And Bill really does think it's a good idea. He said he was deeply touched by my generosity. And there's you. You mean an awful lot to me and I know how much you want a child – and Roman, too – and you'd be a wonderful mother and I know how hard you've tried and how you've been so disappointed. I really admire your courage and I . . . I just wanna do this." She studied her boss' face for some sign of assent. "Please think about it. Talk it over with your husband and your lawyer. And if it's okay with them . . ." Her voice tapered off as she ran out of words to express her feelings.

"Okay," Juliette acceded as she broke into a big grin. "I'll think about it . . . and talk with Roman and Cindy. Okay?" Sally nodded and rose from her chair. Juliette added, "I want you to know, I'm really touched – and surprised." Sally smiled and slowly turned to leave, but before she could open the door she felt Juliette's hand on her shoulders. Turning back around, she saw the streams of tears tracking down her boss' cheeks. In the moment that they hugged, Sally would reflect later, she could feel Juliette's spirit permeate hers, as though for a split second they shared something beyond their ordinary comprehension.

Bonding

After meeting with all the principal parties involved and gathering the necessary data on the surrogate and her family, it took Belatron less than three days to prepare the surrogacy contract. The Marchettis' attorney had insisted that Sally and Bill Rifkin retain separate counsel and had recommended May Lynn Kwan, an able young attorney who also specialized in family law. As soon as a fax of the draft agreement had been received and reviewed by Kwan, she met with the Rifkins. Meticulously, she explained each provision in the contract, discussed their rights, and counseled them forthrightly about their decision. When she was satisfied that they understood the full significance of the arrangement, she faxed over a couple of minor modifications to the draft. Within the hour, the contract incorporating her changes came back through. After a quick review, Kwan telephoned Belatron and set up an appointment to finalize the agreement. On December 18th, both couples drove downtown to meet their lawyers at Cindy's office for execution of the papers. After the signing, Sally and Juliette embraced while the other persons present shook hands. Walking arm in arm to their cars, the two women seemed like the closest of sisters.

Despite the hectic pace of the Christmas season, shopping for her family and planning their holiday activities, Sally ignored Juliette's supportive assurances that the matter could wait for a month or two and forged ahead full speed. "This is going to be my Christmas present to you," she explained during one of their lunch conversations. "It just won't be the same if we wait until February to get going."

At the Marchettis' expense, Sally presented to Dr. Radhavishnu's clinic the end of the week for a battery of examinations and testing similar to what Juliette had endured over the past year and a half. Radhavishnu detailed the full panoply of assisted reproduction techniques available to Sally, whose reproductive system was fully functioning and intact. Like Juliette, she could undergo an in vitro procedure. But additionally, since her tubes appeared to be clear of occlusions, she was a good candidate for both gamete intra fallopian transfer, in which an unfertilized egg and a measure of sperm are surgically implanted directly into the fallopian tube, or zygote intra fallopian transfer, in which an embryo is surgically placed in the tube and left to make its way, in natural course, to the uterus. As the fertility doctor explained, the success rates for both GIFT and ZIFT were two to three times that of IVF. However, there was a definite downside. The pain and discomfort level were greater as well.

After lengthy discussions with her husband, Juliette, and Radhavishnu, and careful consideration on her own, Sally elected to undergo an in vitro implantation. Two weeks later, with all the results in, the doctor started Sally on hormonal treatments to put her at the right point in her cycle to receive a fertilized egg. As the course of hormonal supplements neared the end, he scheduled an appointment for an implantation. Juliette stood by her secretary at each visit, counseling her beforehand on what to expect and consoling her afterward on what she had been through.

On the second Friday in January, the two women and Roman drove to the clinic together. At his wife's urging, Bill had gone on to work, content that there were more than enough caring people to hold his wife's hand through the process. After a short pep talk by Radhavishnu, his nurse showed everyone into the examining room. As Sally disappeared behind the screen to change into a hospital gown, Roman excused himself. "There's still a little modesty left in this world. Maybe it'd be better if you were the only one with her." And with that, he slipped down the hall and back out into the reception area.

As Sally reclined on the examining table, her feet in the stirrups, knees bent, the doctor removed what he gauged to be the best four of the four- to eight-cell embryos from their culture dishes with the transfer catheter and inserted the device carefully through the cervix toward the back of the uterus, where he delicately ejected each cleaving embryo. Tolerating the procedure well, Sally was aglow as she and Juliette joined Roman out front an hour later. Radhavishnu left them with words of hope. "This is very good . . . very good indeed. Let's keep our fingers crossed that this is the one."

The next work week was a study in contrasts. Juliette, the hopeful mother-to-be, seemed to be aloof to the date marked on the calendar, going about her daily endeavors as though nothing much was happening. But Sally was on pins and needles, staring at the large appointment calendar that was part of her desktop blotter like an exhausted employee waiting for the hands to strike five o'clock. The humor of it all was not lost on Juliette, who found herself continually reminding her own secretary about the business appointments, luncheons, and staff meetings on the schedule.

When the appointed Tuesday finally arrived, Sally dropped by the clinic on her way to work so one of the nurses could take a blood sample. Two hours later, the nurse phoned with the good news. "We're pregnant," Sally beamed ecstatically as she stood in Juliette's doorway, holding her arms wide open, inviting an appropriate congratulatory embrace. But their moment of celebration was cut short by an unexpected visit from Fred McManus, the company president, who dropped by to schedule a working lunch with Juliette for the next day. Since the women had agreed not to mention anything about the surrogacy arrangement to their coworkers until Sally was well into her pregnancy, Juliette stifled her exuberance for well over half an hour as she chatted with McManus about publishing prospects that had contacted him about the text they writing.

After her superior left, Juliette tracked Roman down at one of his customer's offices on the west side of Denver. "Ask Sally if she and Bill would like to go out to dinner tonight . . . our treat," he offered after hearing the good news. "I'm going to call that florist and have some roses sent up. Do you have any idea what Sally's favorite color is?"

"Pink," came the quick reply.

"Pink it is," agreed Roman as he signed off. Thirty minutes later, a slightly built delivery boy brought up two sprays of roses – a lustrous pink for Sally and deep scarlet for Juliette.

For the next six months, the two women seemed inseparable – eating lunch together almost every day and shopping for nursery furniture and baby clothes at the malls on the weekends. Roman had to be content with having his wife to himself only during the evenings. But he had no complaints, he mused as he recalled the fervor of their recent lovemaking. *With that burden of failure off her shoulders,* he realized, *she's back to being the same old Juliette again.*

As the weather began to warm, the alpine bushes and trees sprouted their early leaves. The springs and creeks started running at high speed from the melt of the snowpack. Roman yearned for a heart-pounding trek over mountain trails, for the smells and sounds of a roaring campfire, for the feel of cool, rarified air on his face. His mind had been too long engulfed in the constraints of civilization and he needed fresh postcard images of magnificent vistas to reinvigorate his spirit.

One summer night, after his wife had retired early, he sat down at his desk with a calendar, his topographical maps, and his favorite Colorado guide book and scratched out a number of ideas for trips. After supper the next evening, he brought up the subject.

"I've been itching to get up into the mountains again pretty soon," he said as she joined him on the couch. "It's been a while since we've gotten away for a backpacking trip, and I was thinking we might oughta plan something out and get it done this summer before the baby comes, and while Sally is still a month or two away from her due date and all. What do you think?"

"God, it's been that long since we were at Rainbow – what, almost three, no, four years?" she replied, gazing out the window at the rising moon, incredulous that time had slipped by so fast. "Whatever happened to our honeymoon?"

Roman chuckled satirically. "Oh, yeah. Our honeymoon. I'd forgotten all about that."

"Did you have something in mind?" she asked.

"Yeah. Yeah, I did, as a matter of fact." Eagerly, he popped off the sofa and scooted into the room they both used as a home office. Bringing a stack of notes and reference materials back to the dinner table, he shoved the floral centerpiece to the side and called her over. "This'll give us more room to spread everything out," he reasoned as he pulled up a chair for her. "I've got three trips here to different areas – places we haven't been yet. One would take about a week and the other two could be done in two to four days, depending on how much we want to do and how long we'd be willing to stay away."

As they explored the maps and reviewed the notes he had made on each proposed trip, Juliette seemed to drift off into her own reverie until Roman pulled her back with another "What do you think about that one?" Finally, sensing that she was not altogether with him, he threw it back at her. "Are you with me on this? Are you sure you really want to get away for a while, or are you gonna be so concerned about Sally and the baby you'll regret ever having left?"

The candor of his query came out of the blue. "No," she maintained, setting the record straight. "I want to get up into the mountains with you, sure. Sally and the baby will be fine. I mean, what can I do anyway?" She shrugged her shoulders. "I'm not a doctor."

She took his hand in hers and drew him closer to her, speaking softly of their tender times together. "I've been thinking about the last time we did this – when we went to Rainbow. I really loved it there, the hot springs, the canyon, the birds and flowers, the river. It was just great. And we talked to those people who'd gone farther up the trail to the Continental Divide. I was just thinking of that."

She turned to look her lover in the eye, her lips pursed in a pleading pout. "Could we go back there, Roman, just this time? These other trips are really wonderful and I can tell you've spent a lot of time thinking them through and they'd be great to do, but I'd really like to go back to the place where it was such a magical time for us . . . at least this time, before the baby comes and all. Next year or the year after, we can do these treks. But this time, for that honeymoon we've still never had, I want to go back to Rainbow."

"Sure we can," he agreed. "If that's what my love wants, that's what she gets." He disappeared back into the small bedroom, pulled out a large file from the lower drawer of his desk, and dug through the maps until he found the detailed topo of the Weminuche Wilderness. Back at the table, for the next hour the two of them digested every detail of the beat up chart, looking for trails, landmarks, prospective camping sites, and clean water sources, measuring the distances and changes in elevation, and planning out their route by the calendar. By the time they went to bed, they were both so exhausted it was as if they had actually hiked all the trails that only their minds and memories had traveled.

Sally began the twenty-fifth week of pregnancy with a checkup by Dr. Radhavishnu, who pronounced both mother and fetus "very good . . . very good indeed." As they drove back to the office, Juliette invited Sally and her family to join them for a July Fourth barbeque in Castle Rock. "At least barbeque and beer for us and a green salad and protein shake for you," she joked.

Thursday turned out to be a perfect day on the eastern slope. White, puffy cumulus clouds dotted the blue sky, drifting southeasterly on a light wind. The afternoon thundershowers the day before had washed off the accumulation of prairie dust that had drifted over the neighborhood from the grading of a nearby subdivision development, leaving the foliage clean and revitalizing the vegetation. With the relative humidity in the thirty percent range and temperatures only in the mid-eighties, Mother Nature became the principal host of the festivities. Roman's cooking and Juliette's canapes took back seats.

While the two Rifkin children frolicked in the backyard, the four adults lounged on the deck furniture under the shade of a huge umbrella. Roman hopped in and out of his seat every five minutes, checking on the mesquite smoker, which was filled with beef brisket and chicken. Bill sipped his beer and recounted his days in the Navy. The two children, Jacob, age seven, and Tiffany, age four, played with the toys their parents had brought from home. Juliette listened intently to every story Sally related about each child, from tales of her pregnancies to the present day. Every once in a while, Bill would pick up on something in their conversation and remind his wife of "that time when," triggering another yarn or two.

As the holiday wound down, Bill roughhoused on the lawn with the kids, Roman hosed and scraped the grill, and the two women retired to the kitchen to load the dishwasher and store the leftovers. "Roman and I are thinking of getting away for a little while in a few weeks," Juliette announced, wanting to sound out her surrogate about the idea.

"Oh, that's great," said Sally. "Any place special? I've been trying to get Bill to take me to Hawaii for the longest time. He used to talk about his days when he was stationed at Pearl Harbor, but now he doesn't much anymore since it always gets me to talking about the vacation thing again." She chuckled.

"Well, it's a special place all right, but it's not Hawaii. We're going on a backpacking trip up into the mountains."

"Ooh, that sounds romantic," cooed Sally. "Tell me more."

They sat at the kitchen table, sipping cups of peppermint-camomile tea, as Juliette related many of the personal details about the couple's first trip to Rainbow. "So it's going to be the honeymoon we've never quite had," she concluded. "And an anniversary of sorts too. It'll have been four years since Roman and I really got back together. And we're going to the place where he proposed to me."

"It sounds just wonderful," Sally commented, reflecting silently for a moment on her own romantic fantasies. "Maybe next year, when Tiff's a year older, we can get away like that on a family trip – do a little camping. But I doubt that we'd backpack in like you two are going to do. Just too many things can go wrong with children, you know."

"I don't yet, but I guess I will soon enough," replied Juliette, as she reached over and patted Sally's tummy. A sip or two more and Juliette changed the tone of the conversation. "But me getting away for a few days or a week, are you going to be all right with that?"

"Sure," Sally reassured her. "Look, it'll still be weeks before I'm due. And both of my kids were born right on or a day after their due dates. Besides, our little Indian friend says everything is going just fine – *very good indeed.*" Her spontaneous mimicry of the doctor's accent was priceless. "According to him, I don't show any signs of a possible premature delivery. All that's going to happen is that I'm going to keep getting bigger and bigger. Now if you wanna hang around Denver and watch my stomach pooch out instead of going off to a mountain hot springs and making love in a pool of warm water under a starry sky with that hunk of a husband you've got, then every day before we leave the office, we can go into the ladies' room and I'll take off these damn maternity pantyhose and you can stare at my expanding tummy. Okay?"

"I think I get your point," conceded the hostess as she laughed at Sally's hyperbole.

Family Formalities

As Belatron had informed her clients when she first introduced the idea of surrogacy, Colorado was one of the great majority states that had failed to keep its laws abreast of many of the most recent developments in fertility medicine. Although its legislature had passed a provision in 1987 to deal with the problems inherent in the parental rights and obligations of sperm donors, declaring the husband of a woman artificially inseminated to be the father of the child, irrespective of the lack of a genetic relationship, nothing in the law seemed to address the gestational surrogacy arrangement between Sally and the Marchettis. As was often the case when the express legislative intent did not specifically address the facts, creative lawyering of the highest order was demanded.

As the fourth month of the surrogate pregnancy came to a close, Belatron called the Marchettis into her office to discuss her legal plans. After reviewing her file to verify that the Rifkins lived within the boundaries of Denver's Second Judicial District and revisiting the Colorado statutes, she detailed the course of action she had devised. She would file for a declaratory judgment of paternity and maternity in a Denver Juvenile Court, instituting what was termed a friendly suit, in which all parties with an interest in the outcome of the case agree on the terms of its resolution and hope that a judge will see it the same way. To protect their right to privacy, the action would be filed with names of the Marchettis and the Rifkins referred to only by initials. Belatron would ask a judge experienced in juvenile matters to declare that the unborn child being carried by Sally was legally that of Roman and Juliette Marchetti.

"We're going to want to do this in Denver," Belatron explained, "because the district is big enough to have separate courts for juvenile matters like this. And I'm going to want a judge who deals almost exclusively with adoptions, paternity, and family disputes to handle this issue. If this gets filed in the Eighteenth," she reasoned, referring to the judicial district for the metropolitan area south of Denver where the Marchettis resided, "we'll get a judge who handles everything – from murders and rapes to water court disputes to auto accident injury cases. So you'll be the plaintiffs bringing suit against the Rifkins to determine parentage. And since they live in Denver, the Second District will have jurisdiction.

"And we'll wait until Sally enters her third trimester to file. At least under *Roe v. Wade* and its progeny, we can argue that, by then, the fetus would be considered a viable life. And besides, there's precedent in Colorado for declaring the paternity of an unborn child. So even though our state laws haven't been construed by the courts to deal with declaring the maternal parentage of a child before its actual birth, I've found a case or two from other states that we can point to in support of our position. And, of course, the best thing is we're not being opposed by anybody. But that doesn't mean it's a cinch, you understand. We've still got to convince a judge. Let's just hope we draw one who's forward-thinking."

"You mean not retarded?" joked Roman.

"That's one way to put it," Cindy replied with a snicker as she reached for a pen. "In fact, I think I'll write that one down."

The luck of the draw on the day of filing pulled up the name of Judge Diana Marie Fox, a twelve-year veteran of the bench and former legal advocate for abused women. A mother of two and grandmother of three, she was fast approaching retirement age, a milestone she would rather have the privilege to ignore. With a legal mind as sharp as a tack and a wit to match, she was one of the Second Judicial District's most well respected jurists.

After getting copies of a number of opinions and memoranda that Fox had issued and talking to several attorneys familiar with her court, Belatron filed a short supplement to her original legal brief and requested an expedited hearing. At the beginning of Sally's eighth month, on a Thursday morning in mid-August, those with an interest in the matter gathered in the courthouse to present their testimony and other evidence to the juvenile court judge. At Belatron's request, the judge had issued an order closing off the proceedings from the public and sealing all its records – a practice common in juvenile and family matters.

As the hearing commenced, Judge Fox asked for clarification from Cindy. "As I understand this matter, Missus Belatron, you are asking for both a declaration of paternity under C.R.S. section 19-4-105 and a declaration of maternity under section 19-4-125, is that correct?"

"Yes, Your Honor," replied the attorney.

"Well, this'll be a new one for me," Fox commented, her face expressing her sense of wonder. "You may present your evidence."

Belatron opened with testimony from her clients. Juliette gave a brief history of her attempts to become pregnant, from the first ectopic through the last miscarriage, and of the surrogacy arrangement with her secretary. Through her witness, the lawyer introduced into evidence copies of the surrogacy agreement and its related documents. Roman was next, testifying about his marriage, his desire to have a family, and his donation of sperm to the fertility clinic and affirming his desire to become a father.

Dr. Radhavishnu came on as the star witness – his complete files in tow. After drawing out the medical testimony and establishing the chain-of-custody elements required by the courts, Belatron submitted copies of all the MFS clinic's records on Juliette and Sally, including the recent results of DNA testing that Radhavishnu and an outside laboratory had performed. "Based upon a comparison of the DNA analysis of the fetus's amniotic fluid to the blood samples taken from Juliette and Roman Marchetti and Sally and William Rifkin," the doctor declared, "I can state conclusively – and within a high degree of medical certainty – that the Rifkins are excluded as the parents of this female child. The Marchettis, on the other hand, are included within the group to certainties of greater than ninety-nine percent."

"Your Honor will note," Belatron pointed out as she wrapped up her examination of the fertility specialist, "that the DNA evidence admitted conforms in every respect to that demanded by C.R.S. section 13-25-126 when paternity is at issue. And under section 19-4-125, the same genetic testing is admissible to prove maternity."

"Thank you for pointing that out," Fox replied. Then, turning her attention to the witness, she added: "But, Doctor, before you step down, I have a question or two." Halfway out of his seat, he eased back down and spun ninety degrees to face the judge, smiling broadly and courteously.

The judge glanced over at Belatron for a word of explanation. "In reviewing the cases you cited in your moving papers, I noted one of them indicated there was expert testimony to the effect that . . . uh, let me see if I can get it right. I've got a note here somewhere." She shuffled some papers on her desk. "Oh, here it is. In support of a similar position, the doctor in the case testified that the fetus has a blood system entirely separate from its mother's – that her uterus provides only a means of carrying nourishment to and waste away from the baby." Turning back to face Radhavishnu, she framed her question. "Doctor, if you would, please talk a little bit about that and how it relates to the concept of consanguinity, which, as you may know, has been the underlying legal presumption of parentage from time immemorial."

"Yes. Of course," the witness replied. "Admittedly, in many cultures, the cornerstone of what defines a family has been the sharing of a common blood between the parents and their offspring. But modern medical science has redefined consanguinity over the last few years. We now know that a familial relationship is not determined by the blood per se but by the genetic material – the chromosomes and DNA – in the sperm and egg.

"What you stated earlier about the mother's body – or in this case the surrogate's body – having a completely separate blood system from the fetus is true. Think about it for a minute. It's common knowledge that children who have completely different blood types – A, B, AB, O, and so forth – are born to women every day. Only in a small minority of cases do the blood types of the mother and child actually match. So we've acknowledged for many years that a child does not actually share the same blood as the mother or host who carries the baby. And I can testify conclusively – and I think this is what you're looking for – that Missus Rifkin does not have a common blood tie to the fetus growing inside her womb. Of that, I have no doubt. On the other hand, I will state with medical certainty that this child is, how would you say it in legal terms, 'of Juliette's blood'." He paused to read the judge's face. "Does that answer your question, Your Honor?"

"Yes," responded Fox. "Thank you, Doctor." Turning back to Cindy, she added, "If you don't have any other questions of this witness, Missus Belatron, he may be excused."

The attorney nodded to the doctor to step down, then addressed the court. "If I may further illustrate the point before I call the next witness, Your Honor?" Belatron requested.

"Certainly."

"On this idea of consanguinity, am I the blood relation of the person or persons who donated the blood that was transfused into me when I had my last surgery? If Your Honor has given blood or plasma in a blood drive, are you now related in a familial way to every person who might have been given your blood products?" She paused to let the answers to her rhetorical questions sink in. "No matter how ancient the principle, consanguinity has been redefined in modern times by genetics. DNA is determinative of familial relationship, not blood."

"Your point is well taken," Fox interjected. "You may call your next witness."

Sally and Bill Rifkin followed the doctor and gave their own histories of involvement in the surrogacy arrangement with the Marchettis, reaffirming at every opportunity their disavowal of any parental interest in the child. May Lynn Kwan also rose from her seat at the Rifkins' counsel table to assure the court that her clients had been effectively represented by separate legal counsel throughout the surrogacy process. At the conclusion of the presentation of her evidence, Belatron stood before the bench and requested a court decree that the unborn child being carried to term by Sally Rifkin was the natural child of Juliette and Roman Marchetti and an order that the birth certificate be issued which would reflect their parentage of the baby girl.

Judge Fox, who had been carefully studying the documentary evidence, leaned forward in her chair, resting her arms on her desktop. One hand reached up and slid her reading glasses down to the tip of her nose. "Missus Belatron, in your motion, you claim authority under provisions of the Children's Code, but, as you must know, there are no reported cases in this state in which those provisions were applied in the way you envision."

"That's correct, Your Honor. We're not aware of any Colorado court that has applied section 19-4-101, *et seq.*, the way we propose. But, as we've put forth in our briefs, the California Supreme Court was faced with a similar situation in the *Johnson v. Calvert* case and that court applied California's version of the Uniform Parentage Act to the facts. Your Honor will note the table we've attached to the brief in which we set forth the various provisions of the model legislation applicable here – the exact language of each of the statutes for Colorado, California, and Ohio being set forth in the first three columns and the Uniform Parentage Act provisions in the fourth. By comparing the language, you can see that the provisions are virtually identical."

"So you're suggesting that the Colorado courts should follow the California precedent and construe our version of the Uniform Parentage Act to apply to a case in which maternity is at issue?"

"Yes, Your Honor. That's exactly what we're urging," Belatron replied emphatically. "But even if this court did not agree with the reasoning of the California court, alternatively we would urge the court to declare maternity under the common law, as did the Ohio trial judge in the case of *Belisto v. Clark*. Of course, we feel that the *Belisto* case is distinguishable from *Johnson* because the Ohio legislature specifically excluded surrogacy matters from the purview of that state's version of the Uniform Parentage Act. And, of course, the trial judge could not use the same provisions that the *Johnson* court had applied to reach the equitable solution. But, Your Honor, the important thing is this – both courts, no matter which course each one took, arrived at the same conclusion. The woman who provided the eggs in a gestational surrogacy arrangement was the natural mother of the child."

Belatron paused, studying the jurist's face. Years of experience compelled her to continue. The judge could see the right outcome; now she just had to be convinced that there was a sound legal basis for it. "We don't mind going out on a limb, Counselor," one of the district court judges had exhorted Cindy during her first year or two of practice. "Just make sure the branch is thick enough and strong enough to hold the weight." Fox needed more.

"And even if Your Honor regards the reasoning in *Belisto* to be more persuasive," Cindy went on, "we're simply asking this court to recognize that the Colorado legislature did not envision this medical advancement when it last debated amendments to the Children's Code. What my clients are asking this court to do is what courts have been doing for centuries – by fiat of common law, declare what makes common sense. Legislatures are often not able to keep up with the rapid advancements we're seeing in all fields of science and technology, whether it be fertility medicine or computer science, and it falls upon the courts to fashion remedies where the legislature has not acted.

"The simple, incontrovertible facts before the court are these. First, the egg that was necessary to create this living being was taken from the body of Juliette Marchetti. Second, the sperm that fertilized that egg came from her husband, Roman Marchetti. Third, the gestational surrogate, Sally Rifkin, shares no genetic kinship with the baby developing inside her womb. Fourth, Sally's husband, Bill Rifkin, has not made any contribution of genetic material to the creation of the child in his wife's womb.

"A final point I wish to make relates to what will happen if this court does not issue the decree we have proposed. At the time of the birth of this child, Sally Rifkin will be legally decreed its mother. Bill Rifkin will be presumed by the law to be the child's father. In order to enforce the surrogacy contract between the Marchettis and the Rifkins, they will have to file another friendly action, by which demand is made that Bill and Sally surrender all parental rights. At the same time, the Marchettis, will have to file for adoption of the child – their *own* child. The Marchettis will then have to undergo an extensive background check, fitness examination, and screening. Since Social Services is backlogged, they'll have to go through a private licensed adoption agency if they want to expedite the adoption process. And they'll have to pay those fees. When the agency completes its report, the court will have to review and examine the adoptive parents. Yet all that trouble, emotional anguish, legal expense, and court time could easily be avoided by using a little common sense – now, here, today.

"If I may inject a lighter note, Your Honor, my clients have one other option – and that would be to petition the state legislature and lobby for a change in the statutes and, when that's finally accomplished, probably about the time the child is ready to go off to college, they can be recognized as her parents." Everyone in the courtroom chuckled at the absurdity of Belatron's final option.

"Well," the judge retorted, injecting her own sense of levity into the proceedings, "this child may be the result of the miracle of modern science, but if your clients could get our legislature to act that swiftly, now that would really be a miracle." After the laughter had settled down, Fox continued. "But aren't you asking this court to make law here?" she inquired, her expression soured by the thought. "You know that the courts are not kindly disposed to judicial legislation."

"We do understand that Your Honor, but the facts of this case cry for a different outlook. The courts are often called upon to interpret the laws of the legislative body, and frequently the judicial branch has little to go on to determine legislative intent. And on occasion, the courts are called upon to formulate a rule of law when they determine that legislators have not promulgated laws applicable to the facts in a given case. The common law is a rich tradition from which have come many of the legislative codifications of today. If I may illustrate my point with one example. Your Honor is well aware that much of the law of negligence developed over the centuries through the judiciary, not the legislatures. And few would doubt the rich tradition that such forward-thinking judges have given to the development of the legal system we have today."

"A point well made," the judge noted, tapping her pen on the legal pad as she formulated her next question.

"If I may, Your Honor," Belatron requested, "what we're asking the court to do is simple. Sally Rifkin is pregnant. Doctor Radhavishnu has testified about the custody and control of the genetic materials he received from the Marchettis up until the time he implanted Juliette's fertilized eggs in the uterus of Sally Rifkin. He has further testified that Missus Rifkin tested positive for pregnancy within ten days of the implantation, which would indicate that one of the fertilized ova the doctor had implanted successfully attached to the uterine wall. And the Rifkins testified that they had abstained from sexual intercourse during the required time. And most important, Doctor Radhavishnu certified the results of testing on the amniotic fluid of the developing fetus, which proves conclusively that the child Sally is carrying is the biological offspring of Juliette and Roman Marchetti. We are asking the court to build upon the rich tradition of the common law and to use its common sense."

"I do have one other problem I would like you to address, Counselor," added the judge. "And that concerns the right of the Marchettis — specifically Missus Marchetti–to make health care decisions about the baby. And my concern is that legal recognition of their parental rights might be misconstrued to give them some authority to make decisions concerning the health care of the surrogate, Missus Rifkin. And that's something I have been wrestling with."

"We understand the court's apprehensions, Your Honor," Belatron acknowledged. "And neither I nor my clients – and, I dare say, Miss Kwan and her clients – would have any problem with language in the order to the effect that the right to make decisions about the baby's health care shall be held by Missus Rifkin up until the moment of birth." She glanced over her shoulder for signs of concurrence from her clients, then at Kwan and the Rifkins for the same.

Kwan rose briefly to address the court. "We would have no problem with that, Your Honor."

The judge scribbled down her last notes and then thanked those present for their attendance. "I have certainly received an education in both science and the law here today." Turning her head to address the lead advocate, Fox concluded the proceedings. "I will take this under advisement and would hope to issue a ruling within the next two weeks. Missus Belatron, if you have not received my order by then, please feel free to contact my clerk." With that she rose from the bench and left for her chambers.

The order came by fax a week later, with a follow-up copy by mail. By declaration of the court, the child being carried by Sally Rifkin was that of Roman and Juliette Marchetti, the natural parents. The order directed the person who prepared the certificate of birth to reflect the same. That evening was spent in high celebration as the Marchettis took the whole lot, the Rifkins, Cindy and her husband, and Miss Kwan and her date, out for a Friday night of dinner and dancing.

One Last Trek

It was early on the last Friday morning in August. Judging by the cool, crisp feel of the predawn air in the mountain highlands, Summer, with her cloak of greens and golds, was giving way begrudgingly to her more variegated cousin, Autumn. Roman had spent the previous evening doing the final rundown through their checklists and meticulously loading their backpacks, separating the items they would be using the two or three nights they were staying in town from those that they would need on the trail. Meanwhile, Juliette put in extra hours at her desk in the small bedroom finishing her review of the final publisher's pages on the book she had coauthored. Their missions accomplished, they had both hit the sack early, setting the alarm for an hour before their usual rising time. With luck, they assumed, they would be able to put in a few more hours on their last day of work before their honeymoon-vacation back to Rainbow.

Roman hit the shower within minutes after the clock radio switched on, but Juliette hit the snooze button and rolled over, burying her head under the king-size down pillow. Whether she actually got those extra ten minutes was open to question. A gentle shake from her husband finally got her out of bed. While Roman dressed and headed to the kitchen to grab some breakfast and fix his brown bag lunch, Juliette jumped in the shower. As she toweled off, she felt a short series of light stomach cramps. Throwing on her robe, she combed through her hair and went to find her husband. Just as she kissed him good morning, another light twinge struck.

"You okay?" he asked as he slipped two pieces of whole wheat bread into the toaster.

"Just a cramp," she replied, tossing her wet hair to the other side and combing it from the nape of her neck. "It's probably my period coming on," she surmised with a touch of exasperation in her voice, "finally!"

"In here?" He ran his hand across the left side of his stomach below the navel.

"Yeah. About there."

"Me too," he added as he made a face. "I've been feeling a little queasy this morning. Think it was the Thai food we ate at that place in Denver last night? I'd never been there before, but one of my customers said it was good. Maybe there was something in the sauce."

"Maybe," she conceded. Roman poured her a glass of juice. She took it and sipped slowly, still combing. "I've eaten my share of Thai food before, but not that stuff I ate last night." She made a strange face. "I guess it just didn't agree with us." The mere recollection of their evening meal seemed to temper both of their appetites. Instead of going for the frying pan and their usual eggs-over-easy, they settled on the toast and orange juice and headed out for their respective workplaces.

With a heavy box of publishers' proofs under one arm and her purse and laptop computer draped from the other side, Juliette trudged up the routine two flights of stairs from her space in the basement parking garage to her office building lobby, leaving her feeling slightly warm and lightheaded as she waited for the elevator. *A fine time we're going to have backpacking into the high country,* she thought, *if I get whipped climbing two flights of stairs.* But by the time she walked into her office, the dizziness had passed.

Shortly before lunch, a short spasm of cramp-like pains stronger than the ones that hit her in the shower prompted Juliette to call Dr. Sanders, who she had resumed seeing as her regular OB/Gyn after the IVF miscarriage. When she explained to his nurse that she and her husband were going out of town the next day for up to a week, she was able to get penciled in on his calendar as his last appointment of the day. Working right through lunch so she could complete her pre-vacation assignments, she paused long enough on her way out to share a tender goodbye with Sally and made the short drive over to Sanders' Littleton office.

After relating her history and symptoms to the nurse-midwife, Juliette offered the conclusion about food poisoning she and her husband had reached earlier that morning. She also suggested to the nurse that she could be having strong premenstrual cramps since her period had been quite irregular lately. Responding to a question from the nurse about whether Juliette had been under a lot of stress recently, she conceded that the last few months had been a pressure cooker. She had been working late hours for the past three weeks to finish drafting up a new project proposal. And the manuscript on native medicinal plants she had written with her boss and a pharmacology professor in Minnesota was in the final proof stage. Then there was the surrogacy arrangement, with its legal maze of pleadings and hearings.

On top of all that, her husband's aunt and uncle had flown in from New York in mid-July to visit all the Marchetti families in the Denver area. Then her parents had come up from Arizona for ten days in early August. And now she and her husband were trying to get away on an extensive backpacking trip, which had taken hours to plan and provision. "We never did get to take our honeymoon," she reflected. "I started a new job right after we got married and then got pregnant and all."

Just as she finished her explanation, Sanders entered the examining room, receiving the chart from the nurse and glancing over the most recent notes. In spite of a long workday, he still managed his usual charming smile. As he palpated Juliette's abdomen, she winced slightly at the pressure of his fingers. After completing his pelvic exam and taking a smear of vaginal secretions, he scribbled his impressions on the chart and wrote out a prescription. "I'll be back in a minute," he said. "You can go ahead and get dressed."

One minute turned into several as Juliette waited anxiously, fearing that the delay presaged news that could threaten her week's plans. Finally he returned. "Well," he explained, "it could be a slight case of food poisoning, or it could be cramps because you're late. If it's food poisoning, it's quite mild. You haven't been experiencing any diarrhea or significant nausea and I would expect an escalation of those symptoms if it's bacterial in nature. So I don't think an antibiotic is called for right now. And they can do more harm than good if they're over prescribed." He handed her the small slip of paper.

"I normally wouldn't recommend anything for a mild case of food toxicity but a light painkiller, which is what I'd also recommend for the cramps. You don't have a history of strong premenstrual cramps, but you have had them off and on, maybe once or twice every year or so. And given your history of repeated episodes of pelvic inflammatory disease, I want to make sure it's not a recurrence of a strain that might've been dormant for a while. We've taken a smear and will send it over to the lab for a culture. If there's something there, we'll get it."

He paused and flipped through her file until he found the records he wanted.

"I remember we talked a little bit about this back when I did that emergency surgery for the ectopic, but is it possible that your first husband could have given you a sexually transmitted disease?" She appeared stunned by the very suggestion. "I ask that because sometimes they can come and go like this," he explained further. "And that could account for the damage we saw to your fallopian tubes during the surgery."

"I don't know," she replied, digging for an answer into a past life she would rather be able to forget. "If he did, he never told me about it. But as confused and depressed as he was during our last couple of years together, he could've picked up something if he was sleeping around. So I guess it's possible."

The doctor continued to add notes to her chart. "Did you ever have any pelvic inflammations before your first marriage?"

"No, not that I recall. No."

"How about during the first couple of years of that marriage?"

"No. No. I don't think I had one until we first started having problems . . . you know, physically, with the abuse. So I guess I just related the pelvic pain to the kicking and all."

"That may be the case," Sanders surmised. "It could be that the scar tissue I made notes about in these surgical records came from those beatings, but it might have also come from some disease process. So we'll have the lab run cultures for the most common STDs. If that's what this is, we'll be able to control it without any problem. But it's probably what you thought . . . just some bad food or a strong set of premenstrual cramps. Or it could be a low-grade pelvic infection."

"I hope it's just something minor," she said. "We're leaving town tomorrow and heading up into the mountains for a few days. I certainly don't want some kind of infection spoiling our trip."

"Well, that shouldn't happen," Sanders reassured her. Glancing at his watch, he added, "As late as it is, we're not going to get the lab results until early next week. So that prescription I gave you is for an analgesic that's a little bit stronger than what you can get over the counter. There should be enough there for a week, but you might want to take some Ibuprofen or Acetaminophen along with you anyway. This shouldn't be anything that would affect your backpacking trip. In fact, the exercise and lots of fresh air would probably be beneficial, considering the stress you've been under. Your immune system is probably depleted of its reserves, and that could be why you're susceptible to this right now. So don't worry about anything. Take a painkiller if you need one and get out and enjoy this weather. And try to be near a phone Monday or Tuesday so you can call our office and see if we have the lab results back. If there's some kind of pelvic infection, I can call in a script for an antibiotic to a pharmacy near where you are." With that comment, he left her and disappeared into his private office at the end of the hall.

Stopping off at the drugstore nearest Sanders' office to have the prescription filled, she took one of the pills before getting back on the freeway to Castle Rock. Caught up in the mess of end-of-week rush hour traffic, it took her nearly forty minutes to get as far as the Denver Tech Center, the starting point of her earlier trip. Another hour later, she finally made it home, getting the front door unlocked just as Roman pulled into the driveway. After commiserating about their hectic workdays and persistent stomachaches and her horrible traffic, they loaded the 4Runner with the gear they had packed and retired early. After taking a long, hot bubble bath and another one of the prescription pills, Juliette slept soundly through the night without further discomfort.

The crack of dawn filtering through the sheer bedroom curtains woke Juliette up before the alarm clock could sound. Feeling a dull ache, she popped a pill with her morning orange juice, then roused her snoring husband. Hitting the shower but skipping the shave, Roman grabbed a bottle of juice and a couple of bagels for breakfast and announced he was ready to hit the road. Within minutes, they were on the interstate, heading south to Walsenberg, then east on U.S. 160 south of Blanco Peak, across the San Luis Valley, and on toward Wolf Creek Pass.

Passing up the turnoff they had taken to the Rainbow trail head years before, they drove on to Pagosa Springs, where they planned to luxuriate in the foibles of civilization for the nights before and after their back country trek. After registering at The Spring Inn on the edge of the San Juan River and putting a few things in their room, they scarfed down a huge lunch of burgers and fries at a quaint caf□ on the main drag. Roman even topped it off with a hot butterscotch sundae at the ice cream parlor he had spotted back up the highway. "That Thai food left me kinda empty," he rationalized as he recalled how little he had actually eaten over the last thirty-six hours.

"Me too," chimed in Juliette between licks on her cone.

"You sure you're feeling okay?" he queried cautiously. "We can hang around the Pagosa area for a day or two before we hit the trail if you're not ready. Maybe do a rafting trip or something."

"No. I don't think we need to do that," she answered. "I took a couple of those pills I got from Sanders – one last night and one this morning. I was still having a little cramping when I woke up, but it was more like a soreness, not a grinding pain like before." She gave him a studious look. "But how about you? You still having any problems?"

"Nope. All gone." He patted his slightly bulging stomach. "I was still feeling funny last night, but nothing today."

"Well, I guess whatever hit us is going away." She smiled to allay his concerns. "I'll be fine. Not to worry. Besides, I want to get back up to Rainbow. Nothing less will do." Her tone of voice clearly conveyed her sense of determination, and Roman knew better than to press any farther.

They passed the afternoon seeing all the sights of downtown Pagosa, which was no mean feat since the central part of the booming mountain town was only a few blocks long. Popping in and out of local artists' galleries, artisans' markets, jewelry stores, and antique shops, they finished their afternoon of shopping the same way they had started it – with empty hands and full wallets. After a quiet carbo-loading supper of pasta at Castagna's, an Italian eatery a block off the main road, they walked back to their motel, where a very public soak in the riverside mineral bath was followed by a couple of much-needed professional massages. When they finally got up to their room an hour after sunset, they poured themselves into bed and went out like a couple of candles in a hurricane.

To Rainbow and Back

After a large Sunday brunch laden with fresh summer fruits, Juliette and Roman repacked the little bit of gear they had brought into the motel room and sat down on the bed to review their trek plans. They would start with a hike back up to Rainbow Hot Springs, where they would stay for the first two nights. Then they would follow the Rainbow Trail north to Piedras Pass, where they would pick up the Continental Divide Trail. They would camp there a night or two, depending on the site and views, and then head east toward Sawtooth Mountain. Again, they might stay there a night or two before heading back southwest down the Beaver Creek Trail to where it picked up the Rainbow Trail. Depending on how they felt, they might go back to Pagosa for a night or they might head east and stay a night at South Fork. Then home to Castle Rock.

As they reviewed the planned legs, Roman checked over his supply list to make sure they had enough food and other essentials for each day, each campfire meal or trail snack. For her part, Juliette double-checked her list of other supplies, such as water purification tablets, matches, first aid kit, and the all-important essential of the civilized woman – toilet paper. Satisfied that they were prepared for the odyssey, they checked out of the motel and threw their things on the back seat.

Stopping at a service station on the east side of town, Roman filled the tank with gas and disappeared inside to pay. When he returned, he was clutching four ice-cold cans of soda. Tossing one to Juliette, slipping two into the Li'l Playmate cooler behind the driver's seat, and popping the top on the fourth, he justified the unexpected purchase. "These are the last things we're gonna have for the next few days that aren't gonna be either freeze-dried or treated with iodine tablets. So enjoy!"

By the noon hour, they were parked at the familiar trail head. As Juliette rearranged what was being left behind in the 4Runner, Roman lowered the tailgate, dragged his pack out to the edge, and strapped it on. He had almost forgotten about the extra drinks in the cooler when he heard her say, "Think fast!" He turned his head just in time to see the flying can already halfway to him. He reached up to catch it but misjudged it. The can bounced off the tips of his fingers and landed on a patch of soft grass.

"Nice try, Champ," she taunted curtly as she opened her soda and gulped down a couple of big swigs. Then she turned to position her pack for loading.

With a full pack on, he almost lost his balance as he squatted down to pick up his soft drink. He flashed back on the last time he had been at that very spot, how she had made him stumble and fall back onto his pack and how she had teased him about looking like a turtle that had been knocked over onto its shell. A devilish thought of sweet revenge crossed his mind and, in one smooth motion, he picked up the can, raised it high out in front of him, and popped the tab, sending a spray of sugary mist up into her face. As he backed away from what he expected to be a certain retaliatory onslaught, his heel caught a protruding rock. Once again, but this time of his own making, he found himself reclining on his backpack, knees and elbows up in the air.

Initially shocked by the unexpected shower, Juliette did a quick burn to inflamed irritation. But when she caught a glimpse of the source of her exasperation momentarily trapped like the rat he was, she burst out laughing. Ripping off her T-shirt to reveal a braless upper torso, she wiped the soda off her face, neck, and chest, tossed the wet shirt into the back of the vehicle, and pulled a clean, dry shirt out of the front pouch on her pack. All the while, Roman struggled mightily to get back onto his feet, having had the misfortune to fall between two saplings which were preventing him from rolling over onto either side to get up the easy way.

The trek up the trail was both invigorating and exhausting – the former coming only when a momentary pause brought a halt to their experience of the latter. As before, they stopped for a long rest break about halfway to the springs, where the two large bridges crossed the West Fork.

"I'm a bit winded," she said as she slipped out of the backpack and plopped down next to Roman. "I'm afraid I've gotten a bit out of shape over the last few years. Going to a health club just doesn't quite cut it when it comes to getting in shape for these mountain trails."

"Well," added Roman as he offered her the first drink of water, "we've been working out at only 5,000 feet and this trail runs about eight to nine thousand. That's quite a bit of difference when it comes to oxygen content."

"It's not just the oxygen," she explained between swallows. "I can already feel the soreness building in my legs and calves, especially when we climbed that last zigzag."

"We've still got a couple of good ones to go," he cautioned, "so pace yourself. We're in no hurry to get there. It's Sunday and what few people may be there will likely be leaving. And the same goes for the trail over the next couple of days. If we're lucky, we'll have a bit of solitude for a while."

"Just what the doctor ordered," she remarked as she passed him the water bottle and stretched out in the warm sunshine.

After a quick snack, some light rehydration, and a revitalizing deep leg massage from her mate, she was raring to go. "We've got a good hill to start off with," he warned as they both hoisted and strapped on their backpacks. "So take it slow. If we need to stop another time or two along the way, it's no big deal. We've got the whole week ahead of us. I've got no intention of getting burned out the first day."

When they finally arrived at the camping area about an hour and a half later, Roman could tell in a glance that she was whipped. They selected the vacant site that had a sizeable stack of leftover firewood and set up the tent. Roman volunteered to scour the area for additional wood and encouraged her to do something less strenuous, like getting the fire started. By the time he brought back his third delivery, she had dozed off, with her butt and legs on a sleeping pad and her back up against the big log. What she had made of a campfire was all but burned out.

An hour later, Juliette was startled to consciousness by the arrival of an overly friendly golden retriever, whose owners were passing through the camping area on their way down the trail. Roman, who was busy unpacking and arranging their bedding, lunged out of the tent to her momentary screams.

"What did you think it was," he joked when he assessed the situation and shooed off the dog, "a bear?"

"It's not funny," she insisted, still groggy from her nap. "I don't imagine you'd like to wake up to the smell of hot breath and a slobbering tongue on your face." He smirked. But just as he opened his mouth to utter a witty comeback, she stopped him cold. "Never mind!" she insisted, pointing an accusing finger at him. "I know what you're thinking, Bub, so just don't even answer that!"

As she shifted her weight forward to get up, she felt a pain in her left side. "Ouch!"

"You okay?" He scooted over to her side.

"Yeah," she replied as she sucked a little wind to ease the pain. "Just a little sore."

"Is it the cramps coming back?"

"I don't know. I don't think so," she said as she rose to her feet, grasping her husband's extended hand. "I think it's just overexertion from the hike. I began to feel a little stitch in my left hip about three-quarters of the way up that first steep climb after the bridges, but it went away about ten minutes after we got to a more level part of the trail. I'll bet that's what it is."

"You want one of your pain pills?"

"Yeah. That might not be a bad idea. Thanks."

Roman slipped back into the tent and rummaged through the side pockets of her pack until he found the prescription bottle. While she downed the medication, he restarted the fire. With a sumptuous warm lunch in their bellies, they both stretched out on their sleeping pads and dozed off.

When they awoke after another one-hour nap, the sun was already beginning to set behind the steep canyon wall, casting a shadow on their campsite and bringing the usual mountain chill to the area. "How about a dip in the spring?" Roman proposed as he returned from the overlook.

"Anybody down there?" she asked.

"Nope. Got it all to ourselves again."

"Oh, goody," she gurgled as she took a swig of water. "Let's go!"

Roman watched her with a measure of concern as they took the easy long way around down to the river's edge hot pool. Stripping off their dusty, sweat-soaked clothes, they inched into the heated water, letting their skin slowly adjust to the temperature. "Feeling any better?" he asked a short while later.

"Just bunches," she replied. "Calves don't ache; thighs don't ache; hips don't ache; feet don't ache. Everything is just warm and relaxed."

"How about your shoulders? You carried a lot of weight on your back. We haven't tried to pack this much in before. We've got five or six days' rations up there."

She rotated her shoulders and twisted her upper torso. "They do feel a little tight," she admitted.

"Scoot over here," he encouraged, "and lie back against my chest." When she was in position, he stroked the sides of her neck lightly, slowly increasing the pressure, then moved down to the tops of her shoulders, then her upper arms, and around to her back and shoulder blades. When he had finished, she extended her head back as far as she could and invited a kiss.

They stayed in the water for a couple of hours, until even the warmth of the pool could not offset the chill of the night air. Up at the camp, Roman fanned the remaining coals into a flame, the stoked the fire with branches until he had a roaring blaze. When he had a supply of coals to rake out, he set up the trusty, soot-encrusted cooking pot and prepared a masterpiece of chicken, mushrooms, and rice, freeze-dried style. Meanwhile, Juliette steeped two hot mugs of herbal tea. Their bellies full and bodies relaxed, they dozed off in their cozy two-person sleeping bag.

They snoozed soundly until the morning sun rose high enough to break over the canyon walls. Leisurely explorations within a half mile of the camping area revealed additional sources of thermal water, though neither of the two pools they discovered had anything approaching the rustic charm and appeal of the main one. As they trudged through a low-lying area north of the camp and came around a large bush, they were startled by the sight of two llamas grazing in a small pasture. Standing there dumbfounded, they heard the rustle of foliage and looked to the right just as a tall young man stepped from the bushes into the high grass of the pasture. Walking up to the smaller llama, he flourished the staff he carried and made some unintelligible sound, causing the young animal to trot toward its mother. Another call and a swing of the stick and both animals moved along down the trail. Catching a glimpse of the two strangers out of the corner of his eye, the herdsman raised his other hand and shouted another indecipherable expression that somewhat resembled "hello." Juliette and Roman waved back as the man and his hairy beasts disappeared down the trail. *Well, don't that beat all,* Roman thought as he turned to his wife and shrugged his shoulders.

"They're not indigenous," she reassured him facetiously. "I know. I have a Ph.D. in biology."

After another late afternoon soak in the pool, they retired to their campfire for an evening of dry cuddling. As Roman prepared another meal to write home about, Juliette crawled into the tent to change from shorts to the warm fleece pants she had brought for such nights. As she removed her underwear, she caught a glimpse of small spots on the crotch. She attached a panty shield to her fresh pair, slipped on the long pants, and returned to the fire.

"Well, looks like my period may finally be starting," she announced in a disappointed tone, knowing how that would curb their range of sexual activity for a while.

"How's everything else?" Roman asked as he poked around in the fire with a long stick. "No more pains?"

"Nothing to speak of," she explained. "Still a little sore from the exertion, so I've been taking the medicine Sanders prescribed. But another night of rest should take care of that. If you were thinking of heading on up the trail tomorrow, I'll probably be fine."

"Well, we said a night or two here, but we could make it three," he offered. "We'd both forgotten how out of shape we'd become."

"Let's plan on doing the next leg tomorrow," she concluded. "After our little surprise out in the pasture today, I think we've seen about all there is to see here. Nothing could top that!"

Turning in as the last logs burned down, Roman was abruptly awakened in the middle of the night by a stabbing pain in his groin. As his mind and senses sharpened, he realized the source. Juliette was tossing and turning in the bag and had kneed his thigh just below the hip. Grabbing a flashlight, he looked at his watch. Two forty-three. He turned the light on his wife. Her head swung from side to side. He could see small beads of sweat collecting in the thin furrows of her brow and running down her temples. She was breathing deeply through her mouth – almost panting. He reached over to feel her forehead and cheeks with the back of his hand. She was feverish. He ran his hands over her face and down her neck. Still warm. Too warm. Unzipping the middle of the twin bag, he tossed some of the cover to the side. He put his hand up under her T-shirt. Her whole body was warm, from her head down to her waist.

He leaned over and whispered her name in her ear. Slowly at first and then as though startled, she awoke. "What?" Her voice cracked from the dryness of her throat.

"Jules, you're running a fever," he informed her.

"What?" She still was not quite coherent. He could not tell if it was from being awakened from the fever.

"You've got a bit of a fever," he repeated. "I think you'd better take some Ibuprofen or something. Where is it?"

She put her hand to her face, then her forehead. "Yeah. Yeah. Okay." She pivoted her head from side to side to get her bearings. "It's in my backpack, on the left side, bottom pocket."

Roman dug into the pack, pulled out the plastic bottle, and shook two out onto his hand. Reaching the water jug chilling in the night air outside the tent, he handed her the tablets. "Thanks," she said as she gave the water back to him and lay back down. Screwing on the lid and tossing the jug to the side, he reclined on his side, elbow on his camp pillow and head resting on his palm, and stroked her face. "That's nice," she said as he comforted her. After ten minutes, she finally dozed off. Roman readjusted the sleeping bag, rolled over onto his other side, and fell sound asleep.

A Sudden Departure

They both awoke four hours later to a shrill wail. It took each of them a few seconds to realize that the sound was not a nearby screech owl. It had come from Juliette. "What is it?" Roman cried as he reached out to hold her. He could see her wincing, but he could not tell if it was from pain or terror. "What? Did you have a nightmare?"

"My stomach," she moaned as she slid her hands down her body.

"Is it the cramps again?"

"I don't know. It just hurts. Sharp pain, here on the left." She took his hand and slipped it under the elastic waistband of her fleece pants. He could feel an area of increased warmth through her cotton panties.

"Maybe you should take another one of those prescription painkillers," he suggested. She nodded her head as he removed his hand and fumbled through the side pocket on her pack. Pulling the container out, quickly he glanced at the label. "1-2 tablets every 4 hours, or as needed, for pain." He jiggled the pill bottle until two dropped out on his palm. Then he grabbed the water bottle and handed it all to her. When she had downed the medication, he convinced her to lie back down while he gently rubbed her belly. Within five minutes, she murmured that the pain was going away.

"Just stay there a while," he urged her. "Give the medication time to do its thing." She nodded and closed her eyelids.

Roman slipped out of the tent and revived a morning fire, brushing a half inch of white ash from the top of the coals, tossing some dried grass and small twigs on top, and blowing gently until the first flames appeared. After steadily feeding larger and larger branches to the fire for ten minutes, he had it hot enough to boil a pot of water. While the peppermint tea bag was steeping in the mug, he stuck his head back in the tent. "You up to a warm cup of tea?"

She raised her head from the pillow. "Yeah. I think so. The pain is almost gone." Sitting up and putting her hands down across her stomach, she added, "Boy, two of those little pills really pack a punch."

"I'll get your tea," he offered as he turned back toward the fire.

"No, wait. I'll come out there. I need to get up and move around a little bit anyway." She unzipped the outside of the bag, tossed the cover aside, and scooted up to her knees. As she glanced down at the bedroll, she gasped. Quickly slipping out of her fleece pants, she looked down. The crotch of her underwear was soaked with blood and more blood had seeped onto the sleeping bag, leaving a spot about four inches in diameter.

"Roman!" she cried.

"Oh, my god!" he exclaimed when he saw the bloodstains.

"There's something wrong," she said, trying to temper her degree of distress. "I think this is more than just an overdue period. I wore a maxipad last night because the first day of my period is usually the heaviest, but this isn't right. It's too much. I've never had this much." He hadn't seen such fright in her eyes since that ectopic pregnancy years ago.

"It's okay," he said calmly. "It's gonna be okay. We'll break camp and head back to Pagosa. We'll find a doctor there and get you checked out. If things are okay, if it's just your period, we'll think about coming back up here. Or if you're not feeling well, we'll stay in Pagosa or maybe drive back toward home and stay in some of the nice places on the way. Or if there's something wrong, we'll get you right back to Denver. Okay?"

"Okay." She wiped away a tear and forced a smile.

While Juliette cleaned herself from a jug of untreated river water and sipped her tea, Roman collapsed the tent and packed their bags, shifting as much weight as possible from hers to his. After dumping the rest of the jug over the pit and scattering the coals, he lifted the pack onto her back, cinched it down, and then loaded his. *At least I'm mostly going downhill,* he thought as the heavy load settled onto his frame.

They had made it about a mile down the trail when Juliette cried out in pain. Discarding his pack in a flash, he rushed back to her side as she leaned against a tree.

"Same pains?" he asked, motioning to her pelvic area. She nodded and winced.

"Let's take this off," he suggested, popping the waist belt clip, loosening one shoulder strap, and sliding her pack to the ground.

"You think another pill would be okay?" she asked.

"It's been almost three hours since you took the first two. It says every four hours or as needed. I don't think one more would be a problem. You want one?"

"Yeah. I think I'm going to need it if I'm going to make it down this trail."

He unzipped the side pocket where she kept toiletries and medications and pulled out the two pill bottles, slipping the Ibuprofen into his short's pocket. He took a tablet out of the other container and handed it to her with his water bottle. While she took it, he looked around the area. Spotting a large felled tree ten yards off the trail, he stashed her backpack behind it and tossed some leaves on top. Then he marked the spot in the trail with an arrangement of stones. "We'll come back and get it later," he said. "You don't need any more exertion than just getting yourself down."

It was almost another hour before they arrived at the two-bridges crossing. He could tell from her color she needed to rest. As she reclined in the warm sunshine on the bank of the rushing river, Roman desperately rummaged through the bottom of his pack, pushing left and right articles that obstructed his search. Finally, he pulled out a small black plastic case.

"I'd almost forgotten about this," he said as he showed her the cellular telephone. She was too exhausted to open her eyes and acknowledge it. "I don't even know if it'll work in this canyon or not. Probably too much interference. But let's give it a try." He realized he was talking more to himself than to his wife.

He punched the power key and waited. Nothing. He punched it again. Nothing. Again. Two seconds. Four. Six. "Hey, I got a dial tone!" In her state of mind, could Juliette even hear him? Immediately, he punched 9-1-1. "It's ringing!"

"9-1-1 operator," he heard a woman say. "What is your emergency?"

"I'm on the Rainbow Trail near Wolf Creek Pass," he spoke slowly and distinctly. "There's a woman who's bleeding very badly. She needs emergency help."

"Please repeat . . . you said," came the sputtering reply. ". . . breaking up . . . repeat your emer . . ."

He repeated the message forcefully, syllable by syllable. "Rain-bow Trail. Rain-bow Trail. Near Wolf Creek Pass. Near Wolf Creek Pass. Bleed-ing ve-ry bad-ly. Bleed-ing ve-ry bad-ly. Need pa-ra-me-dic. Need pa-ra-me-dic." He waited. Five seconds, ten, twenty. No response. He hit the off button and then tried to power it up again. No dial tone. He waited. No tone. One more time. Two seconds, six, ten. Still no tone. "Shit!" he cursed, catching himself at the last minute to keep from throwing the phone into the river.

He looked down at Juliette. She was ghostly pale. He tried to rouse her, but she did not seem to have the energy to come to consciousness. *Is she going into shock?* he wondered. *Should I leave her here and run back to the car? I'm sure my car phone will work from there. But what if she comes to and I'm not here? Maybe the cell phone'll work another mile down the trail – after we get away from this steep canyon. Maybe I'll find someone on the trail and they can go for help. Maybe the call got through. Maybe they heard something – at least enough to come looking for us. But maybe they didn't.* His mind raced through endless scenarios. Finding no sure answer, he chose a course and acted.

Searching through the first aid kit, he found a small vial of smelling salts, which he broke and waved under Juliette's nose. Coughing from the acrid odor, she became partially conscious.

"Jules, we've got to get going," he said as he helped her to her feet. Abandoning his own backpack right where it had been dropped, he put his shoulder under her right arm and hoisted. Slowly he helped her across the second bridge and up the next climb, dragging her a step from time to time when she lost the pace. Half an hour later, but barely 200 yards down trail from the river bank a hundred feet below, they reached the top of the hill. But they were still two miles from their car. Exhausted, Juliette pleaded for rest.

"I . . . can't walk . . . anymore." She spit out the words with gasps of breath. But Roman could sense the danger another delay would bring on, so he slipped in front of her, crossed her arms around his neck, tied her hands together with his bandana, squatted down, and heaved her up onto his back.

As he took slow, careful steps, he talked to her, trying desperately to keep her from fading back to sleep. Every minute or two, he would gently jostle her as he readjusted her weight on his hips. She would rouse just enough to respond to him. He talked about the eighth grade, about French class. Since she had continued on with her studies of that language through college, he asked her anything he could remember about it.

"What was the word for girl?" he asked.

"*Jeune fille*," she mumbled.

"What's 'boy'?"

"*Garcon*."

"Woman?"

"*Femme*."

"Man?"

"*Homme*."

"Husband?"

"*Mari*," she lovingly whispered in his ear.

And on and on he went, step by step, minute by minute, until his mind could not think of any more words to ask. Then it was on to high school friends. Who dated whom? Who was a cheerleader? Who played football? Basketball?

At times she seemed lucid, at other times almost incoherent. When he turned to the subject of their relationship, she seemed to perk up. The class reunion. Her trip back to Colorado. Their trip down to Taos, then to that first hot springs, then to all those places on the Western Slope.

"Rainbow!" she cried suddenly. And he was off onto their second backpacking trip, when he brought her up that trail for the first time, and gave her his senior class ring, and then surprised her with an engagement ring. With each reminiscence, she seemed to gain a bit of strength and clarity. He could feel her arms snuggle around his neck as she leaned her head forward and placed her lips against his ear"Have we gotten to Oz yet, Toto?" she whispered.

Had his resolve not been fierce, the words would have crumpled him – brought him to his knees. His mind raced as he recalled the fantasy story he had written one night at his computer before she came back for that first trip together, but his survival instincts would not surrender control to his emotions. Step after step. *Another hill. Just twenty yards to the top*. Then downhill for a while. *That'll be easier.* His mental processes all but shut down, and he lost track of the import of their conversation. *Step right. Step left. Right. Left. Watch out for that rock! Can't afford to stumble.*

His energies almost depleted, his senses began to shut down. His sense of smell could no longer detect the pine scent of the forest wafting across the trail with each puff of the gentle morning breeze. His nose served no function other than to suck all of the air that it possibly could, letting his lungs separate out the life-sustaining oxygen and carry it through his bloodstream to his waning muscles.

His intellectual processes began to shut down too. He forgot about talking to his wife to keep her conscious. He did not perceive her body going limp against his back or her arms and hands dangling from his shoulders. He did not detect the warmth of the red liquid mixing with the sweat on his lower back, soaking into the tail of his shirt and rear of his shorts and running down the back of his legs to his socks. All he could see was the trail – step after step. *Right . . . left . . . right . . . left.*

Clouds of powdery dust swirled around the toes of his hiking boots as each footfall pounded down onto the dry trail. The occasional sharp rock jutting from the packed clay drove a searing pain all the way up his body. But his mind shut it out, allowing himself to hear instead only the familiar mental mantra of survival – *right . . . left . . . right . . . left.*

He did not hear the shouts of the two figures running up the trail about a hundred yards ahead of him. All his aural senses could register was the thunderous beating of his own heart as he shuffled his feet. *Right . . . left . . . right . . . left.* And the rasping reverberation of his windpipe as he gasped for oxygen, his lungs strained to their limits.

He did not see the man and woman running full speed toward him. All he could see through the eyes partially blinded by the streams of salty sweat was his right foot. Then his left. *Right . . . left . . . right . . . left.*

When the two members of the search-and-rescue team finally reached Roman about half a mile from the trail head, he collapsed to his knees, then onto his side, as the paramedics lifted Juliette off his back. Out of the corner of his eye, he saw the tall man put his hand to Juliette's carotid artery. He could see their lips move as they spoke to each other, but his ears and brain could not make the low sounds into intelligible words. Roman gasped for another breath and caught a glimpse of the female attendant as she felt up and down Juliette's wrist. Another deep breath and his mind began to clear. As he raised up to support himself on his hands and knees, he saw the woman lean over and put her ear to Juliette's chest. With another deep breath, he managed to push himself into a sitting position, placing his hands on his hips. He breathed deeply again, salvaging just enough air to force out a single question. "How is she?"

He panted rapidly as his head dropped down. He slid his hands to his thighs to keep from falling face first back into the dusty trail. One more deep breath. As he looked up, he saw the female paramedic unfold the lightweight metal-framed stretcher and lay it out on a flat part of the trail beside Juliette's motionless body. Without so much as a word, the two strangers moved in perfect synchronization, the man slipping his hands under her shoulders and the woman firmly gripping her ankles, lifting her onto the litter. They both picked up their gear, slung the straps over their shoulders, then squatted to grab the handles on the stretcher.

The woman spoke to Roman as they passed by. "Can you keep up with us?"

He reached out for a nearby boulder, steadied himself, and forced his legs to lift him back up to a standing position. "Yeah," was the only word he could muster as he took his first plodding step.

Questions and Answers

He sat in the waiting room of the local hospital for an hour, then two – a forlorn and despondent figure, his elbows on his knees, his head cradled in his hands, small pools of moisture collecting between his feet on the pale linoleum floor. The search and rescue team had hurried Juliette down to where the private road joined the first part of the foot trail and loaded her into the back of their vehicle while Roman kept pace right behind them. At the trail head, the woman spoke again.

"Can you drive your car?"

"Yeah," he replied.

"Stay right behind us," she ordered, then hopped into the back of the van as her partner started the engine.

They rushed Juliette to Mary Fisher Medical Center in Pagosa Springs, where the surgeon on call, who had been summoned to the hospital by the search-and-rescue dispatch, was waiting for them. Their duties discharged, the emergency personnel paid their respects to Roman and disappeared down one of the passageways. Occasionally, a nurse or elderly hospital volunteer would approach the beleaguered and unkempt stranger to ask if there was anything she could do. Clean and bandage his scrapes and cuts? Show him where he could clean up? Get him some coffee or food? Once he was able to lift his head and manage a polite smile as he said "No thanks," but the other times he could barely manage a grunt and an almost imperceptible shake of his head.

Mostly, he just carried on his own internal debate, mumbling a phrase every now and then, second-guessing each decision he had made during the last week, planting within his own soul the poisonous seeds of blame for what had happened to her. Never had he felt so alone as he did during these few hours. He had no family in southwestern Colorado – and no friends or business acquaintances either, to the best of his recollection. Aside from the masseuse from

The Spring Inn or the female paramedic who drove the makeshift ambulance back to town, he had never spent more than ten minutes with anybody in the area. Twice he composed himself enough to stand up and shuffle over to the pay phone to call a close friend or a family member, but as he got part of a number dialed, he broke down. What would he say? Was she going to make it? She had to, he kept telling himself. She couldn't die. She just couldn't. Not now. Not when their dreams were just about to be fulfilled.

After his second attempt at making a phone call to his family, he decided he had to collect himself before he talked to anyone. He had to know what had happened. His mind raced through the events of the past four days – the Thai food Thursday night, their stomach cramps Friday morning, her visit to Dr. Sanders Friday after work, their strenuous hike up the trail Sunday morning, her sudden fever in the middle of the night, her cries of pain that jolted them awake Tuesday morning, her valiant struggle to make it down the trail, the weight of her body on his back, that final whisper in his ear. Each incident was etched in minute detail on his memory – like a series of slow speed video images. He replayed each vision over and over, at times pausing to inspect the minutia of each still frame. And at the end of the trail, still lacking an answer, he automatically began to recycle it all – one more time.

A world away but only three doors down the corridor, the surgical team worked at a feverish pace. The choreographer of the medical miracle makers was a balding man in his early sixties, short in stature with a noticeable bulge around his mid-section. Dr. John Crenshaw had left a lucrative, big-city, private practice after nearly thirty years to go into semi-retirement in a small rural county. After having sold his interest in a small Denver surgical clinic to the two other surgeons with whom he had partnered for over two decades, Crenshaw had bought a 200-acre horse ranch about ten miles west of Pagosa and retired – well, sort of. Although not quite up to the level of challenges he had taken on in the past, his twenty-hour-per-week office practice offered him the opportunity to keep his medical skills sharp without having to devote an exorbitant amount of time to the profession.

Minutes into the surgery, he opened the region of apparent injury. Carefully he cut through the subcutaneous layers below the abdomen, exposing Juliette's reproductive organs. Having identified the source of the hemorrhaging and stopped the bleeding, he probed the area with slender forceps. Within seconds he found what he was looking for. He snipped off several tissue specimens, placed them in two vials, and handed them to the OR nurse. Then he sutured the incision, stepped away from the table, and slipped the two specimen containers into the right pocket of his scrubs. After peeling off his surgical gloves and gown, he walked through a labyrinth of corridors to the waiting room to speak with the next of kin.

"I'm John Crenshaw," he said as he extended his hand to Roman, who rose from his chair.

"Roman Marchetti," were the only words Roman could muster.

The surgeon gestured toward the sofa. "Let's go over there. It'll be more comfortable." Like a human puppet with its will stripped away, Roman followed the doctor and took a seat on the couch.

"What I'm going to tell you is preliminary, you understand," explained Crenshaw. "I won't prepare my final report until I get the results back from our lab. I've got some specimens we'll need to take a look at along with our hospital pathologist, but . . . " He measured his words with precision. ". . . everything I've seen to this point indicates that your wife had a major rupture of her left fallopian tube, which was caused by an ectopic pregnancy."

For the first time in the past several hours, the wheels in Roman's mind began to spin with thoughts other than those of personal fault or self-pity. He stared at the doctor in disbelief. "That can't be," he argued. "She had her tubes tied a few years ago – after her first pregnancy. She'd hemorrhaged back then because the pregnancy turned out to be ectopic and she lost that tube, so we decided to tie the other tube."

"I suspected as much," remarked Crenshaw. "I examined her reproductive organs during the surgery. I could tell from what I saw that the right tube had been damaged previously. The two ends had been tied off and buried in an abdominal fold. But her problem this time wasn't on the right side. It was on the left. The embryo had gotten lodged in the tube about a third of the way down and continued to grow. When it got too big, it ruptured the tube. That's what caused your wife to bleed internally – and massively. She lost a great deal of blood before she went into shock. And now her kidneys have shut down. And she's lapsed into a deep coma." He reached out and put his hand on the husband's shoulder. "If she lost the right tube years ago and the doctor tied the left tube, how could she have gotten pregnant? Something's not right."

"As I said, Mister Marchetti," Crenshaw reminded him, "these are just preliminary findings. But I should be able to be more conclusive after I take a look at the lab tissues. Something caused your wife's left fallopian tube to rupture. It appears to have been internal pressure, not an external source – like a fall. You were hiking, right?"

His mind swimming in confusion, it took Roman a second to realize a question had been directed at him. "Yeah, right. Up by Wolf Creek Pass."

"That's what I'd been told," the doctor confirmed. "Now, the tissue samples we're going to look at in the lab will be able to tell us positively whether there was anything of an embryonic nature in your wife's abdominal cavity. If it was, then my suspicions will have been confirmed – that she suffered a severe hemorrhage of the left fallopian tube as a result of an ectopic pregnancy, causing massive internal bleeding that put her into a coma" Glancing at his watch, he added, "So if you'll excuse me, I'll get down to the lab and confer with our pathologist. It's possible I may have some more definitive answers for you within the hour. I know you'll want to see your wife, so I'll have a nurse come down and take you to her room." Noticing Roman's disheveled condition, he inquired: "Do you want to use one of the bathrooms to clean up?"

"No, I'm okay," Roman insisted, glancing down at his arms and legs. "Just a couple of scrapes. They'll be okay." He looked back up at Crenshaw with an air of resignation. "I need to be with my wife."

"I'll send the nurse down," Crenshaw stated as he gave Roman's shoulder another squeeze, rose from the sofa and disappeared down the corridor.

In the lab, the surgeon and the pathologist scrutinized the contents of the vials with great care, first by naked eye, then by microscope. Easily identified were the remnants of the left fallopian tube from about a centimeter from the fimbriated end to the mid point of the tube. Also collected from the abdominal cavity were quantities of blood, which, the microscope revealed, contained cytoblastic tissue, indicative of a developing embryo. But most curious to both doctors was the excised tissue that had affixed to it two small plastic clips, parallel to each other about two centimeters apart. As the hospital pathologist dictated his report into a microphone, Crenshaw slipped over into the doctors' lounge and logged his impressions into one of the staff computers. As soon as the pathologist notified Crenshaw that the lab report was ready, he picked up a copy and walked through the corridors to the recovery room.

Roman rose from the chair beside Juliette's bed as the physician opened the door. "Have you finished your reports already?" Roman asked dubiously.

"Not a real busy place, as you can tell," Crenshaw responded. "Not too many emergencies around here, so these things get top priority." The surgeon pulled up a chair from across the room and they took their seats, turning to face each other.

"As I indicated to you before, Mister Marchetti, my first impression was that your wife suffered massive bleeding as a result of tubal rupture from an ectopic pregnancy. We've now examined some of the tissue we recovered from her abdomen, and I'm able to state conclusively that your wife was pregnant. Embryonic tissue was found in her pelvic area. There's no doubt about that."

Roman shook his head. "But how? Her doctor in Denver specifically recommended that she have the remaining tube tied so she wouldn't have to run the risk of a second ectopic pregnancy. He told me she could've died from the first one she had three years ago. I thought she couldn't get pregnant that way. That's why we'd been working with the fertility clinic trying in vitro implantations. And that was over a year ago. This just doesn't make sense!" His tone and temperament exhibited noticeable agitation.

"There were some other interesting findings from the lab exam that may answer some of your questions," Crenshaw interposed. "Give me a minute to go through all of our findings, and then I'll try to answer your questions."

"I'm sorry Doctor," Roman apologized, lowering both the pitch and volume of his voice.

"In addition to the presence of embryonic tissue, both the hospital pathologist and I observed a definite rupture of the left fallopian tube wall. We were able to identify with a reasonable degree of accuracy the initial point of rupture and subsequent tears. These observations are important because, combined with the evidence of embryonic tissue, it leads to only one opinion, which we share concurrently – that is, the fallopian tube ruptured because of the growth of the embryo within the confined space of the tube, which led to massive internal bleeding. In other words, your wife hemorrhaged internally and only as a result of the ectopic pregnancy. As I've indicated to you before, her body shows no signs of external trauma, such as if she'd fallen while hiking or climbing and severely injured her pelvic area. There are no bruises, abrasions, or contusions anywhere between her waist and her mid-thigh – and certainly nothing that would have accounted for the extensive internal bleeding she has suffered."

Crenshaw paused to let the medical jargon sink in. Roman resisted the impulse to restate his previous question. The doctor continued. "In addition to those findings, I removed a small piece of tissue from the left side of your wife's reproductive system. I had my suspicions when I first observed it in your wife's body while she was on the operating table, and that hunch has now been confirmed by microscopic examination. The two spring clips that had been affixed to the left tube during that tubal ligation you spoke about were attached to the peritoneal tissue immediately adjacent to the tubal lumen – but they were not occluding it."

"Something about that sounds familiar," Roman said, "that stuff about the lumen and occluding. I vaguely remember her OB/Gyn talking about that when she had that surgery. But that was years ago."

Crenshaw slipped the reports between some of the sheets in his notepad, flipped over several sheets, and drew a sketch on the first blank one he found. Holding the clipboard and attached pad up against the back of the sofa, he pointed to the lines with his pen. "This is a rough diagram of a fallopian tube. This flowered-looking end here is the fimbria or outside end of the tube. It hovers near the ovary, which is this oval shape here. The tube itself is this double line, running back toward the uterus in the center of the body. The lumen is just the name for the hollow part of the tube. During a normal conception, an egg leaves the ovary, and enters the fallopian tube through the fimbria. If coitus takes place at an opportune time in the woman's monthly cycle, the sperm swim up the lumen of the tube where they meet with the egg as it's descending and fertilize it. Then the fertilized egg, or embryo continues to travel down the tube until it reaches the uterus. There it affixes to the uterine wall, where the fetus grows and develops. If the embryo gets lodged in the tube – stuck – often due to adhesions or scar tissue, its continued growth will eventually cause the tube to rupture.

"If a woman wants to have her tubes tied to prevent future pregnancies, or for whatever reason, there are several acceptable methods available to accomplish those ends. The tubes can just be cut in the middle and the ends buried in an abdominal fold. That's what your wife's surgeon apparently did with what was left of the right tube after the first ectopic. Or the surgeon can fold the end of each piece back against itself, sort of like folding a garden hose when you want to temporarily stop the water, and then tie the folded tube. Or a surgeon can use a pair of plastic clips, which snap together over the tube and effectively block, or occlude, the passage of sperm up the tube. If the sperm can't get to the egg, there can't be a conception." Crenshaw scribbled a line here and a dash there as he illustrated each point of his exegesis.

"What the pathology exam confirmed is that the clips put in on the left side were not on the tube. They were attached to a piece of peritoneal tissue adjacent to the fallopian tube, and they were touching the tube, but they were not blocking or occluding the space within the tube. So theoretically, and practically speaking as well, sperm could swim up the length of the tube without any impediment from the birth control device."

Roman appeared to be getting quite disturbed by the doctor's revelations. "Why weren't the clips across the tube?"

Crenshaw shrugged his shoulders. "I can't say definitively," he admitted, "but it appears to me that the surgeon put the clips in the wrong place. He identified what he thought was the tube and slipped the clips around it and snapped them down, but what he clipped was not the tube." Roman stared at the surgeon in disbelief.

Crenshaw paused, glanced down at his feet, took a deep breath, and looked back up at his patient's husband, lifting his shoulders and open palms. "He just missed."

Rights and Remedies

The next day, Roman followed the ambulance carrying Juliette's motionless body all the way back to metropolitan Denver, where arrangements had been made for her long term care. He had recovered all of their gear from the search-and-rescue team members, who had gone back to the area after they left the hospital to retrace the couple's steps and retrieve the abandoned packs. Having gotten a few of the answers he needed, he finally had been able to contact both families from his motel room late Tuesday evening, refusing his younger brother's offer to fly into the Durango airport, sixty miles to the west, and accompany Roman on the return drive.

When he pulled into his driveway after seeing Juliette settled into her hospital room, all of the Marchettis – his parents, brother, sister-in-law, and their two children – were waiting anxiously for him in the house. His mother was already firmly ensconced into the guest room, having brought enough clothes and personal items to last a few nights. "I'll take care of things," she insisted, referring to meals, the housework, and whatever else came up that Roman needed her for. "And there's no arguing the point."

The patron of the Marchetti family pulled his older son aside as his wife fixed tea in the kitchen. "Don't fight her on this, Roman," he counseled. "It's just something she's got to do. It's her way of saying how much she cares for you and Juliette. You understand?"

"Sure, Pop," he replied. "It's okay. I understand."

After a fitful night of sleep, with dreams so vivid he felt he could touch Juliette's smooth skin and smell her sweet fragrance, Roman began the unwelcome task of apprizing the remainder of those closest to Juliette of the events of the past few days. First on the list was Sally. He had wanted to call her the evening before, when she was at home, but visits from Juliette's brother and sister, along with their families, made the privacy he needed impossible.

Sally answered the phone with her usual effervescence, surprised to hear his voice, her mind spinning as she wondered what trifle necessitating a telephone call must have sprung into Juliette's mind while soaking in a hot pool. Or maybe it was just an anxious expression of unnecessary concern about the baby. But as Roman fed her the dire story, piece by piece, she crumbled. When he hung up, she rose from her desk and quietly closed the hallway door to the secretary's office. Then she retreated to one of the wing chairs and sobbed herself into sobriety.

After soliciting assistance and emotional support from the office manager, Jane, the two women complied with Roman's request and flipped through the Rolodex on Juliette's desk, picking out the names and numbers of those business associates whom they thought should receive special notice about her condition. Just before noon, Jane called McManus, the company president, and asked him to drop by Juliette's office before he headed out for lunch. When they broke the news to him, his face turned ashen white. Assessing Sally's stress, he called a cab and sent her home for the day while Jane finished calling the last few names on the short list.

Shortly after lunch on Friday, Roman's brother and sister-in-law dropped by to accompany him to the hospital. Gazing at her body lying motionless in the white-sheeted bed, his emotions overwhelmed him. Tears flowed from his eyes, rolled down his cheeks, and dropped from his chin to the crisp white bed sheets below. When they brought him home, the answering machine was beeping with one telephone message that his mother had missed when she ran back home to pick up a few more things.

"Roman. It's Cindy Belatron. I got a call from Sally this afternoon. I wanted to convey my deepest sympathies to you. You know we all hope Juliette pulls through. She's such a special woman." There was a pause as the attorney cleared her throat. "If you have time, give me a call this afternoon or tomorrow morning." Muttering something to himself about how stupid he was to have forgotten to call her, he dialed her office. The secretary put him through immediately.

After the additional appropriate best wishes, Belatron put on her lawyer's hat. Apologizing for having to discuss business at such a time, she brought up the baby. "How is this going to affect the surrogacy arrangement?"

"I . . . I don't know," he stammered. "To tell you the truth, I haven't even thought about it."

"Have you spoken with the Rifkins?"

"Just Sally. She's so close to Juliette, you know," he explained, "I called her the day I got back into town. But we didn't even talk about the baby." He hesitated as that part of his mind began to get into gear. "I just assumed everything would stay the same. Am I wrong?"

"I don't want to alarm you," Cindy replied, "but I don't know. I really don't. This has been such a unique situation from the beginning. If the law was settled, I could give you all kinds of assurances, but it's not. We've been breaking new ground with this from the beginning. So I guess the best answer is that a lot of it depends on what you really want to do."

"What do you mean?"

"I know you want to hope for the best and that Juliette will pull out of this coma, but if she doesn't, are you prepared to raise this newborn as a single parent?"

"Why wouldn't I be?" His attitude conveyed a touch of indignation.

"Good. Good. That's what I needed to hear. Let me do some more thinking about this overnight and we'll talk more tomorrow if you have the time."

Early Monday afternoon, Roman sat quietly in his recliner in the den and stared at the surgeon's report and pathology laboratory records, trying to make sense out of his candid discussion with Doctor Crenshaw. His mind replayed the advice of Cindy Belatron, who had counseled with him at her office earlier that morning. She had listened carefully to her client's recreation of the events of that fateful day, especially to the comments ascribed to the Archuleta County physician. "When you've had some time to adjust to things," she urged, "you should speak with an attorney about what you've told me. I don't do personal injury cases. Never have. But you need to counsel with someone who practices in that area. Like you said, 'Something went wrong.'"

She rose from behind her desk and came around to sit in the chair next to him. "And I'm not telling you this because I think someone ought to be sued every time something goes wrong. But you've got more to think about than just yourself. Sally is still carrying Juliette's baby. And I have every confidence that the birth will go smoothly. She and her husband have been very candid that they have their hands full with the two they've got, so I have no reason to expect that Juliette's condition will change their commitment. And it's not just Juliette's baby; it's yours too.

"I've been thinking about our telephone conversation yesterday and I want to make sure we can get around any legal complications that could arise because of what happened to Juliette. But I have no reason to believe Judge Fox will disturb her previous order or impede Juliette's dream of giving you a child. I'm going to meet with the Rifkins' attorney next week and talk this thing over, at least from a legal point of view – whether we need to inform the court about Juliette and what else you might have to go through in terms of legal proceedings. While I'm working on that end, you need to speak to someone about Juliette – not only on your own account but as the legal guardian of the child yet to be born. And if you don't know where to turn to find an attorney, call me. I'm sure I can come up with someone."

Now there he sat at one-thirty on a Tuesday afternoon, just a week after his wife collapsed on the mountain trail, in the reception area of a twelfth-floor law office in downtown Denver. "Frey, Cooper & James, P.C." the brass doorplate read. His high school buddy, Glenn Matson, had reminded him that one of the girls they had graduated with, Veronica James, had gone on to law school and was practicing in Denver. Feeling uncomfortable about laying the intimate details of his and Juliette's lives on the line to a total stranger, he had telephoned Ronnie – as she had been called in high school – to find out if she could meet with him. She had agreed and scheduled an appointment for early the next afternoon.

A pretty blond secretary came out to the lobby and introduced herself as Ellen, then showed Roman down a hall and through the third door to the left. James rose from the seat behind her desk and came around. She was wearing a smart dark blue pantsuit with a bright yellow silk blouse underneath. Thirty-seven years old, just a couple of months younger than Roman, her raven black hair was beginning to show an isolated strand or two of gray. With bushy eyebrows, high cheekbones, and full lips, she was much more attractive as a mature woman than the image of the gangly girl of the mid-seventies imprinted on Roman's memory. From the picture window behind her desk, he could see the vast expanse of the Civic Center Plaza.

Knowing little about his story other than that it concerned a former classmate, she put her arms around him warmly and offered her consolation before inviting him to be seated with her on the leather sofa. After grabbing a legal pad and pen off of the end table, she listened intently as Roman gave her a brief history of his marriage to Juliette, the first pregnancy and tubal ligation, the failed in vitro implantations, the surrogacy contract and successful implantation, the undiscovered second ectopic pregnancy, and Juliette's tragedy in the high country. After she completed her last of five pages of notes, he handed her copies of the surgery and pathology reports, which she had requested that he bring. She disappeared from the office for a minute or two and then returned, handed him back his copies, and sat back down on the couch. With a yellow highlighter, she marked pertinent sections of the copies she had made.

Clipping the pen onto the side of her notepad, she turned to face Roman. "These tissue samples mentioned in the lab report," she asked, "do you know where they are?"

"I guess they're still at the hospital in Pagosa," he replied. "Why?"

"According to what Crenshaw said," Ronnie explained, "the surgeon who did the tubal ligation affixed the clips to the wrong tissue. I'm certainly not an expert when it comes to surgery, but if this Doctor Sanders mistook the peritoneal tissue for the fallopian tube, that sounds like negligence to me."

"That's what I thought," Roman concurred. "The whole purpose of the tubal ligation was to prevent her from getting pregnant again. Sanders had said both tubes were so messed up that, if she ever did, it was very likely to be another ectopic. I didn't want to take a chance of losing her so I convinced – well, that may be too strong a word – urged her to have the remaining tube tied."

"One of the first things that needs to be done is to make sure those tissue samples are preserved," James advised. "I'll make a phone call about that right away. Now, what Crenshaw said about the surgeon 'just missing,' how strongly did he voice that opinion?"

"Well, he was pretty sure about his facts," Roman replied.

"That's not exactly what I meant," Ronnie stated. "How should I explain this?" She searched for the right words. "Lots of doctors give you their frank opinion when they're talking to the patient or to a family member, but when it comes to repeating those opinions on the record, either in public or in a deposition or in court, they suddenly hem and haw and beat around the bush – worse than the most artful of politicians." Roman chuckled at the comparison. "So what I'm getting at is how strongly did Crenshaw feel about his opinion?"

"He seemed quite confident about it. And his tone of voice was quite emphatic."

"Did he express any doubt about the clips not being in the right place?"

"No."

"Was he forceful when he said the surgeon 'just missed'?" Ronnie inquired.

"He sure sounded forceful to me."

"If he took the stand to testify, do you think he'd talk to the jury the same way he talked to you?"

"I think so," Roman declared. "Yes, I think he would."

"Good. Good. We'll definitely have to talk to him about this and to that pathologist too."

"So is this something you'd be able to look into?" queried Roman.

"I've got to talk to my partners about it first. Let me explain a little bit to you about lawyers and their practices. Most of what we do here is criminal law. The head of the firm is Mark Frey. Perhaps you've heard his name."

Roman shook his head. "Can't say I have."

"He's been involved in a number of high-profile cases in the Denver and Colorado Springs areas during the last five or ten years, but he's been doing criminal defense almost exclusively for the last twenty. But whatever he does, he does it well. He's a great trial attorney – one of the best I've seen.

"Evan Cooper is number two on the door. He did a lot of divorce cases for a number of years, but he teamed up with Mark a little more than two years ago on a child sexual abuse case, and they've been together ever since. I don't know if Evan handled any personal injury cases before he joined Mark, but I'm quite sure he hasn't handled one since. While Mark projects a certain flamboyant and confident persona in a courtroom, Evan is our legal researcher and tactical planner – Mister Meticulous – Doctor Detail.

"I joined the firm about six months ago. Before that, I'd been a prosecuting attorney in the D.A.'s office for about eight years, handling everything from misdemeanors to rapes." She snickered, prompting a look of confusion and curiosity from her prospective client. "I'm sorry. That's rude of me – laughing at an inside joke. I was just thinking back to that case I mentioned where Evan first teamed up with Mark. The prosecutor's butt they kicked was mine." Roman smiled and nodded in recognition. "And to tell you the truth," Ronnie added, "I think the jury came back with the right verdict. But that's another story. Anyway, after another year or so kissing up to too many politicians, I decided to leave the D.A.'s office. When Mark got wind of my intention, and he's never told me how he found out since I hadn't made it official or even really told anyone, he asked me to come join him and Evan.

"Anyway, I've gotten a little far off track, but I wanted you to know that our experience in personal injury cases is limited. If, after thinking it over, we don't think you'd be well served by our firm, I'll find you a top-rate medical malpractice attorney." She paused to collect her thoughts. "So, I think we've covered all the bases for now," she added as they rose from the couch and stepped toward the office door. "I'll get back to you as soon as I can with our decision."

A Legal Analysis

Early Friday morning, after their usual review of pending cases, James introduced the new matter she had been researching over the past couple of days. "So that's why you were working all weekend," Evan Cooper teased, directing his snipe at her in the direction of Mark Frey. "And I thought she was hanging around on the chance that she could score some brownie points if you happened to wander in."

Just a hair more than six feet tall, athletically trim, and always dapperly dressed, Frey, now in his early fifties, was the most recognizable and celebrated member of the firm. His white hair contrasted sharply with his deeply tanned face and dark business suits. His expression always projected the depth of his thoughts and feelings – whether one of sober concern or light amusement. Through his quarter of a century of legal practice, he had earned every bit of his reputation as a persuasive courtroom advocate, pulling the rabbit out of the hat on more than one occasion when the evidence seemed stacked against him by convincing the jury of the innocence of his client with the force of his oratory and depth of his conviction.

Cooper, on the other hand, was a master of minutiae. More than a dozen years younger and about four inches shorter than Mark, he was widely regarded as a litigator and legal researcher of exceptional quality. Tinker Toys was the analogy he used to refer to his treatment of a case. "You take it apart, break it into its smallest components, then put it back together again until you've got something recognizable. And if it doesn't look right, you break it apart and do it all over again."

The only member of the firm who had a spouse, Evan's taste for marriage had survived being fouled by his ten years of practice as a divorce attorney. Mark, however, had lost his appetite for marital life after a costly break up. In contrast, Ronnie had never quite gotten close enough to the wedding table to even smell the aroma of the cake.

"Very funny," retorted James, still unsure of the true nature of Evan's wit.

"Don't pay any attention to him," Mark advised. "When we first started this firm, the boob told me in no uncertain terms that he didn't work weekends – that he was an avid cross-country skier during the winter and mountain biker the rest of the time. He said he'd only had to go into his office on weekends or holidays three times during all those years he practiced solo and that he didn't intend to change his tune, not for me or anybody. So the first month after he joins me here, I drop by on Saturday morning to pick up the mail and I find him in the library, with ten or twenty books stacked up around him. I must've stood in that doorway for five minutes before he even saw me and, then, when he did, it just about scared the shit out of him."

"Now you're getting a little carried away with your description," Evan insisted. "A little startled, maybe, but that's all."

"Anyway," Frey went on, "every time I catch him in the office on weekends, I tease him about trying to score brownie points with me. So he's not picking on you. He's teasing himself. Now, what about this new case?"

"Okay. Where do I start?" she wondered out loud. "First, it's a civil matter, not a criminal one. So I haven't signed up the client yet. I told him I wanted to look into a couple of things and then talk to the two of you. I realize our experience here is almost exclusively criminal, with the exception of Evan's track record in domestic relations, which he takes great pains to remind us that he hated." She gave Evan a smirk as if to pay him back for teasing her – or teasing himself.

"I've only been with this firm for about six months now," she continued, "and I wasn't going to jump the gun and commit to a civil damages case, no matter how interesting, if it's not something we want." She glanced down at her notes from the meeting with Roman. "This is a personal injury case – medical malpractice to be precise." Over the next ten minutes she detailed her former classmates' marriage, Juliette's first pregnancy, the tubal ligation, her collapse in the wilderness, the pathologist's and surgeon's reports, and the opinions of Doctor Crenshaw. Mark and Evan listened intently, reviewing and marking extra copies of the reports she gave them.

Mark interrupted. "What was the date of that tubal ligation again?"

"Uh, just a second," Ronnie replied as she flipped back to the first page of notes. "In September of 1993 – the 27th."

"Well, you're right, I haven't handled a civil case in years," Frey admitted, "but I think we've got a problem right off the top with the statute of limitations on personal injury actions. Isn't it two years? That'd be September of 1995 and here were are in September '96."

"Yes, there's a two-year statute, but the legislature codified the old common law discovery rule, which allowed an action to proceed if the injured party, with the exercise of reasonable diligence, couldn't have known of the nature and cause of the injury."

"That rule generally came out of those lost surgical instrument cases, didn't it?" asked Cooper.

"Yeah. Those were the kinds of cases that caused the courts to first toll the running of the statute," she agreed, "when patients didn't find out until they got x-rayed or opened up again that the cause of their problems after the first surgery was an instrument or a sponge or something that had been inadvertently left in."

"How 'bout that?" remarked Evan. "I actually remembered something from law school."

"Will wonders never cease?" razzed Frey. "Okay, we can get past the statute of limitations, but what about the statute of repose?"

"What's that?" queried Cooper.

"When the legislature enacted tort reform back in the late eighties," Mark informed his colleague, "they put in a special provision for doctors that said they couldn't be sued under any circumstances if three years had passed since their negligence caused the injury."

"I thought you said you hadn't practiced any civil law for years?" James inquired.

"I read *The Colorado Lawyer* avidly," Frey replied, "every month. And the new updates that are coming out online too. Gotta keep up with all the code revisions and case law – even if it's not criminal. Besides, you couldn't miss all that hullabaloo about tort reform when the legislature was debating it back then – what with all the newspaper articles and all that damn junk mail from the political action committees, the insurance people, and our brethren trial lawyers. So I know a little something about limitations and repose. But 'little' is the operative word."

"Well, I researched both over the weekend," Ronnie told her proteges. "And I can't say it's clear sailing on the repose question. Problem is, I can read the statute both ways, to allow an exception under the discovery rule or not."

"You lost me," Cooper conceded.

"The language can be read both ways," James added, "to allow someone like our client to file after the three years has lapsed or to bar such a filing. And, as we might expect, there haven't been any appellate decisions construing the wording."

"Well, that's certainly a case of legislative clarity," sniped Evan sarcastically.

"But on the whole . . . ," Mark said, leaving a blank to be filled in by James.

"On the whole, I'd say that it means never past three years, for any exception," Ronnie conceded.

"Okay. Things are up in the air on that one," Mark concluded. "But one thing we should be able to agree upon . . . that is, if we take the case, and I say 'if' . . . we've got to bring the lawsuit immediately. We're not going to have time to plan this thing out for six months before filing. There's not gonna be any lag time to try to settle the claim and avoid the courts. We've got less than two weeks before the statute of repose would kick in, if it actually does, and we have to assume it would bar the action completely." The other two counselors nodded their assent.

Directing his follow-up to Ronnie, he added, "Have you got time on your calendar in the next thirteen days to handle this? With the date of the botched surgery being September 27, 1993, we're going to have to get this filed no later than the twenty-sixth."

"If we want the case," she assured them both, "I can make the time."

"Okay. Good." Frey was on the edge of his seat, scribbling his thoughts down on his notepad. "Parties. I assume we've only got the husband to deal with here. With this coma and all, hopefully she had a durable power of attorney naming her husband. And of course, as her husband, he'd be her guardian and conservator. What about all that?"

"According to her husband," James replied, "all of that's been taken care of."

"Has he got someone handling the guardianship/conservatorship work?" asked Cooper.

"Yeah. Betsy Fuller down in Castle Rock," answered Ronnie. "She prepared their joint wills and medical powers of attorney right after they got married."

"Good. We're okay on that one," remarked Frey as he scratched through a line of the notes he had been making as Ronnie had laid out the facts. "We'll only need to sign up the one client."

"Maybe," interjected James. "Sort of." Both Cooper and Frey stopped writing and looked at her inquisitively.

"You didn't say anything about either of them having children from previous marriages and you told us about all those unsuccessful in vitros and now she had this second ectopic that ruptured," Mark reasoned. "She can't still be pregnant!" he added begging a denial.

"Oops," Ronnie added, realizing she had missed the notes about the surrogacy arrangement.

"Oops?" Mark inquired. "Now what does that mean?"

A wry smile broke across Ronnie's face as she watched her two colleagues wrestle with the mental puzzle she had inadvertently created. "Well, I'd guess you could say she *is* still pregnant . . . sort of," she replied.

"Sort of pregnant?" Evan scoffed incredulously. "Someone can't be 'sort of' pregnant, Ronnie. Didn't you take high school biology?" He looked over at Frey, laughing at what he thought was a great joke. Frey chuckled with him, but James just smiled politely.

"Well, in this case, that's exactly what she is – a little bit pregnant," Ronnie retorted, really relishing the torture her fellow partners were suffering. But as the smiles faded from the faces of the two men, James finally offered a complete explanation. "The Marchettis entered into a surrogacy contract with one of her coworkers. The fertility specialist implanted Juliette's eggs, which had been fertilized in vitro with Roman's sperm, into the uterus of the surrogate about eight months ago. The surrogate is now carrying Juliette's child. According to Roman, the surrogacy contract will be fulfilled. Sometime in the next three or four weeks, mid-October or so, he'll become a father to his comatose wife's baby."

"Whew!" exclaimed Frey, his breath whistling out his pursed lips. He turned to Cooper. "She was right, partner. The lady's 'sorta' pregnant." Directing his attention back to Ronnie, he asked, "Okay, now what's the law on that situation? Can an unborn child have a cause of action or does it have to wait until it's born? And how do the statutes of limitations and repose affect that? I mean, it's clear that this child has been damaged. If Juliette never comes out of that coma, for all intents and purposes it's going to grow up without its natural mother. Or is she its natural mother? Do the Marchettis have to wait until the contract has been fulfilled before Juliette becomes a mother?" He paused for a second as if to catch his breath. "Man, you can go around in circles on this one, can't you?"

"Well, I didn't say it was easy," conceded Ronnie, "but there's already a court order in place directing that Juliette's name be listed on the birth certificate when the child is born."

"When did that get issued?" asked Frey as he made ready to scribble another significant bit of information on his legal pad.

"About a week or two before the Marchettis took off on that backpacking trip," James added, glancing at her notes. "Came out of Denver juvenile Court – Judge Diana Fox."

"Assuming that holds up, at least it's her child, legally," Cooper interjected.

"Who could challenge it?" Ronnie appealed. Mark and Evan looked at each other blankly, then shrugged.

Frey picked it back up. "Okay. What about damages limitations? As I *recall,* that was a big part of the tort reform package – limiting the amount a person can recover against a doctor?"

"Right again," James responded. "There are damages limitations for health care professionals, and that diminishes the attractiveness of the case, no doubt. There's a million dollar cap on economic and a quarter to half a million cap on noneconomic."

"Was she working before all this happened?" Mark questioned. "What kind of economic damages do we potentially have here?"

"According to her husband, she was making in the seventies," Ronnie answered.

"And how old?"

"Thirty-seven."

"Seventy-thousand-a-year times twenty-eight years of remaining work life expectancy," Evan mumbled, doing some quick math on his pocket calculator. "So we're easily above the cap with just lost earnings."

"Easily," concurred James. "In most states, we could probably start at two million in lost family income."

"Well," Evan commented, "there's another case of our legislators screwing the victim to favor a powerful lobbying group."

"Not to mention the influence that political contributions from the medical community can gain," James added, reflecting on her own years in the D.A.'s office, where politics mixed with the law like homogenized butterfat.

"Then there are the future medical bills," Ronnie added. "What if she stays in this coma for years? That kind of medical care can't be cheap."

"We'll need to get some estimates on that from the hospital she's in now," Cooper suggested as he punched more numbers into his calculator, "but I'd bet it would certainly run in the tens of thousands, if not hundreds, per year. And over five or ten or twenty years, that could be another million or two – maybe more."

"And if and when she does come out of the coma," Ronnie added, "she could be partially disabled."

"True," Cooper agreed. "Very true."

Mark tossed his pen on the conference table, spun his chair, rose, and walked over to the window. When he hitched up his pants and rested his chin in his hand, both Evan and Ronnie knew enough to cease any further conversation. Mark was thinking – hard. He had heard all he needed to hear and was ready to make a decision. After a minute or so of complete silence, Frey whirled around on his heels and smiled – like a kid about to get on a thrilling carnival ride for the first time.

"I like it. It's an interesting case, with some legal issues that could be ground-breaking. That's one thing I've fantasized about since law school, being involved in a case that made new law or set new precedents. That's all we read in those law books, cases that established precedents and made the law what it is today. And I always kind of envied the attorneys who brought those cases to trial and then took them up to the appellate level. Not that I necessarily want this to o up on an appeal, you understand." He paused while the wheels whirred.

"So, I'm for taking it on. I assume you are too, Ronnie, or you wouldn't have brought it up." She nodded in affirmation. Turning to Cooper, Frey inquired, "Evan, what about you? If we're gonna sign this one up, it oughta be unanimous. It's Ronnie's case, but I've got a feeling you and I will have a little something to do with it."

"Sure," the younger man answered without a moment's hesitation. "It's a good case for us. I enjoy the criminal work, but now that we're growing as a firm, I'd like to see us broaden our practice a little bit. I haven't kept up with too many civil damages cases, but the facts seem really unusual to me. We've got a woman whose fallopian tubes are so messed up that getting pregnant poses a risk to her life. So a doctor talks her into getting a tubal ligation to prevent that risk from happening, but then he slips up and fails to sterilize her. She gets pregnant and it damn near kills her. Anything like that out there in the case law, Ronnie?"

"No, nothing in Colorado, not in the reported cases at least," she answered. "And nothing at all that I've found where the woman almost died as a result of a botched sterilization. But I did find some cases in other states where a child was born as a result. Those cases generally refer to the tort as wrongful pregnancy. It's really nothing more than a standard medical malpractice claim in nature, but it's been given a special name because the women who've brought the lawsuits sued for not only their time lost from work, their hospital expenses, and the pain and suffering of another childbirth, but also for the cost of bringing up a child they had taken definite measures to avoid having."

"Boy, I'll bet the courts have had a whale of a time with that issue," remarked Cooper. "After all my years of doing family law and listening to endless preaching about what serves the best interests of the child, I can just hear all those stodgy old justices trying to deal with an unwanted pregnancy issue. I'll bet there's a bunch of crap in those decisions about how the birth of a healthy child into a family can't constitute damages *per se,* how such a characterization would stigmatize the child, and so forth. Right?"

"On the button," Ronnie concurred, surprised at her cohort's intuitive perceptions. "But those are decisions from other jurisdictions. So, since there was nothing in Colorado, I called a couple of personal injury lawyers I know. They told me they'd heard of a handful of wrongful pregnancy claims that had made it to trial and probably a number more that had been settled before getting to trial. But usually these kinds of failed sterilization cases lead to the successful birth of a child, not a near fatal injury to the mother. So the big fight in the law has been over what kind of damages should be allowed and in what amount. If the child is not healthy, say retarded or malformed, there are often big damages awarded if the doctor should or could've done something that would've prevented conception. But if the child is normal and healthy, the controversy centers around whether the cost of raising a child which had been placed against should be taxed to the doctor who screwed up the sterilization procedure. A lot of those issues are going to be a long wav from what we've got."

"True," cautioned Frey, "but they set the tone for cases with similar fact patterns. If the courts don't like – quote – wrongful pregnancy –

unquote – cases, we've gotta start thinking about this case in simpler terms. All this talk about wrongful pregnancy is just gonna screw things up. And that's probably what all those justices on the various appellate courts of the states you were talking about have done – gotten everything screwed up with confusing words."

"What do you mean?" asked James.

"Well, the term 'wrongful pregnancy' is all wrong," Mark argued. "It's oxymoronic to most people. Pregnancy is a good thing – perpetuation of the species, keeping the bloodline alive – so it doesn't make sense to call it a 'wrong.' See what I mean? You give something a label like that because it accurately describes the legal dispute, but it's all wrong from a sales point of view. It's like calling an item on your restaurant menu slop or puke or something like that. Society views pregnancy as good, not bad, not wrongful. So when you try to sell the idea to the public, or to a jury, or to the press, or to bunches of justices who oughta know better that your client was wronged by becoming pregnant, it runs counter to our basic instinct."

"So what do we do about it?" asked Evan.

"This is just a medical malpractice case," Frey explained. "Just that simple. We're not gonna even use the term 'wrongful pregnancy.' Strike it from your lexicon. This is just an ordinary personal injury case, which happens to have extraordinary circumstances surrounding the negligent act and subsequent injuries. That's all. Think of it like a bomb. This doctor got careless. But he might as well have surgically implanted a bomb in her womb, a bomb with a three-year fuse. And when the bomb finally went off, it just about killed her."

Pressing Matters

Not even two hours had elapsed since Ronnie James walked the personal injury complaint over to the County, & City Building and filed it with the District Clerk that her telephone rang. The court beat reporter from the *Rocky Mountain News* wanted to know more about the case of *Roman P. Marchetti, individually and as next friend of Juliette A. Marchetti, v. Paul '. Sanders, M.D.* Since the Colorado Rules of Civil Procedure called only for notice pleading, stating just enough facts to apprize the opposing party of the basis for the claim, the journalist wanted to know how Juliette Marchetti had been injured, how long she and her husband had been married, whether there were any children, and so forth. But James told him she could not release any more details at this time, apologized for her brevity, and hung up the phone. The next morning, another reporter, this time one from the *Denver Post* called. To similar questions, Ronnie gave the same abbreviated response.

The three lawyers had conferred about the possibility that the press would pick up on the unique facts of Roman's claim – a failed sterilization procedure, a second ectopic pregnancy, Juliette's injuries and subsequent coma – and had decided it would be best to do everything they could to protect their clients' privacy. The opportunity for publicity would come in due time.

Besides, Cooper rationalized, things would not get any easier if the birth of the Marchetti's baby came off as expected and they added the name of a newborn as a plaintiff in the lawsuit along with its parents. It would probably not take the press too long to decipher the pleadings and discern the extraordinary circumstances of the child's conception and birth. "God, I can see the tabloid headlines now!" exclaimed Evan as he and Ronnie enjoyed another of their routine Thursday lunches at Duffy's. "'Woman In Coma Becomes Mother!'"

"Tabloid, Hell!" retorted James cynically, obviously irritated with the voracious and unrelenting natures of the two journalists who had telephoned her so far. "That'll probably be the headline in the mainstream papers."

Unfortunately, the trio of attorneys had underestimated the ravenous appetite of the local press for the uncommon story. Later that Thursday evening, only five minutes after Roman had returned home from another lengthy visit to Juliette's hospital room, the same *Rocky Mountain News* reporter who had contacted James called the Marchetti home number. Although he was somewhat taken aback by the intrusion into his privacy, Roman maintained his composure and simply told the journalist he would have to talk to his attorney. With the young man still entreating him for "just a comment," Roman hung up and called Ronnie. After relating the events of the last couple of minutes, he asked how the press got his telephone number.

"Probably right from the telephone book," she speculated. "You know, it doesn't take much investigative skill now, what with computers and the Internet and all the personal data out there that's accessible in an instant, to take your name off the complaint I filed, input it, and come up with a whole bunch of information on you – telephone number, home address, employer, workplace, car license plate number, make and model, date of marriage, and so on. I'd like to say we can insulate you totally from this sense of grim curiosity that seems to dominate the press these days, but it's impossible."

"Isn't there anything I can do?" he pleaded.

"Only thing I can suggest right now, other than going into hiding somewhere, which I know you're not going to do, is call the telephone company and see if you can get an unlisted number."

"Yeah, I guess I could do that." She assumed from the silence that he was making a note. "Hey, wait a minute!" he exclaimed. "I've got an extra line in my house that I use for my fax and computer. And I wouldn't think it's published anywhere, like in the phone book. I'll bet I could just switch them – plug the telephone into the fax line and vice versa."

"That'd be simple enough if it'd work," James added.

"Yeah. I'm sure I could. I did it once before when my telephone number went on the fritz down at the central switching station. And I remember the phone was dead and I thought there might be something wrong with the phone set so I plugged it into the fax line and got a dial tone. Then later that day I tried it back in the other jack arid it worked fine. I called the phone company later, and they said they'd had some computer equipment failure in a bank of numbers, so that must've been it. Yeah, that'll work."

"Great," replied Ronnie. "Is your home fax number on your business card?"

"Yeah, it is."

"Good. Then I'll tell my secretary and Mark and Evan when I go in tomorrow."

"Thanks, Ronnie. I appreciate you talking to me about this after hours. I hope I didn't disturb your evening."

"No problem," she reassured him. "And if you get any more calls, just remember to refer them cordially to your attorney and just hang up." She added with a giggle: "And if they call back after that, tell them you're going to call the telephone company and report them for phone harassment."

Roman's quietude was short-lived however. The next morning, when he arrived at his place of business a minute or two after eight, he saw a van emblazoned with a television station logo parked right out front. Lurking on the sidewalk were a reporter with a microphone and a man with a video camera. Before Roman could even put the gearshift in Park, the young woman scurried up to his car door, her videographer trailing a few feet behind. She positioned the camera into her favored angle with hand signals over her shoulder, then turned to address Roman. "Mister Marchetti," she asked as she glanced down at her notepad, "could we ask you a few questions about the lawsuit you filed against a Denver doctor?"

"No comment," he politely replied to the backpedaling journalists as opened the door and emerged.

"Why do you believe that her doctor was responsible for your wife's injuries?" she probed, following him up the walkway toward the office door, the cameraman scrambling close behind.

"Please," Roman said, waving his hand at her to stop, "if you want a statement, you'll have to talk to my lawyer."

"We're not interested in hearing from your lawyer," she snapped as she let the microphone slack down to her waist. She gathered her thoughts for a moment and then raised the mike back to her mouth. "Our viewers want to hear from you," she implored. "They want to hear your story about your wife. How was Doctor Sanders responsible for what happened? And what *did* happen to her?"

Roman spun as he reached the front door, trying as hard as he could to control his sense of exasperation. "I've said all I'm going to say. If you want anything further, you'll have to talk to my lawyer, Veronica James. If you don't have it, I'll have one of my staff bring her phone number out here to you." He turned and grabbed the door handle.

"Can you tell us about your wife?" the reporter persisted. "How was she injured? Is there some way we could talk to her?"

Roman whirled, his face reddening with rage. "Don't you people have any respect for privacy? What if this were your wife or sister? Would you want someone like you pushing a camera and mike in your face? Hell, no! So what gives you the idea that you can do to everybody else what you wouldn't think of doing to yourselves?" He paused for a moment as he glared at both of them. "You're just a bunch of buzzards, feeding off the flesh you find rotting at the side of the road. And don't give me that crap about the First Amendment. You don't give a shit about the dignity of the Constitution and the liberties it protects. All you're concerned about is getting a big headline or the lead story. If you just gave a damn about the people behind the stories you prostitute . . . " He choked on his emotion as he spit out his last words, paused, and then calmly entered his building, leaving the stunned journalist visibly shaken.

Inside, Roman was anything but the picture of surgical composure the TV reporter had seen only a second or two before. Hardly acknowledging the "good mornings" of his staff, he stalked directly back to his office and slammed the door with a bang that made his employees recoil. Tossing his valise onto its customary space on his credenza, he picked up the phone and dialed his lawyer's office. When the receptionist told him James was in court for a hearing, he could not restrain the "Shit!" that a burst of temper forced out of his mouth. Apologizing to the young woman on the other end, he asked if he could leave a message for Ronnie to call him – urgently.

"Mister Marchetti," came the sweet response, "if you have a moment, I can try her cell phone number. If she's not actually in the courtroom, she'll probably still have it turned on."

"That'd be fine," he replied sheepishly, embarrassed by his loss of control. But thirty seconds of an Abba tune playing in the background did little to assuage his ire.

"Mister Marchetti?" a slightly older female voice inquired.

"Yeah. I'm here."

"This is Ellen, Miss James' secretary. I'm sorry. We weren't able to reach her. She has to turn the cell phone off when she goes into court. But if you could tell me what the problem is, I'll make sure she calls you the moment she gets back. The receptionist said you seemed quite upset."

"I'm sorry about that," he said again. "But there was a TV reporter sitting out in front of my building when I pulled up this morning and she was sticking her microphone and camera in my face and it just kinda got to me."

"I understand, Mister Marchetti," Ellen said supportively. "Would you hold just a minute more?"

"Yeah, sure." Back on "hold," the song had changed, if not the musical era. Now he was treated to a sixty-second segment of one of the Carpenters' greatest hits. *God,* he mused, *if they put me on hold again, it'll probably be the Captain and Tenille.* His mental wanderings were brought back to the center when a deep male voice came on the line.

"Roman? This is Mark Frey. I understand you've been having some problems with the press?"

"Yeah. Hi, Mister Frey. How're you doing?"

"I'm just fine, thanks. So what's going on with the press? They bugging you?"

"Yeah. Started last night with a phone call. I told the guy to talk to my lawyer, but he just kept asking questions. So I just hung up on him. Then I talked to Ronnie and I figured out a way to hold the phone calls at bay, for a while at least. Then this morning, I drive up to my building and there's a van for one of the TV stations parked out in front and a reporter and cameraman rushing up to my car. So it's got me a little ticked off."

"Hey, I know it's tough," Frey said, "but it's the price we pay for having public courts and a public press. It'll die down in a few more days. First time man bites dog, everybody's running around to interview everyone about everything. But the story gets old quicker than roadkill steaming in the summer sun. Everybody wants to get the story first. When they realize they can't get the big scoop, they'll go looking for another one. I assume Ronnie told you to just say 'no comment' and to refer the press to us, right?"

"Oh, yeah. She did. But that doesn't seem to deter their questions. I told the TV reporter that, but she just kept asking questions. Must've fired off three or four as I was walking away from her."

"Anything particularly upsetting about the questions?"

"Well, yeah. Looking back on it, I guess that's what pushed my button."

"What'd you do?" asked a concerned Frey.

"Well, I gave her a good tongue-lashing."

"Oh?"

"Yeah," Roman conceded, now feeling a bit chagrined about his conduct. "I kind of laid into her."

"What'd she ask?"

"I remember her asking me something about the way Juliette was injured – you know, more details about what happened. But then she asked if she could talk to Juliette, and the pot just boiled over. I mean, I can't even talk to Juliette. Geez!"

"You didn't take a poke at her, did you?" Frey asked, a smile invisible to his client across his lips.

"No. No. I didn't touch her," Roman replied defensively, unsure of whether the attorney had asked the question in a serious vein.

"Well, that's a relief. You know, you're not one of those big Hollywood stars who can afford to punch out one of the paparazzi – like Frank Sinatra or Alec Baldwin. You don't make their kind of money – either to afford the lawyers it'll take to clear you of the charges or to pay the civil judgment the jerk's likely to lay against you."

"For the first time in my life," realized Roman, "I have some sympathy for what those celebrities go through."

"What'd the reporter look like? Was she someone you recognized from the news?"

"No. I hardly ever watch the local newscasts. I'm a CNN and PBS viewer."

"Did you catch which channel she was from?"

"I think it was nine. I remember seeing the logo on the side of the van and thinking, 'Oh, boy, here we go,' and I'm pretty sure it was a nine."

"Okay. I'll give the station a call and talk to their news editor. I'll give them a piece of my mind about the questions the woman asked you – how they were inappropriate and just a little rude and smacking of sensationalistic journalism. There's nothing that gets a good editor more on edge than accusing their station or paper of having a slightly yellow tint to their coverage. And if that doesn't work, I'll get through to the manager and threaten the station with a restraining order. Unfortunately, getting a judge to issue one against the press isn't too likely. But we could have some fun threatening them with the challenge."

"That last idea sounds really good to me," said Roman enthusiastically.

"I hate to tell you this," Frey continued, "but it's only going to get worse before it gets better, especially once your child is born in a few weeks. Right now, the press doesn't know about that part of the case and they won't until we make the child a party, and that won't happen until the baby's been born. But sooner or later, your wife's condition is going to become more well known. And it's likely the press could figure a few things out when we get into the discovery phase of this lawsuit. We're going to have to produce your wife's medical records to the defense pretty soon here."

"Yeah, I see what you mean," Roman realized.

"So, the best thing to do is just calm down," Mark advised. "Ignore them. They're like those little gnats that swarm in front of your face. If one of them gets careless and gets too close, you'll probably breathe it in, but it won't do any damage. You're frustrated because your emotions are still raw as a result of your wife's condition. Just don't let your temper bubble over and get the best of you.

"All you need to do is be polite to the reporters, say, 'no comment,' refer them to us, and then turn your back on them. They get frustrated when you do that because now, to get any kind of story, they have to put lawyers on TV. And they seem to hate to do that – first, because we're professionally removed from the emotional part of the conflict, so we don't punch out photographers or scream or cry, and that's what they want for their newscasts – raw emotion;.and second, we're living, breathing advertisements for our law Practices, and those jerks can't stand to give free commercial time to anybody, especially lawyers. So do your best to ignore them. This'll lose its luster in another couple of days."

Family Reinforcement

The next two weeks elapsed without any further intrusions by the press into Roman's personal or business life. He never knew whether Frey's call to the television station had tamed the wolves or if the frenzy of a breaking story had just petered out, like Mark had predicted. But he really did not care. He just wanted to get through each day with a minimum of conflict and a maximum of work.

His daylight hours were consumed with keeping his business prosperous, ever more difficult in the face of steadily-growing competition from all directions. After work, he would drive directly from his building to the hospital, where he would spend an hour or two at his wife's bedside, talking to her about the events of the day as though she could hear every word. By seven-thirty, he would be over at Rifkins' house, working through the last details of the delivery and planning for the new arrival.

Beginning back in the fourth month of the surrogate pregnancy, Roman, Juliette, and Sally had started attending twice-weekly classes on natural childbirth at the YMCA. Their presence at the first few sessions had drawn perplexed gazes and whisperings from the other participants, but as the other couples learned that Sally was a surrogate for the Marchettis' baby, the trio became the object of great fondness. At the end of each evening, a different group of classmates would invite them for a cup of coffee – a hot cup of herbal tea or a cold glass of milk being the customary fare for the expectant mothers.

It was somewhere about the fifth week that the class instructor, a licensed midwife who had been through four childbirths of her own, affectionately nicknamed them the *"menage a trois."* Now with Juliette out of the birthing picture, Bill had stepped in to take Sally to the classes during the remaining weeks. When Roman regained some semblance of control in his personal life and rhythm to his daily schedule, he joined the couple for the last few Monday and Thursday evening sessions. By that time, Bill had assumed the responsibility as head birthing coach, explaining the reasons for his presence to the instructor and other class members, thus sparing both his wife and Roman the discomfort.

Although the press coverage had been limited to the initial blurbs in the two Denver daily newspapers, any possible TV story having been scuttled for lack of exploitable footage, the legal significance of Juliette's condition was not lost on Judge Fox, who had read one of the small stories with some measure of contemplating her course over the weekend, she sent a letter to Belatron, with a copy to Kwan. The last sentence of the first paragraph caused Cindy's heart to pound just a little faster for a few seconds. "To the extent that the untimely and unfortunate injuries to Juliette Marchetti will have a significant effect on the remaining parties in the matter, I would like to schedule an informal hearing in chambers at the earliest convenient date before the birth of the child."

Roman's concern matched that of his lawyer. "What do you think she's going to do?" he queried when his lawyer called him at home that night.

"I don't think you should worry about her changing the order," Belatron reassured him. "That is, unless Sally is beginning to have second thoughts."

"No. No. That's not going to happen," Roman insisted. "I've been over at their place quite a bit during the last week or two, and everything is going great. She's been teaching me all kinds of stuff about babies you know, diapering, bathing, feeding, stuff like that. And sometimes, when she thinks I'm watching TV with Bill and doesn't know I'm listening, I hear her talking to the baby, about Juliette. It's like she's trying to prepare my daughter psychologically or something. It's kinda weird in a way, but, on the other hand, it's really quite touching."

"That's comforting to know," Cindy said. "But I've got a feeling the judge may be more interested in having a little talk with the two lawyers in this matter than with their clients."

"How so?" Roman asked.

"Well, I hope I'm wrong," Belatron commented, "but she may be a bit miffed at May Lynn and me for not notifying her formally right after we learned of Juliette's injuries. Has a little something to do with the lawyer's code of ethics about candor before the tribunal. But May Lynn and I talked it over the week, and we just didn't see any reason to stir things up. We both took a look at the code and concluded that it didn't call for us to go running to the judge all of a sudden. But Judge Fox may see it a different way. I don't know. I'm probably worrying unnecessarily."

"We probably both are," Roman concluded.

The original setting for an October 4 hearing had to be canceled at the last minute by the court when an urgent juvenile criminal matter bumped the Marchetti/Rifkin matter. The next Monday, when Belatron finished up with her early morning hearing in another courtroom, she made it a point to stop by Judge Fox's offices to inform her clerk of the urgent need to reschedule as soon as possible before the baby's birth. "The judge and the baby may not see exactly eye to eye on timing," she quipped. So late that next Wednesday afternoon, with Sally's due date drawing closer by the hour, Belatron, Roman, Kwan, and the Rifkins returned to the courthouse to meet with the judge and allay her concerns.

"Thank you for coming," Fox began as soon as her court reporter had finished setting up. "I hope my letter has not alarmed you unnecessarily. That was certainly not my intention. But given the tragedy that befell Missus Marchetti, I felt it was important that we supplement the record in this matter. Hopefully, this will not take more than a few minutes of your time."

Turning first to Roman, she offered her condolences. "My heartfelt sympathies to you, sir, for what you must be going through. I want you to know how very impressed I was by your wife when she appeared before my court. I'm certainly praying for her full recovery." Looking over at Sally, now bulging at the seams with expectant life, she added, "And I know this must have affected you greatly as well. It was quite apparent from your testimony that your friendship with Missus Marchetti is of great importance to you."

"Thank you, Your Honor." Roman forced out the words, but Sally could manage no more than a nod as she wiped away her tears.

Looking over at her court reporter, Fox directed, "Let's go on the record." Turning back to the attorneys and parties, she explained her decision to convene their gathering. "I've called this informal hearing today *sua sponte* because of the recent injuries sustained by one of the principal parties to this court's order of August 23, 1996. Because of the events that occurred about a month ago to Missus Marchetti and in light of her current medical condition, which I understand to be comatose, this court wanted to give the principal parties — specifically Missus Rifkin and Mister Marchetti – the opportunity to reaffirm their previous testimony and to inquire whether this court should take any measures to its previous order."

"No, Your Honor," Belatron replied. "Miss Kwan and I have consulted separately with our clients and neither party has any reason to request a modification of the order as a result of what happened to Juliette Marchetti. If his wife does not recover, Mister Marchetti is fully prepared to raise his child as a single parent. He has expressed that intention with quiet resolve ever since the first few days after his wife slipped into a coma. Furthermore, the Rifkins acknowledge that they are not the natural parents of the child and do not have any desire to impede Mister Marchetti's custodial rights."

"For the record, Mister Marchetti," the judge requested, "did your attorney correctly state your intentions? Would you intend to raise this child as a single parent should your wife not regain her health?"

"Yes, Your Honor," Roman responded. "She's my daughter. She's Juliette's daughter." His visage spoke volumes. "I haven't even considered any other possibility."

"And Missus Rifkin," Fox added, "do you wish to change any of your previous testimony regarding your disavowal of any claim of parental rights to the child you're carrying?"

"No, Your Honor," Sally said emphatically as her hands traced nervous circles on her distended abdomen. "This is still Juliette's child, not mine."

Looking over at Belatron, the judge continued. "Is there anything in the order as it now stands that you believe needs to be changed?"

"No, Your Honor," Cindy replied. "Both Miss Kwan and I have reviewed this court's order carefully, and we do not believe the order, as worded, has been affected by Juliette Marchetti's current medical status. And we have no reason to request a modification. However, the parties have discussed the effects that Missus Marchetti's condition will likely have on the first few months of the child's life, and they have amended the surrogacy agreement previously filed with the court to cover those changes. And we'd like to file a copy of that with the court at this time." Fox nodded and Belatron handed her the papers.

"As Your Honor will note," the lawyer went on, "the principal concern of this amendment is compensation to Missus Rifkin for her services as a surrogate mother after the child's birth, services which would have been performed largely by Missus Marchetti. We had previously calculated a compensation figure based on the number of days Missus Rifkin was projected to lose from her current employment as a result of the childbirth and postpartum recovery. Now that figure has been increased to compensate for these additional services. Miss Kwan obtained the figures in consultation with various professionals . . . health care, nursery, and so forth . . . and Mister Marchetti has approved them. As we've done with all other papers that concerned this surrogacy arrangement, Your Honor, we are filing these with the court to avoid any suggestion of the baby-selling charges that have tainted surrogacy agreements since they first began."

"The court appreciates your candor, Counselor," Fox stated, "and this will be accepted and made a part of the record." She handed the papers to the court reporter, paused long enough for the clerk to mark them, then turned back to Cindy. "Unless someone has something to add, I'll bring these proceedings to an end. The order will stay in place as is. Juliette Marchetti's name will appear on the birth certificate as the natural and legal mother of the child."

"Ooh!" exclaimed a startled Sally. Looking down at her belly and then up at the judge, she explained. "She kicked." Then, recalling the formality of the setting, her face turned a shade of pink as she apologized. "I'm sorry, Your Honor. It's just that she kicked really hard."

"Then it's unanimous," Fox chuckled. "My ruling has been affirmed by a higher authority." Glancing around the room at the smiling faces, the judge wrapped up the matter. "If we have nothing else, this hearing stands adjourned." Rising from her seat, she extended her hand to Roman. " Good luck to you, Sir."

"Ow!" Sally suddenly cried as she started to rise from her chair. As those gathered looked on, Bill leaned over and spoke softly to his wife. Looking up at Roman, he nodded, then explained to the judge. "We're going to need to get going."

"Are you going into labor?" Fox asked.

"I've been having a few contractions here and there," a game-faced Sally revealed.

"How long?" inquired the judge.

"Oh, about three hours," the surrogate replied, shrugging her shoulders as though it were no big deal.

"Oh my goodness!" Fox said, becoming more concerned and anxious with each tidbit of information. She glanced at the clock next to the bookcase. "Do we need an ambulance? It's getting close to five o'clock. The streets may be getting a little crowded."

"No, Your Honor," replied Bill. "We've got it all under control. Sally's a real pro at this. But if we could, we'd like to alert her doctor."

"Well, by all means, then," Fox assured them as she pointed to the extension on a table by the door. "Dial nine first," she instructed as Roman picked up the handset. "And don't let me keep you any longer," she added, directing the comment to Sally.

Radhavishnu on notice, the *menage* zipped down Broadway in the 4Runner before the rush hour homebound traffic began to plug up the major arteries, pulling into the Swedish Medical Center parking lot just about five. Having prearranged all of the paperwork, Sally was whisked up to the labor and delivery floor and comfortably situated into a birthing room, tastefully painted in peaceful pastels. After a nurse took Sally's recent history of the labor and her vitals, timed a couple of contractions, checked her for dilation, and telephoned her report to the doctor, she came back in with some words of wisdom.

"We're still hours away," she explained to the three of them, "so you might as well get comfortable for the long haul."

Roman and Bill alternated as Sally's attendants-in-waiting, helping her with breathing and focusing techniques as the contractions came and massaging her back and hips during the intervals of rest. Sally's immediate essentials had been packed in a small suitcase for three weeks and had been lugged with her by either Roman or Bill everywhere she went, with a degree of security and attention rivaling that of the Secret Service agents who follow the President. Since Sally could not have anything to eat during labor, she sucked on the miniature cubes of orange juice packed frozen in the thermos. Meanwhile, her ex-sailor husband slipped down to the hospital cafeteria first to "chow down" When Bill returned, Roman followed his lead at the next appropriate inter-contraction rest break.

It was sometime near two in the morning that a familiar voice roused a sleeping Roman, who had dozed off for about forty-five minutes of his allotted hour on a sofa just down the hall. "It's time, Mister Marchetti." Roman squinted and blinked rapidly to clear away the dull film of sleep. Then he made out the affable face of Mary Ann, Radhavishnu's top nurse.

"Sally's fully dilated now – ten centimeters – and the contractions are coming less than a minute apart."

Finally pulling himself together, Roman bounded out of the makeshift bed, tossing the hospital blanket to the side, and followed the nurse down to the birthing room, now softly lit by muted table lamps, the bright fluorescents hovering overhead having been doused for the expected event. Sally's favorite music played on the tape deck Bill had lugged up from the car, and the sweet smell of a strawberry-scented candle wafted in the air. Even Radhavishnu was in the mood, having traded the usual blue scrubs he wore when performing procedures at his office for a surgical frock decorated with teddy bears, lambs, and kittens.

Bill stood resolutely by his wife's side, holding her hand, counting and puffing heavily along with her as he coached her through the descending phase of another breathing cycle. Beads of perspiration popped out of the pores on Sally's forehead, converged in the shallow furrows on her brow, and then trickled down in short streams when the buildup exceeded the cohesive strength of a droplet of human exudate. The hospital staff nurse on the other side of the bed reached over with a damp washcloth as each contraction terminated and mopped the patient's brow. Sally's sweat-saturated bright red hair appeared jet black in the dim light, her familiar front curls replaced by half a dozen clumped spikes shooting which shot out in every direction.

As Mary Ann helped Roman into his birthing garb, Radhavishnu kept a close eye on the vaginal opening. Catching a glimpse of the activity at the door, he orchestrated the final set of pushes. "Mister Marchetti," he welcomed the expectant father warmly. "You're just in time. Come over here," he directed. "We're starting to see the crown of the baby's head now. So it should be just another few minutes." Now fully alert, Roman took his place next to the doctor.

"Sally and Bill tell me you're wanting to catch her, correct?" Radhavishnu inquired for confirmation.

"Yes," Roman replied, his heart racing with anticipation. Out of the comer of his eye, he caught sight of the eight-by-ten portrait of Juliette that Sally had positioned on her bedside table. *We're both going to catch her, he* thought.

"Good. Very good," the doctor commented. "Since you've been rehearsing this at your classes, I don't need to tell you anything but the when. So when I give you the signal, you just do what you've practiced." He looked up at the expectant father, whose nervousness was obvious in his face and his body language. "You'll do just fine," he reassured Roman.

With each subsequent contraction, the crown of the head became larger and more evident, eventually filling up the entire circumference of Sally's cervix. Three more contractions and hard pushes and the head emerged fully. Two more contractions and pushes and the first shoulder popped through, then the second. And at the doctor's signal, Roman dropped his arms and hands into position just as the final contraction squeezed the child's hips and squirted her free of the constrictions of her captivity.

Without uttering as much as a single whimper, the newborn was placed at Sally's breast, where she lay in quiet stillness for several minutes, gulping in small breaths of air and opening her eyes for a second or two as they adjusted to the light. At the doctor's cue, the new father snipped the umbilical cord, leaving the remains for Radhavishnu to tie off. As the delivery nurses finished cleaning baby Juliet and picked her up, the infant made a soft gurgling sound, blinked widely, and looked fixedly at Roman.

The depth of that gaze broke through all pretense of the calm composure he had been able to maintain through the ten-hour ordeal. Looking into those two pools of soft light, he sensed the depth of his connection with this newborn soul – and he felt the spirit of his wife surrounding them. The emotional emptiness in his heart from the loss of Juliette's conscious presence was instantly restored through the eyes of a child.

Pre-Trial Preparations

When the luster that followed the filing of a new lawsuit faded to drab, it was time for James and company to hunker down to the hard work of preparing the case. The day before Roman's next scheduled meeting with Ronnie, the three lawyers gathered in their firm's conference room for the first of what would become many brainstorming sessions. Through his attorneys, Doctor Sanders had answered the complaint, denying both counts of negligence – the first for the failed sterilization and the second for not diagnosing the second ectopic pregnancy. No surprise to anyone in Ronnie's office. And among other defenses, he pleaded the statute of limitations as expected.

"By the way," queried Mark, "who's on the defense?"

"The firm of Powell, Kaminsky & Rader," replied Ronnie. "Curtis Powell signed the answer as lead counsel. He's also listed one of their junior partners, Megan O'Brien, in the signature block, so I assume she'll be handling some of the pleadings and discovery – and maybe second chair at trial."

"So what do we know so far about them?" asked Frey. He had learned from his many years of combat in the criminal courts that knowing everything possible about an opponent was as valuable as having a complete grasp of the evidence and the witnesses. He considered it of even greater importance since his firm was now treading on the less familiar ground of the civil justice system. "I assume you've called around to some of our friends who do these kinds of cases."

"I've talked to a couple," said James. "The Powell firm is one of the five medium-sized firms in the Denver metro area that handles a lot of medical malpractice defense work. Seems that the major med mal carriers like to spread it around when they assign cases. So no one firm gets too much of a stranglehold on an insurance company's business."

"Keeps the lawyers' fees down too," added Cooper. "Five firms all trying to outdo each other and get that little extra bit of work. Snip a bill here, cut a fee there. Legal surgery of a sort."

"So true," admitted Mark. "But the insurance companies know how to play the game better than most. That's one reason I never got into insurance defense work. Anyway, we're getting a little off track. Back to the lawyers. What have you heard about that lead counsel?"

"Good trial lawyer," replied James, glancing at a note or two she had made during one of her conversations with a top personal injury lawyer. "Fairly dry in presentation. More of a 'gee guys, doctors save lives' kind of approach. His firm's practice is about fifty percent med mal and fifty percent other types of insurance defense work, . . . auto collisions, property liability workers' comp, and so on. And they tell me that Powell handles almost nothing but malpractice cases now. So he's got a lot of experience defending doctors and has developed a really good rapport with them. Personality-wise, he's very sedate. He doesn't get riled up at trial."

"We're a long way from trial," interrupted Frey. "What about discovery and motion practice? Are we going to get bombarded with motions and discovery disputes, or is this likely to go smoothly?"

"Other than the issues we talked about before we ever signed on the case?" replied James with a question.

Cooper interrupted. "You mean when we bring in the baby as a party?"

"That's certainly one of the bigger ones," agreed James, "but we've talked about a couple of others." The other two lawyers nodded as recollections of their previous conference came back. "But to answer your question, Mark, I don't think we'll be dealing with an unusual number of motions on spurious issues. Powell doesn't have a reputation as a Rambo litigator – contending every point, no matter how minor. To the contrary, he leans heavily toward full and open discovery and expects the same courtesy in return. According to one plaintiff's attorney who went up against him in a med mal case just last year, he thinks Powell really strong-armed his insurance claims person to settle before trial. Powell will take it to trial if he thinks he's got a winner, but he speaks his mind clearly if he thinks the defense has problems.

"And he seems to have the respect of his insurance companies and their claims departments," she continued. "If he advises settlement and gives them a figure they can live with, they'll give him the authority to settle. But I also hear he's a shrewd negotiator when it comes to settlement. More than one attorney has walked out of a mediation or settlement conference with a feeling that Powell had more money available than the top figure he offered."

"Good. Good," commented Mark. "It's nice to know he's got a favorable track record when it comes to settlement. From the figures we talked about a few weeks ago, it looks like our damages are easily going to exceed the limits of the doctor's insurance policy. If Powell gets that message early enough, that we can justify our demand for the limits, then we can settle before we get too deep into the costs of a trial. And though it won't be adequate compensation for our clients' losses, hopefully we can spare them the ordeal that a trial is certain to be. Now, who've we got for a judge in this case?"

"It's been assigned to Beth Williams' court," replied Ronnie.

"She must have a civil-only docket," said Evan. "I've never run into her in a criminal matter."

"Right," James confirmed, reading directly from her notes at times. "Civil trials only. She's been on the district court bench for four years. Originally from Denver but went back east to law school, Pennsylvania. Hired by one of the big firms downtown right out of law school. Actually she was the first black woman in the firm. Spent seven years there. She left to go solo for a while. Then hooked up with Peter Claxton and they partnered in a general civil practice for about ten years. She's happily married and a mother of two, both in high school. She's in her mid-forties, very active in charities but not politics. Was a bit of a surprise to have been appointed by the Governor since she had no real political track record. Talk was he felt her race and sex made for good politics. Of course, she was eminently qualified too, not that that seems to make much of a difference in some circles. But her lack of a political agenda or dues to pay to anybody have turned out to be big assets. She's well respected in most circles as a fair-minded jurist."

"Anything give us an indication of whether she's progressive or conservative in her legal philosophy?" asked Frey.

"Couldn't get a feel for that," Ronnie replied. "I assume you're talking about some of the unique issues presented by this case?"

"Yeah. Statutes of limitation and repose – surrogate child – those kinds of things," acknowledged Mark.

"Nope. Nothing yet. But I'll keep looking – and asking."

"When we bring in the child as a party, any chance she'll do something contrary to that juvenile court judge's ruling?" Frey wondered.

"I expect Powell might try to challenge the daughter's standing, just to try to get her noneconomic damages for loss of society and consortium out of the picture. But I don't have any reason to think it'll work. Sure, the facts are a little unusual, what with the surrogacy and all. But things like this happen every day when a prospective father gets killed or severely injured while his wife is still pregnant. And once the child's been born, it's added as a plaintiff. Seems like the equal protection clause should require similar treatment when it's the mother who dies before the baby is born." She glanced at Evan for a pearl of research wisdom.

"Yeah," Cooper affirmed, tapping his eraser lightly on his legal pad. "Ronnie's right. This isn't really quite on point, but I remember reading a case where a pregnant woman died a few minutes after they got her to the ER. The doctors managed to keep her body on life support and delivered the baby a couple of hours later. The court recognized that the surviving child still had full legal rights as a survivor and derivatively for the wrongful death of its mother."

"Pull up that case and anything similar," Frey directed, "and save them for a rainy day. I've got a feeling we're likely to need them down the road." Frey looked at his notes and checked another item off his agenda. "Now for planning our case. What are you thinking about in terms of medical experts?"

"First, we've got that Pagosa Springs surgeon," answered James. "Strong opinions – and very cooperative. I doubt that there'll be a challenge on his factual findings, but we may have a problem stretching the boundaries of his expertise to an OB/Gyn practice. I certainly wouldn't want to rely on him as our only expert in that area."

"What kind of experience does he have as a general surgeon?" inquired Frey. "He's not some small-town schmuck that they're going to beat up on, is he?"

"No. Not at all. He's got great credentials," she said as she handed out a couple of copies of his resume. "He worked here in Denver for many years before retiring to Pagosa Springs, so he should feel quite comfortable in the city if we want to bring him here to testify at trial. Of course, we could always do him by video."

"Looks fine to me," surmised Mark, scanning the biographical data. "Who else you got on your first list?"

"I don't think we'll need him, but there's the hospital pathologist in Pagosa who did the lab report on the tissue specimens – notably the clips and the left tube. And I've gotten the name of an OB/Gyn expert who teaches at CU Med School." Ronnie tracked down her notes with her pencil, looking for the name. "Here it is. Doctor Benjamin Steinberg."

"Is he board-certified?" questioned Frey.

"Sure is," Ronnie replied.

"Good. Gotta have someone who's board-certified in that specialty."

"Any other medical people we're gonna need?" asked Frey.

"Not that I see right now. We may want to think about the fertility specialist, Doctor Radhavishnu, if his expertise is required to explain the presence of this surrogate child. But nothing more as far as medical experts go."

"Okay," said Mark. "What about an economist?"

"I've talked to one – a professor at the University of Denver. She taxed me over her C.V.," Ronnie added as she handed a stapled set of six sheets to her colleagues. "She's listed the cases she's worked on the last page – six in the last four years."

"Any other hired experts we're gonna need?" Mark asked.

"No others planned at this time," Ronnie replied.

"Good," remarked Frey. "What about the physical and documentary evidence?"

"I've acquired all of Juliette's medical records – from the family doctor she had growing up, all the doctors and hospitals she went to when she lived in Austin, the university health clinic in Lawrence, Kansas, as well as those from Sanders and Radhavishnu. Roman has collected all of the photographs he's got of his wife – their wedding pictures, some he took and a bunch that she'd put into albums before they got married. It's a sensitive area, but I've talked to him about doing a day-in-the-life video of Juliette now and the therapy and all she's going through.

"We've also gotten copies of her entire personnel file and her payroll records to show her earnings over the past four years or so. I don't think we'll need to get any of those from her previous employer in Texas, but we can if we need to. I've got several authorization forms signed by our client. And, most important, we've secured the specimens from the Pagosa pathology lab."

"Evan, anything come to mind that Ronnie might have missed?"asked Frey.

"Seems quite complete to me," Cooper answered. "I don't know that we'll even need them, but we should check with Swedish Hospital where Juliette had the emergency surgery for the first ectopic and see what tissue evidence their lab might have preserved in paraffin or on slides. I'm sure we'll come up with other thing as we start to work with our experts."

"We've got a case management order in place now," Ronnie added. "That'll set the pace of discovery over the next couple of months. First thing I'm going to want to do is take the deposition of our defendant, Paul Sanders."

"Any dates in the works?" inquired Cooper.

"Powell and I have tentatively agreed on a week from this Thursday. I'll do Sanders in the morning and then present our client for Powell to depose in the afternoon. Then on Friday, I'll do the certified nurse-midwife in the morning and Sanders' other nurse that afternoon. I want to try to get these out of the way before Christmas. It looks like our client may be bringing his daughter home by then."

"Wonderful," Frey commented. "Anything from the doctors about Juliette?"

Ronnie shook her head. "No. Afraid there's no change there."

Evan raised a finger in the air, signaling his intent to interject himself into the conversation. "Back to Sanders' deposition a minute. I've been reviewing Juliette's medical records, especially her last visit to Sanders," Cooper informed his colleagues. "Be sure you cover that last presentation thoroughly. Find out why the doctor didn't diagnose the second ectopic pregnancy before Juliette went off on a backpacking trip. We've really got to flesh that out."

"I agree," replied Ronnie. "I sent the first wave of records I got from the local doctors and hospitals to Doctor Steinberg shortly after I received them, and he's taken a quick look at them. I spoke with him briefly the other day just to get his first impressions before I depose Sanders. He said he'd reserve final judgment until he'd reviewed all the records, but he had a hunch that there was some additional carelessness there. He said Juliette presented with many of the classic signs of an ectopic pregnancy. Other than the fact that both fallopian tubes were thought to be nonfunctional, he can't figure out why Sanders didn't cover his bases and do the blood serum test. Then, if anything came back positive, do an ultrasound."

"Did Steinberg have any idea why those tests weren't done?" asked Evan.

"If he had any guesses, he didn't offer them," James explained. "Who knows – maybe Sanders had a golf game to go to. Roman said his wife had made a last-minute appointment and sneaked in late in the afternoon. Maybe the doctor was in a hurry – or just plain tired. But whatever the case, I've got a face-to-face meeting with Steinberg set for that Tuesday. We'll go over everything in detail then so I'll be ready to interrogate Sanders on Thursday."

"Whatever the reason, you'll probably need to dig a bit on that one," commented Mark. "If he's a well-prepared witness, he'll answer your questions as succinctly as possible. So it's gonna be up to you to pull the facts and opinions out of him." The room fell silent as the attorneys looked over their notes, the rhythmic drum roll of Cooper's pencil the only sound.

"What a shame," Evan spoke up as he shook his head slowly. "She goes in with the classic signs of another ectopic and the guy doesn't give her anything but some painkillers. I mean, geez, she could've bought a home pregnancy kit at the drugstore for ten bucks and gotten better medical advice than this guy gave her by peeing on a stick!"

"Yeah, I know," agreed James. "It's a shame that something so simple could have alerted her even to the possibility that she had another ectopic. But according to our client, there was nothing . . . nothing at all. With all she'd been through over the last three years, one ectopic, three in vitros that failed to take, and then a miscarriage of the fourth one, you gotta know she'd have been very sensitive to the slightest suggestion that her pelvic cramps could have been more than a bad meal of Thai food. But, anyway, that's what we're here to find out – why Sanders didn't seem even to consider another ectopic as the reason for her complaints."

Frey glanced at his watch as James finished her last comment. "Oops. Time's a wastin'. I've got a client meeting in about ten minutes. What else have we got to talk about before we wrap this up? Any other depositions scheduled?"

"Not yet," replied Ronnie. "I expect Powell's going to want to depose Crenshaw and the hospital pathologist down there in Pagosa, and maybe the search and rescue people too. Since I believe the surgeon is going to be favorable to us and I've already gotten his records and a sworn statement, there's no need for us to do it. But I expect Powell's going to regard Crenshaw as a damaging witness, so he's going to want to know what the guy is likely to say at trial. And while he's down there, he'll probably figure it won't hurt to talk to everybody else too. He's listed all of them as possible deponents on his contribution to the case management order."

"If you've already submitted your proposed order to the court, have we got a trial date yet?" asked Mark as he rose from his chair and sidled toward the door, anxious to prepare for his upcoming appointment.

"Yep, sure do," said James. "Got it yesterday as a matter of fact." She pulled the pleadings file out of a red accordion folder and flipped over a couple of sheets. "Here it is. A year plus five days away. 'Trial will commence on Monday, the 8th day of December, 1997, at 8:30 a.m.'"

"Good," Mark commented. "Let's do everything we can to keep that date."

A Doctor's Story

The next week and a half flew by rapidly. Late each afternoon, James shut the door to her office and pulled out her set of copies of Sanders' office records on Juliette. For the next few hours, she poured over the records again and again, examining them carefully with her own mental microscope. Her conference with Doctor Steinberg proved to be of great assistance. He was able to decrypt virtually all the medical symbols and shorthand that appeared throughout the office notes and hospital records – inky scrawls that, at times she thought, resembled chicken scratches more than intelligent attempts at communication. Cooper, meanwhile, had drafted and attached to Sanders' notice of deposition an exhaustive subpoena duces tecum, a legal paper which commanded the doctor to bring various documents and other items in his possession or under his control to the proceedings.

On a mid-December Thursday morning, promptly at nine o'clock, Curtis Powell and his client arrived at James' office. Accompanied by a female associate, the three were shown to the conference room by Ronnie's secretary. Standing two inches shorter than his client, the sixty-two-year-old defense attorney's mien projected the quiet dignity of a confident counselor – albeit one arguably a few years behind the times in grooming and fashion. His wavy, gray hair, cut short around the sides, had a slicked-down sheen, leaving Ellen to wonder if Powell was still taking his daily dab from a super size tube of Brylcreem he had bought back in the fifties. His tortoise shell rims held bifocals and perched on the end of his nose so tightly it seemed as though he might have trouble breathing. His suit was a three-piece navy pinstripe, one hundred percent worsted wool, of course, with a heavily starched white oxford cotton shirt underneath the jacket and vest. Deliberately understated, as the civil defense lawyer's dress credo commanded, his tie was a thin tricolor stripe of navy, gray, and burgundy.

Sanders, on the other hand, was dressed to the nines. Wearing a light beige silk sport coat and dark gray slacks, with a lavender cotton dress shirt and a brightly colored, flowered silk tie, he fit the playboy image James envisioned from what the sources in her rapidly expanding network had said. Even his shoes – brown tasseled ostrich loafers – spoke volumes to those who read significance into such things.

Passing on the complimentary soft drink or coffee, the two attorneys and their client conferred in private at the south end of the room for a few moments while the court reporter finished setting up her equipment. A minute later, James entered the room with Roman and Mark behind her. After all those present exchanged introductions and business cards, Powell took a chair next to his client, who had been seated close to the court reporter for her convenience. The female associate sat down next to her superior. Ronnie and Mark took positions on the other side of the conference table, James directly across from the witness and Roman next to her. Mark took a chair at the end, out of the way.

On cue from Ronnie, the court reporter swore in the witness and James began her questioning. Methodically, she began with Sanders' background, getting more detail than the curriculum vitae Powell had produced showed. She examined him on his training since medical school and residency, obtaining details about the continuing medical education courses he had undertaken during the last twenty years, especially those that dealt with ectopic pregnancy and sterilization.

"I probably diagnose one or two ectopics a month," he replied to one of her questions. "It's not something we keep statistics on, you understand. We'd have to spend hundreds of hours going back through all our records to determine an exact number."

Without requiring Sanders to divulge confidential information about other patients, James inquired about the number of cases which were similar to that of Juliette Marchetti, both in terms of diagnosing ectopic pregnancies and performing tubal ligations. "Same thing on the number of tubal ligations I've performed as on the number of ectopics," Sanders said in response to another question from Ronnie. "It'd take hundreds of hours for my staff to go back through our records and count the number of tubal ligations I've done. But as far as a best guess estimate is concerned, I'd say I average about two a week."

"How many of those are performed for therapeutic purposes?"

"By therapeutic, you mean to protect the health of the woman, like in Missus Marchetti's case?"

"Yes. To protect the health of the woman as opposed to purposes of birth control or family planning."

Sanders tapped his temple with his right index finger as he considered the question. "Of course there are those rare cases where the two overlap – where the woman doesn't want to have any more children and there are medical reasons as well. But if I'm just giving you my best estimate, I'd say of the hundred or so I do a year, one or two are done exclusively as therapeutic sterilizations. And then probably less than one a year for dual purposes. Obviously the great bulk of sterilizations performed today are for birth control purposes."

Running down the items on the subpoena duces tecum like a checklist, she asked Sanders to produce the original of his file on Juliette. Thumbing through it briefly, she handed it to Mark, who carefully compared each original document to the copies they had previously been sent. Meanwhile, James continued interrogating the witness about his experiences with similar cases. After about an hour, Powell seized upon a pause between questions to recommend a short recess.

The session resumed ten minutes later with James delving into the details of the day of Juliette's surgery. Without revealing the intent behind the direction of her inquiry, Ronnie took special note of the fact that the witness' narrative lacked any mention of a discussion about tubal ligation with the patient while she was in his office. But that would have been expected since the surgeon's recommendations at the hospital had been largely based on his observation of the scar tissue in the abdominal cavity an hour or so later. Before Ronnie steered the deposition toward the specifics of the subsequent surgery, she caught sight of the name of the assisting surgeon on the operative report, the one potential fact witness her office had not been able to locate.

"Doctor, do you know the current address and telephone number of the resident who assisted you in the operating room that day – Doctor Trisha Hill?"

"No. I don't," he replied. "I haven't seen or spoken to her since the last time I ran into her at Swedish – maybe a couple of years ago. As I recall, she was about to finish up her residency. But that's all I remember. Haven't seen her in quite a while now."

"Have you heard anything about where she might be practicing now?" James pressed.

"No. No, I haven't," he declared. "But it's been a while, you understand."

"Of course, Doctor," Ronnie conceded as she pulled out a set of questions she had prepared with Steinberg's assistance. After eliciting a detailed description from the witness about the initial surgery to terminate the ectopic pregnancy and stop the internal bleeding, James turned to Sanders' conversations with the Marchettis before the tubal ligation. "Did you ever speak to Missus Marchetti without her husband present after you began the surgical procedure?"

"No," replied Sanders, "I don't think I did. I believe we talked about the first surgery and what I'd found while they were both in the recovery room. As I recall, he was with her while she was awake."

"Did you ever discuss the alternative methods of performing a tubal ligation with the Marchettis?"

"Oh, sure. I remember specifically talking about how we weren't going to be able to save the right tube and how I'd have to tie that one off. And then I told her what I thought were the reasons she had an ectopic in the first place, of the danger it had posed to her life, and I said what I thought were the chances that she'd have another ectopic pregnancy if conception were to occur through the left tube. I recommended doing a tubal ligation of the left so there'd be no chance that she'd have another life-endangering situation like that one."

"Doctor, when a surgeon performs a tubal ligation, there are several methods available from which to choose, are there not?"

"Oh, if you mean techniques, like Pomeroy, cauterization, silicone bands, spring clips, and the like, yes, there are several."

"Did you discuss the variety of techniques with the Marchettis?"

Sanders put his finger up against his temple again and tapped. "Hmm. Let me think. It does seem like I did mention something to them about the use of clips. Yes, I'm sure I did. It's coming back to me now. Missus Marchetti was still a young woman and obviously very distraught over the failure of that pregnancy. And I could tell that she and her husband," the doctor continued, nodding in courteous acknowledgment toward Roman, "were very much in love and very much wanted to have a family. So I told them I could try to suture the good ends of what remained of the right tube together and that I could then put clips on both tubes. And what with all the advances in fertility medicine, it might not be too long before we came up with a way to remove the adhesions and other damage from Missus Marchetti's tubes. That might allow her to have a normal conception and uterine pregnancy. I told them that the clips afforded the best chance of reversibility down the road, while any technique that involved actually severing the tube lessened those chances."

"Did either of the Marchettis say anything in response?"

"Well, yes. I recall that the patient did. She said she understood and that she trusted my judgment and approved of using the clips." He glanced over at Roman, whose face showed his agitation. Suddenly Sanders backtracked. "But I'm not sure whether Mister Marchetti was actually in the room at that time. He might've already left." He paused again and rubbed his temple. "You know, I'm not sure."

Just as she was about to follow up on that testimony, Ronnie felt a light tap on her arm. She leaned toward Roman so he could whisper in her ear.

"Can we take a break?" he requested, muffling his emotions.

Ronnie turned and looked at her client. Sensing his distress, she glanced at her watch and looked over at Powell. "Counselor, we're nearly at the two-hour mark. Let's take a recess now and maybe I can wrap this up before lunch." With a nod from Powell, the plaintiff and his two attorneys stepped down the hall and slipped quietly into Ronnie's office, shutting the door behind them.

"What's up?" she asked Roman.

"That son of a bitch is lying!" he exploded. "He never said anything to us about methods or techniques for doing the sterilization. And he was never alone with Juliette except before he opened her up or between the two procedures when she was still knocked out from the anesthesia. They let me go into the recovery room while they brought her out and I was there from the time she was roused to consciousness until they put her back under. I never heard anything about reversibility or any of that stuff he was spouting off."

"We know that," Ronnie reassured him. "But he doesn't know what you remember about those conversations. And if he can testify persuasively before a jury, he can convince them of it. He's a doctor. He knows all these medical terms and speaks in that language every day. You're a layperson and you don't routinely speak all that medical-ese. So his lawyer can argue to the jury that you didn't understand some of the lingo and, therefore, don't remember it. Or he can argue that the doctor, being a medical professional, was calm and composed during this crisis, while you, being an average person, were all wigged out by what was happening to your wife. And that has clouded your memory."

"So what you're saying is the jury is going to believe him and not me?"

"We don't know which one of you a jury is gonna believe," Mark interrupted. "But what we do need to know is what Sanders' story is. This is just fact-finding. We're not cross-examining the guy before a jury. We're not trying to make him sweat bullets so a jury will think 'this guy's a liar.' We're just trying to get him to give us as much detail as he's willing to give about what took place that day. If he gets a little too inventive, as I think he's been doing in those last few minutes, he'll end up stepping in his own bullshit. Whether it's your testimony that contradicts him and the jury thinks you're more credible than Sanders is, or whether we find a recovery room nurse who says Sanders wasn't alone with Juliette, or we find a paper record that contradicts his time line, or whatever – invariably people who talk too much and volunteer all the details he's putting on the record end up regretting it when they have to eat their own words."

"Oh, I see what you mean," said Roman.

"One other important thing," added James. "Keep a hold on your emotions in there. We don't need to be giving out free information to the other side and that might have been what you just did."

"How so?" asked Roman, puzzled by her comments.

"By reacting to his testimony," she explained. "We don't know what Powell knows and, likewise, he doesn't know what we know. But this process we're going through right now is called discovery because it's the opportunity for each side to find out as much as it can about the other side's case. The rules say it's supposed to be *open*, but that doesn't mean that you just give everything away. No, you still have to do the work to find out what the other side has." She could tell she was losing him. "It's like going fishing. All the fish are out there, free for everyone to catch. Now you can row your boat out into the middle of the lake and sit there and hope all the fish will jump into your boat, or you can bait your hook and cast your line and hope you catch something." Her discourse was interrupted by laughter from Mark.

"I'm sorry, Ronnie," he apologized. "Your analogy caught me by surprise. I never imagined you using fishing to illustrate your point."

"I was thinking of you," she quipped, "knowing how avid a flyfisher you are."

"So what was I doing?" asked Roman, still uncertain about how all this discussion of the legal rules applied to him.

"Okay. Let me explain it this way. Powell may not have known or even suspected that there is a factual dispute over whether his client fully informed his patient about the use of clips. And we might have completed all our questioning without Powell being tipped off. Then again, maybe he had it all figured out before we sat down. We don't know. But what we should now assume is that he's observed your emotional reaction to certain subject matter his client has just testified about and, if they weren't whirring before, his wheels are certainly turning now. Understand?"

"Yeah, I think so," replied Roman. "It's like what you were telling me yesterday when you prepared me for my deposition this afternoon. Never volunteer anything. Make the lawyer dig it out of you. Don't be evasive; don't lie. Just listen to the question and answer only the question that's asked. Answer as briefly and succinctly as possible. Yes and no are the best answers because they're the shortest possible. Right?"

"Precisely," Ronnie commended her student. "Now, the whole point of this is, don't volunteer anything – either words or emotions. Make Powell cast that fly out into the lake. Don't just jump into his boat." She ignored the chuckle and smirk from her elder colleague. "If discovery were any other way, we'd send you over to Powell's office and let him talk to you for as long as he wanted and he'd send Sanders over and we'd talk to him for as long as we wanted, but that's not the way it works. Understand?"

"Suddenly, I feel like I'm back in seventh grade and you're Missus Brashears."

"Who?" Ronnie asked.

"Missus Brashears," Roman repeated. "My seventh-grade English teacher. I think she was a refugee from an all girls' Catholic school, or maybe reject would be a more appropriate description. We figured she couldn't hack the celibacy thing so she didn't become a nun. She was a terror with a wooden ruler. She always had in her hand, slapping her desk with a loud 'whap!' every time someone gave a wrong answer. She was really old, at least she looked that way to a bunch of seventh graders, and she had long black hair that she tied in a bun. And she had these prominent white patches on her temples that ran like streaks along the side of her hair all the way back to the bun. We called her the skunk lady."

"Sounds terrifying," Mark interjected sarcastically, obviously amused by his client's vivid recollection. Directing his comment to James, he added, "Sounds like Ronnie all right."

"Okay, enough horsing around," she countered as she pulled open her desk drawer.

"Oh, God," mocked Mark, leaning back in his chair and throwing his hands up in front of his face, "she's going for the ruler!"

Roman laughed at Mark's antics, but Ronnie only glared. Rummaging through the drawer, she located the evasive object of her search, pulled out a roll of breath mints, and popped one into her mouth. Rising and cavalierly tossing the roll to Mark, she curtly advised her partner, "Take a hint, suck a mint."

A Doctor's Surprise

Back in the deposition, James picked back up with her line of general questions on sterilization. Sanders admitted that the medical literature contained case histories in which procedures had failed. In those extremely rare cases, he acknowledged, nature prevailed over modern medicine, and a woman became pregnant in spite of a properly performed sterilization. The doctor also admitted to taking pride in his surgical performance record. He claimed he was not aware of any tubal ligation he had ever done that had failed. His best estimate was that he had performed more than 1,000 successful procedures in his more than twenty years of private practice.

Defending himself against an aggressive attack by James, he denounced James' assertions that his arrogance interfered with sound medical judgment when he examined Juliette on that Friday afternoon some three years after the tubal. He emphatically denied Ronnie's contention that he elected not to test his patient for an ectopic pregnancy because he refused to consider the idea that he might have made a mistake during the surgery. Relentlessly, James persevered, digging and digging until she found what she wanted.

"Doctor, you do admit, do you not, that Juliette Marchetti presented to your office late that Friday afternoon with many of the classic signs and symptoms of an ectopic pregnancy?" Ronnie insisted as she leaned forward ever so slightly.

"Yes. Yes, she did."

"She gave a history of having had pelvic cramps that came and went over a period of two weeks, did she not?" Her tone was becoming much more argumentative.

"Yes, that's what my office notes indicate."

"She told your nurse that she had related the cramps from as far back as two weeks ago to her period, which was late in coming, did she not?" One by one she checked off each item on Steinberg's list of signs and symptoms.

"Yes, that's what's indicated here."

"Is it not the case that when a woman who is known to be sexually active misses a period, one probable cause is that she is pregnant?"

"That's true. Of course, there can be many other causes . . ."

James cut him short, knowing that his full explanation of the many other medical possibilities would only waste time. "And would it not be standard medical procedure to test a woman for pregnancy if she presented two weeks late in her menstrual cycle?"

"Under most circumstances, yes."

"And Missus Marchetti also complained of some light spotting during that time, correct?"

"Right. The nurse's notes mention that."

"And they also indicate, do they not, that Missus Marchetti said the spotting and cramping had intensified over the past twenty-four hours?"

"Yes."

"You read your nurse's notes on the chart before you examined Missus Marchetti, did you not?" Her tone was cynical – lying halfway condescension and accusation. She had to draw him out and if getting him pissed off was the only way to do it, so be it. Powell might complain, but her methods were within the realm of acceptable examination technique.

"Of course," he insisted. "I always do."

"So you were aware of the history your patient had related before you conducted a physical examination, right?"

"Yes, that's correct."

"And when you examined her, you found her sensitive to palpation on the left side more than the right, correct?"

"Yes. That's what I put down on the chart."

"And that, too – pain and tenderness on only one side – is one of the classic signs of an ectopic pregnancy, isn't it?"

"Yes, it is."

"But with all those factors – menstrual period two weeks late, cramping, spotting, tenderness more on one side – you chose not to test Missus Marchetti for pregnancy, right?"

"Right. We didn't do a pregnancy test."

Quickly glancing back up the list to confirm her check marks in the column, she flipped over to the next sheet. It was time to pin him down. "If a woman who did not have Missus Marchetti's history of sterilization presented with all of the same symptoms, would you have ordered a pregnancy test?"

Sanders became noticeably more uneasy, shifting slightly in his seat and fidgeting with his hands. He looked intently at James as if about to speak, then leaned to his left and whispered in his attorney's ear.

"May we have a moment, Counselor?" requested Powell.

"Of course," she replied. "Do you need to step into an office?"

"No, that won't be necessary," the defense lawyer replied as he rose from his chair. "We'll just go out in the hall for a second." The female associate to Powell's left began to get up but the senior attorney motioned for her to stay put.

While the doctor and his counsel murmured inaudibly just outside the closed conference room door, Mark leaned over to offer a few encouraging words to Ronnie in private. "There's something he's uncomfortable about," Frey analyzed. "Keep on it till we find out what it is."

Thirty seconds later, the two absentees returned to the proceeding. James brought the witness back to where they had left off. "Do you recall the prior question or should I have the court reporter read it back?"

"No, that's fine," replied Sanders. "I recall the question."

"Then what is your answer, Doctor?"

"The answer is yes. If a patient who did not have Missus Marchetti's history of sterilization presented with the same signs and symptoms, I would have ordered a pregnancy test."

"Then why did you not order such a test in Missus Marchetti's case?"

Again, Sanders hesitated, then leaned over to whisper in Powell's ear. After a quick response from his attorney, the witness turned to face James. "It was my understanding that a pregnancy test for a woman who has been sterilized falls outside of the treatment guidelines . . ." He paused as though he were only mid-sentence, then looked at Ronnie as though he had finished with his explanation. But she was not about to let him bury that thought.

"What treatment guidelines are you referring to?"

Again Sanders leaned over to confer in private with his attorney. This time, after only an affirmative nod from Powell, Sanders faced his questioner. "The treatment guidelines set forth in the HMO manual."

"Are you saying that the health management organization which administered Juliette's health plan directed doctors such as yourself not to perform a pregnancy test on a woman who had been sterilized?"

One more time, the witness leaned over to whisper to his attorney. Ronnie had put up with the hesitations and private consultations long enough. Turning to the court reporter, she put it on the record. "Let the record reflect that for the last three questions, the witness has conferred with his counsel before attempting to answer the question." Powell glanced at her and acknowledged the statement, all the while listening to his client's muffled voice.

After another nod from the defense attorney, Sanders spoke up. "That's correct. Since Missus Marchetti had lost one tube from a prior ectopic and had had a tubal ligation of the remaining tube, the managed care people indicated that a pregnancy test was *not* called for."

"Now you just added something there," Ronnie said. "I'd gotten the impression from what you initially said that the guidelines set out in black and white something like 'don't administer a pregnancy test to a sterilized woman,' but now you just said the 'managed care people indicated that you shouldn't administer the test. So my question is, do the guidelines state specifically and expressly that you shouldn't perform that test?"

"No, they didn't," replied the doctor. "That's what I was unclear about and that's why I called the company."

"So you called the HMO while the patient was in your office?"

"That's correct."

"And which HMO are we talking about?"

"Union Health Management . . . Inc.," the witness replied.

"And based upon your conversations with the Union Health Management personnel, you concluded that the pregnancy test wasn't necessary?"

"Not exactly. Based upon the phone conversation, I was directed to not perform that test."

"Directed by the Union Health Management personnel you talked to?"

"That's right."

"Do you know the name of that person?"

"No, I don't recall his name. I don't know if he ever gave it."

"But this person was a man?" James inquired.

"Yes."

"Tell me about the conversation," Ronnie directed. "What was said?"

Sanders glanced over at Powell, then back at James. "I dialed the same number I'd called many times before for situations like this . . . like when I had questions about the treatment guidelines or what was covered under the plan and so forth. I told the switchboard I was a participating physician and had a question about the treatment guidelines and the operator switched me over to a young man . . . or at least he sounded young on the phone. I explained the situation about Missus Marchetti's history and her signs and symptoms. I said that I was planning to do a blood test just to make sure she wasn't pregnant, but that the guidelines gave me the impression I had to clear it since the patient had been sterilized. Then the guy put me on hold for maybe five or six minutes and when he came back on, he said that he'd consulted with his superior and that a blood test wasn't called for under the circumstances. He thanked me for calling in and we hung up."

"Was this man a doctor?" Ronnie asked.

"I assume so," Sanders replied curtly. Then, reflecting on the telephone conversation, he backtracked a step or two on his answer. "I don't know."

"Did you get the name of the superior he talked to?"

"No, I didn't."

"Do you know if the superior was a physician? Did the man say anything that indicated that?"

"No, I don't know. I don't recall him saying anything that indicated he'd talked to another physician." Sanders shrugged and added sheepishly, "I just assumed he had."

James glanced at her watch – 11:45. Turning to Powell, she offered a suggestion. "Counselor, I see we're approaching the noon hour. I was hoping to finish the deposition by then, but your client's most recent responses have opened an area that I had not anticipated. My best estimate is that I'll need another thirty to forty-five minutes to wrap this up. We can break for lunch now and finish after we get back, or I can push on and we can take lunch a little later than we might have anticipated. What's your pleasure?"

Powell glanced at Sanders, who shook his head apathetically. "Why don't we take a break now?" he decided. "I'm sure you're an exception when it comes to estimating how much time you've got to go, but I've known many an attorney who said 'just one more question' and then went on for an hour or two." Everyone in the room appreciated the light touch of humor as they rose from their seats and stretched.

Ronnie had hoped to hobnob with Mark and Roman on the significance of Sanders' taciturn disclosures about the call to the HMO, but both potential luncheon companions had made other plans. Since Roman had two business meetings set for that evening and an early morning flight to St. Louis for a computer expo, Sally was bringing his daughter downtown for a midday visit. And Mark had shifted a client appointment from 10:30 to noon so he could sit in on the round of civil depositions. Almost desperate for someone to talk to about this new information, Ronnie went looking for Evan. But he too was unavailable, having signed out for most of the day to the University of Denver law library to research transcripts of legislative hearings on a recent amendment to the state penal code. Bottled up with her own thoughts and frustrated by the building pressure of internal intellectual discourse, she took it out on her waistline, forgoing her usual grilled chicken salad for a double cheeseburger, large fries, and a strawberry milkshake at a greasy spoon diner a couple of blocks away. Stuffed but psychologically sated as she sat in the corner booth, she looked back over her notes from the morning, trying to formulate her next line of questioning.

When the session resumed at one o'clock, James turned toward Sanders' professional opinion about the guidelines. "Do you, as a licensed medical doctor, agree with a guideline that directs that pregnancy tests not be performed on women who have been sterilized?"

This time, all the conferring the witness had to do with his attorney, presumably, had been done over their steaks and salads. "No, I wouldn't agree with the guideline."

"But you're the one who has a license to practice medicine in this state, not the insurance company, right?"

Sanders was puzzled by the circuitous nature of her question. Cutting through to the heart of it, he replied. "If you're asking whether I believe that an HMO or an insurance company halfway across town or hundreds of miles away should substitute its judgment about what's medically necessary for the health and safety of a patient for that of the treating physician, the answer is 'No, I don't.'"

"Yet as I understand your testimony, Doctor, you allowed someone at the health plan offices to dictate what methods you would use in your diagnosis of Missus Marchetti's condition, didn't you?"

Sanders winced at the words, clearing his throat of its emotional obstruction before answering. "Yes."

Ronnie fought the temptation to continue the attack. *This is only a discovery deposition,* she thought. *It's not cross examination at trial. You've made your point. Don't need to beat him over the head with it.* She backed off a step or two and reassessed her situation. Then she recalled Evan's meticulously prepared request for documents. Scanning it, she found the wording she needed.

"As I understand it, Doctor, this volume of treatment guidelines sets forth what will and what won't be paid for under the health plan, correct?"

"Generally speaking, yes. That's correct."

"And you previously testified that you consulted these guidelines during Missus Marchetti's last presentation to your office?"

"Yes, I did. After I examined the patient, I went into my office to look at the guidelines manual."

"Did you bring that volume with you today?"

"No." He glanced over at Powell with a question in his eyes. Powell just looked down at his legal pad. Sanders turned his attention back to Ronnie. "No, I didn't."

Ronnie had hardly opened her mouth before her opposing counsel anticipated her next request, which she was about to toss in his direction. "I discussed this at lunch with my client," Powell explained. "I've looked back through your subpoena duces tecum and I certainly consider that volume to fit within one of the categories of documents you requested. I'll represent to you that I'll get a copy to you within the next two or three days, if that's all right with you?"

James leaned back and motioned to Mark, who wheeled his swivel chair to within whispering range. Then turning to the defense attorney, she addressed his offer. "Counselor, if it's agreeable to you, since we don't have a copy of the guidelines here with us now, I'd like to recess the deposition of Doctor Sanders until such time as we have received and reviewed the volume in question. As you can well imagine, I'm at a severe disadvantage in questioning your client about a document I've not even seen."

"As long as you're not going to go back into areas you've already covered and try to get a second bite at the apple. . . ."

James interrupted him. "With the stipulation that any further questioning will relate only to the HMO guidelines and your client's practice in regard to them, that would be fine." Hearing a soft hiss, she caught sight of Frey scooting his chair back in her direction. After a brief conversation, she added to her proposal. "And that stipulation also would include any other new matters divulged through your supplemental production of documents."

"That'll be fine, Counselor," Powell stated. "If we turn up any other documents that we haven't disclosed, you can question him about them." With an agreement on the record, the parties took a fifteen-minute break before Roman's deposition began.

A New Party

One of Cooper's law professors at Vanderbilt had taught his students that every case should be envisioned as though it were shaped like an hourglass. From the wealth of evidentiary facts and legal theories that each side could present, represented by the sand in the top half of the glass, only a very few would turn out to be critical. In every case, the professor asserted, the lawyer's challenge was to identify the crucial facts and points of law and to see that they passed through the narrow middle of the funnel, just like so many grains of sand. The wisdom behind that lesson became evident at a hastily called firm meeting the next Monday. The legal import of the revelations made during Sanders' deposition were the sole item for discussion.

While Ronnie had sat through two hours of Powell questioning Roman the previous Thursday afternoon, Mark had briefed Evan about the defendant's conversations with the HMO employee and requested that Cooper research the issues. He left his junior partner with a scribbled sheet of questions. "Can we also bring a claim against the health plan company?" "Would we have to bring it under the federal Employee's Retirement Insurance Security Act?" "Would that require transfer of the case from state to federal court?" "How would that affect the amount of damages? Or would it?"

Contrary to his best laid plans to get in his first cross-country skiing trek around Winter Park, Evan ended up spending not only most of Friday but all day Saturday, in the office library, pulling cases and articles off the Westlaw computer research service. What he found was an unexpected bonanza of recent rulings and heated political controversy. During the past year several federal courts, both at the district and appellate levels, had allowed a cause of action by a patient against his or her employer-funded health plan to go forward. Plaintiffs long denied effective remedy pressed on while the insurance companies lobbied Congress for reform that would undermine the courts' decisions.

When Mark joined his junior partners in the conference room that morning, his expectations were running high about the prospect of bringing Union Health Management in as a defendant. "It gives us another pocket – maybe one that's a little deeper – that our state legislature, in its infinite exercise of wisdom, hasn't sewn shut with the threads of tort reform." Evan and Ronnie smiled with approval at Mark's metaphoric hyperbole. He's turning into a bit of a plaintiff's lawyer, Cooper thought as he organized the fruits of his weekend labors into orderly piles.

Yielding the floor to Evan, Frey asked their research specialist to brief them on the case law. As Cooper began to outline his major points on the chalkboard, he tossed out copies of the cases he had pulled off line, pertinent sections of which he had conspicuously highlighted in bright yellow. "There were three cases that made it up to the federal circuit courts in 1995, all cases of first impression. The first one to have been decided was announced in June, in the Third Circuit, *Dukes v. U.S. Healthcare, Inc.*," he explained as he bounced his pencil eraser on the table top like a drumstick. "It's a case out of Pennsylvania. It started off in their state court system as a typical medical malpractice action, but one of the defendants, a managed care company removed it to federal court on a theory of complete federal preemption under ERISA. The plaintiffs moved to remand it back to the state court and the federal district judge denied their motion."

"Hold on there, Jack!" Ronnie complained. "Let's remand you back to explaining some of these procedural technicalities to me. I don't recall ever running across these kinds of issues while I was with the D.A.'s office, at least not with the type of cases I handled."

"Okay. Sorry," Evan conceded as he mentally backtracked. "We could probably all use a little refresher in some of the differences between the federal court system and the state court system." He thumped the eraser another time or two. "When Congress passed the Employee's Retirement Income Security Act back in the mid-seventies, they put stringent limitations on the remedies a person could obtain if his or her claim related to an ERISA plan. Employer-provided health insurance plans generally fall under ERISA. And what it boils down to is that a plaintiff under ERISA can only recover the benefits he or she would have been entitled to. In this case, that'd be the value of the pregnancy test the HMO refused to pay for. There have been all kinds of personal injury and even wrongful death cases brought under ERISA, and the courts have said that the plaintiff is not entitled to any damages for pain and suffering, loss of spousal income, and so forth."

"In other words," Mark interjected, "a penny on the dollar?"

"More like a penny on each thousand dollars!" Evan retorted.

"That's awfully harsh," commented Ronnie.

"To say the least," added Evan as he went on with his mini-lecture, tapping as he talked. "What frequently happens after a plaintiff files the usual kind of medical malpractice or wrongful death complaint in state court is that the HMO removes the case to federal court, claiming complete preemption under ERISA."

"You're going to have to run through preemption for me," said James. "There's something familiar about it back in the recesses of my memory, but it's been a while since I took that fed courts class in law school."

A quick glance and expression of mild irritation caused Cooper to park the pencil over his ear. "Preemption means that one set of laws takes precedence over another – in this case precedence to the point of exclusion. If our clients' claims fall under ERISA, that's the only law they can sue under. They can't sue for medical malpractice or negligence or any other common law or state statutory provisions. They can only sue under ERISA, can only get the paltry damages it allows – which essentially amounts to nothing – and can only do it in federal court."

"So let me see if I understand what you're saying," said James. "If this medical malpractice claim ends up in federal court under ERISA, all our clients could get from Union Health Management as damages would be the value of the fifty-dollar blood test she should've gotten?"

"That's about it," Cooper agreed. "That's what ERISA preemption is all about. If this turns out to be an ERISA claim, it preempts the usual state law medical malpractice cause of action."

"Whew," Mark sighed, his balloon of high expectations dropping precipitously fast. "Sounds to me like pursuing a claim against an HMO would be a big waste of time."

"Used to be," replied Evan, as a slight smile formed on his face. "Used to be, but no more. That's what these recent cases were all about. In the first one I gave you, *Dukes*, an HMO removed a couple of separate medical negligence lawsuits to federal court and the plaintiffs tried to remand them back to their own state courts. But two different federal district court judges said no and the plaintiffs appealed. So the Third Circuit Court of Appeals heard them both at the same time back in 1995, reversed the district courts' rulings, and sent the cases back to their respective state courts."

"Now that sounds promising," commented Mark. "How'd the plaintiffs do it?"

"That's what I've highlighted on that opinion I gave you," Evan pointed out. "The appellate court distinguished between quality care issues – like malpractice and negligence claims – and health plan administration decisions. If a complaint is based on the latter, it's preempted. But if it's a quality of care issue, it's not."

"So did the HMO appeal that decision up to the U.S. Supreme Court?" asked Ronnie.

"Yeah, it sure did," replied Cooper, "but certiorari was denied. They refused to review it."

"Since the basic holding still hasn't been reversed by the Supreme Court with the rash of other cases that have come up lately, I'd say the holding is firm," Evan reasoned. "Of course, a defense firm with a well-funded client could always fashion an argument that might turn it around."

"Not to mention the insurance company's lobbying power with Congress," added Mark. "So what else? What are these other cases?"

"As far as date of decision is concerned, *Dukes* was the first one. But about three weeks later, in early June, the Tenth Circuit released its decision in *PacifiCare of Oklahoma, Inc., v. Burrage*." Cooper handed out copies of that case.

"Well, that's right out of out of Denver. At least that's our federal circuit," said Mark. "Favorable case?"

"Similar to *Dukes* as far the result is concerned," replied Evan. "State court claim was brought in an Oklahoma court, then removed to federal court. The federal district judge granted the plaintiff's motion to remand so the HMO sought a writ of mandamus from the Tenth Circuit here in Denver to force the district judge to rescind the order sending the case back over to the state court. But the court of appeals refused to issue mandamus. Slightly different facts from those in *Dukes,* but the Tenth Circuit reached the same general conclusion as the Third – certain kinds of medical malpractice claims may not be preempted by ERISA. Then there was another case just a few months later out of the Seventh Circuit – *Rice v. Panchal.* Again, same result," he added as he passed out another set of marked copies.

"So what's been the history of this *PacifiCare* case in this circuit?" inquired Ronnie. "Any Colorado federal cases out there?"

"None that are reported," Cooper responded. "I've been searching around to find one by a member of our local federal bench but haven't heard of one yet. Considering that such a decision would be a case of first impression in this federal district, I'd think a district judge would leap at the chance to get it published. So, I assume that's a good indicator there isn't one. But I'll check around and see if anyone knows anything about one."

"So what type of claim do we assert?" asked Ronnie as she digested the highlighted sections of the cases Cooper had selected. "From what I see here, it looks like that could make a big difference."

"Absolutely," replied Evan. "For one thing, we definitely don't want to assert a breach of contract cause of action. That would surely be preempted because it relates to the administration of the plan. However, in those cases that have been remanded back to the state courts for trial, they've succeeded in avoiding preemption by asserting claims of vicarious liability and negligence."

"Give me an example," requested Frey.

"Okay, sure. Let's take this case. If Sanders had come out and told Juliette he wanted to perform a pregnancy test to make sure nothing strange had happened since the tubal ligation, but the health plan wouldn't pay for it, she could have sued to force Union Health to pay the bill. Now that would have been under ERISA because she was trying to affect the administration of the plan or recover some benefit to which she believed she was rightfully entitled. Any claim brought in state court under contract law or something like that would've been preempted, completely.

"But given the facts as we now believe they occurred, we're saying that the plan employees' interpretation of the treatment guidelines failed to give their agent, Doctor Sanders, sufficient latitude to decide whether the test was reasonably necessary, to protect the health of his patient. As such, Union Health Management was, in effect, making the treatment decision. Therefore, it can be liable for the negligent practice of medicine, especially since, we assume, their decision was based only on statistics – the odds, so to speak – and not on their observations and personal impressions of the patient. I doubt that there's a doctor around in this litigation-rich environment who'd say that he or she would forgo a fifty-dollar test in this kind of case – even if the odds were one in a hundred or one in a thousand that it would come out positive – especially if the one chance could result in life-threatening injuries to the patient."

"So is that what we claim," Ronnie queried, "that Union Health was directly negligent in setting or interpreting a cost-saving guideline that prevented Juliette from getting adequate medical care?"

"That and the vicarious liability theory," Cooper added, "that Sanders was an agent of Union Health and that they're responsible for his failure to diagnose the second ectopic. I'm still contemplating whether we should also assert a vicarious liability theory for the botched tubal ligation."

"I don't understand how we're going to get vicarious liability," James reasoned. "I've looked through Sanders' contract with the HMO, and it clearly labels him an independent contractor."

"Yeah," agreed Cooper, "but keep in mind the basic law of agency. It

won't matter what the contract says if, at the time the work was being performed, Union Health was controlling the details of the work."

"So you're saying that because Union Health effectively made the treatment decision, it was dictating the details of the work to Sanders?" Ronnie questioned. "And *voila*, that made the doctor the agent of Union Health?"

"Something along those lines," replied Evan. "Add to that is the fact that seventy-five percent of Sanders' business comes from his participating physician's contract with Union. At least those are the figures he put in his answers to our written interrogatories."

"Okay. Let's go back to something we just touched on," Frey directed. "About those treatment guidelines. Seems to me I recall reading or hearing about something not too long ago, maybe just last year, where a managed care company had a guideline or standing directive that women in their plan who gave birth were supposed to be discharged from the hospital with their babies within twenty-four hours after giving birth. And some of the babies got sick. So some members of Congress were proposing legislation that would mandate a minimum forty-eight hour stay. Didn't a committee hold some hearings on that?"

"Yeah, they did," agreed Cooper. "I saw mention of a case or two with similar facts on some of the news line services, but I didn't see where anything like that had gotten to court yet. However, I did run off a couple of the articles, and they're in here somewhere." He thumbed through his stacks, pulled out a few sheets, and slid them across the conference table to his colleagues. "In one case – the first one there that led to some congressional committee hearings last fall, a newborn died because it developed a disease that would've been diagnosed and treated if the health plan had allowed the mother and baby to stay forty-eight hours instead of twenty-four."

"That's horrible!" cried Ronnie.

"That's what a few members of Congress thought," replied Evan. The conference room fell silent as James and Mark perused the stories, then glanced over their notes.

Frey spoke up. "So if we drag Union Health into this lawsuit, we've got some good authority to stand on, right?"

"Right," replied Evan, "as far as getting them in. But we still don't know how the facts are going to play out on the treatment decision. The HMO may have a story substantially different from what I understand Sanders told you."

"But if we do add Union Health Management as a defendant, at least we know we stand a chance of keeping this thing in state court," concluded Frey.

"A good chance," Cooper agreed.

"We want to do everything we can to keep that trial date," Frey insisted, "and the defendants are going to want to do everything the can to delay it. We might as well plan for the removal and remand. Evan, what say you go ahead and draft the amended complaint and motion for leave. And when you're through with those, get a motion for remand ready, at least in draft form. I think we have to assume that whoever defends Union Health is certain to give removal to federal court a shot. And I'd like to be ready to file a remand motion the day after they remove it." He turned toward James. "Ronnie. Why don't you give Roman a call and explain this stuff about Union Health to him. We'll want to get his approval on this."

"By the way," Cooper asked, shifting the focus a few degrees, "in terms of calendaring these projects, now that our clients' baby girl has been born, do we have a schedule for adding her as a plaintiff?"

"No. Roman's been pretty well tied up with his daughter for the past month or two, as well as getting over to see Juliette as often as he can,"

Ronnie answered. "What time we've spent together was to prepare him for his deposition. We didn't get around to adding his daughter and signing a new fee agreement."

"Well, let's do that as soon as possible," Mark urged. "He'll just have to make some time within the week. He'll need to come in to sign the papers as her guardian so you can discuss the Union Health matter with him then too. Do we have any reason to think he might not want to go after the HMO as well?"

"None that I know of," Ronnie replied. "We didn't have time to visit much after his deposition last Thursday, so I don't know if what Sanders said really sank in. But our client has a bit of the crusading spirit in him. That's why he's going after the doctor, and I've got a feeling he'll look at the health plan the same way."

"Good," Frey remarked. "Then let's go ahead and prepare our motion for leave to amend and the proposed amended complaint, bringing in Union Health Management as a defendant and adding the baby, with Roman as next friend of the minor."

"You know what's going to happen when the press sees the amended complaint, don't you?" Ronnie commented rhetorically.

"You mean about adding the baby as a plaintiff?" Mark asked. "Yeah, I know. It's unfortunate in a way, but we've gotta put enough information in the complaint to state a cause of action. And I'll bet one of the reporters who's contacted us before about this case is going to pick up on the oddity of it. Let's just hope it doesn't get too far out of hand."

"We've done the best we can to prepare everyone for it," Ronnie added. "I can't think of anything else we can do."

"No. I think you've covered all the bases," Frey remarked. "You've laid out a good plan. Let's just hope everyone cooperates."

"Yeah, let's hope," she replied.

"By the way," Evan inquired, "do we know the baby's name? We're going to need that for the pleadings."

Looking up from her notepad, James responded to the question. "He named her after her mother. Her name is Juliet Abbott Marchetti."

A New Birth

The mild case of local media frenzy that had broken out for the two or three days after the case was filed in late September paled in comparison to the epidemic of national press delirium that followed a court beat reporter's discovery of the motion to amend and proposed amended complaint. That part of Ronnie's plan – filing the pleadings late in the afternoon on the Friday before Christmas – did not turn out to be a smashing success, but it was a valiant effort. The rest of it, she hoped, would protect her clients' privacy.

Not only were the taste buds of the press corps titillated by the uniqueness of a newborn being a party to a lawsuit, but this new wrinkle had two folds. First, the child had not even been given birth to by the mother for whose personal injuries she was suing. And second, the baby had been born over a month after her genetic mother lapsed into a coma. Within hours after the Saturday morning edition of the *Denver Post* broke the story, reporters from every local TV station were calling any telephone number they could dig up to get more details for their own version. But with the law offices closed and all three of Roman's attorneys out of Denver for one type of winter activity or another, all the press could get were answering machine recordings.

Roman had been prepared for the onslaught, holing up with his daughter for the entirety of the two-week holiday season at the ranch house just north of Castle Rock which had been the site of Roman's wedding years before. With a few exceptions, he had arranged to leave his business affairs in the capable hands of his office manager, a gruff-mannered matron in her late fifties who could stare down a pit bull, as the journalists who strayed onto the business locale that next Monday morning soon discovered.

The Rifkins also had benefitted from Ronnie's foresight and maintained their anonymity. On December 18, Sally had parted from the newborn she had nurtured for the first ten weeks at her home in southeast Denver. To help Roman ease into full-time parenthood, he hired on a nanny, Lucille Hagan, a lonely graying grandmother and longtime widowed friend of the Abbott family whose own son, daughter-in-law, and two grandchildren had been transferred back east nearly a year before. Try as they might, the press was never able to find Roman, his child, or the surrogate mother.

While Roman savored the experience of fatherhood and the miracle of life reborn through the holiday season, his attorneys brought in the new year by fighting the expected battles over removal and remand with the lawyers hired by Union Health Management. Lead counsel for the managed care company was Sylvester P. Willis of the law firm of Haskins, Pulaski, McIlhenny & Sturgis, a large Chicago-based firm with more than 300 attorneys nationwide. With satellite offices in Denver, Omaha, Des Moines, Kansas City and Minneapolis, it was well equipped to pursue every legal theory and procedure on behalf of its clientele.

The Denver office been established in 1983 and had grown to more than thirty attorneys in the intervening thirteen years. Willis was the managing partner of the Denver office and a voting shareholder in the national leadership committee. Formerly a partner with one of the largest Denver-based firms, he had been stolen away by HPM&S when the firm's directorship voted to expand into its fourth city. However, the coup was not without controversy. Willis' former firm threatened to file suit against both their ex-partner and his new firm over a large portion of the business Willis took with him upon departure. Although the matter was settled without further publicity about three months later, the talk around the Denver bar was that Willis had been forced by his new Chicago partners to drop many of the clients when several of them related certain misrepresentations that had been made by Willis and the four other attorneys he had brought with him to the Haskins firm.

Sylvester Willis was not a man of large stature, standing about five--foot-eight-inches tall if he wore his dress cowboy boots, which he always did, even when in Chicago for management meetings. Of course, he was the only one of the managing partners so shod and probably the only one who felt he needed to gain a little standing with his Windy City cohorts. In his late fifties, his salt and pepper shock of curly hair was trimmed close, replete with sidewalls and sideburns that dropped a scant quarter inch down the ear. His emerald eyes had a penetrating quality, perhaps because they were set deeply into their sockets. His clean-shaven face had begun to take on that discolored appearance that some men get from small blood vessels bursting right below the surface. "Varicose Face" one rather ill-tempered personal injury attorney had called him during an argument in a deposition – an on-the-record comment which cost the repentant lawyer $500 in sanctions when it somehow came to the attention of the presiding judge. The ever-rounding shape of Willis' girth was matched by the bulbous shape of his nose, which, somewhat like the fabled Pinocchio, seemed to keep on growing – if only a micrometer or so a year. But for all of his distinguishing physical characteristics – some almost comical – his overall appearance was quite distinguished and he conveyed an air of authority and professionalism exceedingly well, it seemed, to the juries which sat on his cases.

On the Monday of the first full work week after New Year's, Willis fired off his removal papers and accompanying motions to dismiss, landing the controversial case right in the lap of U.S. District Judge Thomas A. Glickman. Hardly had the ink dried than James and Cooper retaliated by submitting the motion to remand, which Evan had essentially completed researching and writing three weeks before. At the conclusion of the motion, the plaintiffs' attorneys had requested an expedited hearing on the matter, citing the complexity of the case, the need for ample discovery time, and the trial setting eleven months away. Before Willis and his horde of young defense attorneys could even file their response to the motion to remand, the court clerk for Judge Glickman scheduled the hearing for a Thursday afternoon, three weeks later. But on the last Monday in January, as Ronnie was reviewing the briefs and the cases cited by both sides in preparation for her upcoming oral argument, Ellen interrupted her to deliver a just-transmitted fax from the federal court.

"ORDER-MEMORANDUM," it was titled. Ronnie quickly skipped over to the last page, looking for the ruling. The final two paragraphs gave her the information she sought.

> Plaintiffs' claims relate solely to quality of care issues, which are not completely preempted by the civil enforcement section of ERISA. Plaintiffs do not claim that the insured party was improperly denied benefits due under the plan. Instead, they claim that medical treatment decisions were decisions were negligently made by plan employees and agents.

Accordingly, it is the decision of this court that Plaintiffs' Motion to Remand is hereby GRANTED and the action is remanded to the Second Judicial District, State of Colorado."

"Yes!" James cried as she reached for the phone. Scanning back through the rest of the opinion, she buzzed Cooper's office. No answer – just voice mail. Try the library, she thought.

"Yeah," came the voice on the other end.

"Evan, we're being remanded back to state court."

"What? Have we got an order already? I thought you had the hearing later this week?"

"I do. We did. But I guess we don't – at least not anymore," she giggled as the words stumbled out. "Just got a fax from the court. Glickman's remanded the case."

Cooper shot down to her office in a matter of seconds, grabbing the edge of the door frame to brake his speed, letting his momentum spin him in. While Ronnie stepped out to find Mark, Evan digested each of the judge's points, each case the ruling cited. Returning alone, James stepped out of her shoes and plopped down on the couch, a cold Diet Coke in her hand. "I'd blocked off the whole day to study the pleadings and do some preliminary prepping for the hearing. Now I'm thinking about taking the rest of the day off."

"This is good," Cooper interjected, deep into legal rumination. "This is really good. He's studied the cases thoroughly and made a strong fact-based analysis. Distinguished the facts of those cases Willis had put forth and found strong similarities in those cases we cited." He turned to look at his colleague. "This may actually hold water!" he exclaimed excitedly. "It's as strong an opinion as the best ones I've read . . . and stronger than many of the others." But Evan's effervescent enthusiasm was lost on Ronnie, whose mind was already drifting down a slow river in a sun-drenched canoe – even if it was the dead of winter.

While one lawyer sunned her mind on an imaginary stream and another chewed on legal thought as though it were filet mignon, the media circus rolled into Denver in full force, staged only by its own frustration. Thinking that their local colleagues might not have sufficient journalistic expertise to sniff out the facts, most of the major news organizations had dispatched more seasoned reporters to the Mile High City. But even the presence of national news teams did little to unveil the cloak of privacy that blanketed the coverage. All, of course, was to Roman's great satisfaction.

The best attempts of the swarm of reporters to locate the new father and baby were foiled by the protection of doctor-patient confidentiality and a series of effective court gag orders. And that part of James' plan was working to perfection. After Ronnie and Cindy had paid a visit to the office of the attorney who represented the hospital corporation – coincidentally, a member of its board of trustees and the Belatrons' neighbor – one of the hospital executives called a meeting of all records, labor and delivery, postpartum, and nursery personnel and warned that they could face the loss of both job and license if they violated privacy rights. For the month after the public filing of the amended complaint, all the press was able to acquire was the birth certificate, which listed the father as Roman Marchetti, which they already knew, and the mother as Juliette.

Even the personnel of Fox's court were mum on the subject. Long before Juliette's tragedy injected an element of macabre curiosity into her clients' legal affairs, Belatron had requested that the matter be sealed. And the court had complied with the wishes of those involved. A few days before the child's name was added to the lawsuit, James and Belatron visited with Judge Fox. After the meeting, the judge spoke quietly to each member of her entourage who might be a source of information. The three clerks who had had some contact with the case all agreed to respect the privacy of the parties. And at the urging of James, Judge Williams had recognized the juvenile court's authority to seal such personal matters and issued her own gag order in the civil damages trial. Even Powell was fully cooperative, a point which he made completely clear to all the members of his team.

James had also spoken directly to each of Juliette's coworkers, all of whom had put two and two together and come up with Sally as the surrogate. But, out of their love and respect for Juliette and her family, they agreed to avoid the press. By the time the attorneys put the last piece into place, the stone wall was higher and more structurally sound than anything even Richard Nixon could have envisioned.

The one piece of information that the press was able to deduce from the denials of other fertility physicians was that Dr. Radhavishnu and Mountain Fertility Specialists had been involved in the conception of the child, a report which the MFS staff and its prominent doctor would neither admit nor deny. Armed with only a birth certificate, the press mounted an all-out assault on the birth hospital. But all inquiries were referred to the Swedish Hospital spokesperson, who steadfastly refused to divulge any information whatsoever without the proper signed authorization forms. Nobody could make any headway in discovering the name of the surrogate or the current location of father and child. Attempts to got the information outside of normal channels escalated as virtually every hospital nurse, technician, or orderly connected with the birthing center was contacted. But story after story was killed by editors and producers because of a lack of vital information.

In fact, the only story related to the surrogate birth to make the front pages and the nightly newscasts proved to be a great embarrassment to the media itself. One tabloid reporter, anxious to make a name for himself, offered to pay $1,000 to a records department employee for the name and address of the surrogate mother. Unfortunately, his selection of a prospective spy was poorly planned. She went straight to her manager, who recounted the incident to the administration offices upstairs. The hospital's attorney immediately called James, who, with the cooperation of the Denver Police Department and the Colorado Attorney General's Office, set up a sting.

Equipped with a video camera hidden behind a screen and a microphone that looked like a pen, an undercover policeman, Detective Ernie Mayfield, posed as an ambitious records custodian with a need for some quick cash. When the reporter, Charlie Puckett, dropped by a day later to see what his clandestine contact had come up with, she whisked him down to an out-of-the-way employee snack room to introduce him to Mayfield – a person, she claimed, who had access to records that were not in her department. The camera and mike caught it all, from their initial handshake to the exchange of a fake set of hospital records for the cold hard cash. With scenes at times reminiscent of the John Gotti tapes but at other times more like something out of a Keystone Cops movie, Mayfield played his part as though he were shooting a Hollywood screen test. Darting his eyes left and right, jerking his head around suspiciously at the slightest sound, and moving the reporter to more favorable camera position, like a pawn on a chessboard, the officer was careful to avoid any shade of police entrapment.

"So lemme git this straight. You want me to find the hospital records on this birth?" the CU-educated Mayfield asked in his best homeboy accent as he studied the copy of the birth certificate.

"Right," Puckett confirmed. "Get me at least the admission forms of the woman who gave birth to her. But you can't go by the names on the certificate. The baby was adopted by these people – the Marchettis – when she was born and so the doctor put their names on the certificate. But the woman who gave birth to the baby has another name and that's what we want to find out – who she is, where she lives. All that information should be on her admission forms."

"So why do you want this stuff?" the undercover cop asked.

"That's not important," the young reporter answered. "We just do. Can you get it?"

"Probably," he replied. "I got access to all kinds of labor and delivery records. Sure, I can get this. No problem."

"Great. Great. How soon? Could you have the records here by this time tomorrow?"

"Yeah. I think so. Sure. No problem."

"Great."

"But you know all these hospital records are confidential and stuff? I mean, if I get these things for you, you can't let anybody know where you got them. Right?"

"Oh, sure. Right. No. Your identity will be protected at all times. Reporters can't be forced to disclose their sources. Everybody knows that."

"Well," Mayfield remarked sarcastically, "I sure as Hell hope so 'cause my identity won't be protected much at all if your people have someone like *me* running around their offices."

Puckett took the humorous commentary most gravely. "Oh, no, Mister Mayfield! We take the protection of our sources very seriously. Reporters like me have spent time in jail rather than divulge their sources."

"'Cause what you're asking me to do ain't all that legal, you understand? Our bosses come by every once in a while and lecture us on that, you know? I mean, you know all these hospital records here are confidential?"

"Yes, Mister Mayfield. We're aware of that."

"So what you gonna do if I get caught? What if I get fired or get arrested or something? You got lawyers who can take care of me then?"

"We always protect our sources, Mister Mayfield. Let me assure you of that."

"Okay. Okay." The detective hesitated to make sure he got his next series of lines down right. He looked carefully to his left, then his right. He turned just slightly and bent forward. Puckett did the same. Now they were both three-quarters facing the camera – no longer a profile shot. Even the sound of the reporter's breathing was being picked up by the microphone in Mayfield's shirt pocket.

"So Louise tells me you offered to pay her two thousand bucks if she could get these records for you?"

"No. No. Only a thousand. That's what I told her. A thousand dollars."

Mayfield jerked his head back and feigned disbelief. "What'd you mean only *one* thousand? That's not what she told me. She said you offered her two."

The young journalist was perplexed. He knew he had said one; now, he concluded, this con artist was playing the con on him. "I only offered her one thousand," he insisted, shaking his head from side to side in his most sincere fashion.

Mayfield leaned back in his chair, crossing his arms over his chest, mindful not to block the mike. "No way. No way. I'm not gonna do it for no thousand dollars. No way."

"But that's all I've got," the reporter exclaimed.

"Then you'll just have to get more," Mayfield proposed. "I ain't risking my job for no thousand dollars. What if I get them and then you don't show up? No way."

"What if I can get you two? Will you do it?"

"For two . . . ?" The detective paused as if he was thinking it over really hard. "Yeah. Yeah. I'd do it for two. But I want one now and one when I get them to you."

"I can't do that," Puckett whined.

"Then find me someone who can," Mayfield insisted, "and I'll do it."

The reporter rubbed his brow and sat back in his chair. "Give me a minute to make a call."

"Call who?" the detective inquired suspiciously.

"Just some people," Puckett replied as he pulled a flip phone out of his jacket pocket and started to get up.

"Some people who?" Mayfield reiterated as he as he grabbed the man's arm. "If you're gonna call somebody, you can call 'em from here. How do I know you're not someone working for the hospital trying to get me fired? All you've shown me is some old business card."

Puckett sat back down and contemplated his next move. Flipping open the cell phone, he punched in a telephone number. "When the receptionist answers," he explained as he handed the phone to Mayfield, "ask for Dennis Chalmers. He's my editor. If they ask you who's calling, give them my name. But then give it back to me and let me do the talking."

Mayfield did as instructed, and by the time the telephone conversation was over, the reporter had fully implicated himself, his editor, and even the tabloid's senior management. When the reporter started to pull out his wallet, the officer hopped up from his chair and scooted over to bar the door. Then back in camera range, he held out his hand as the young reporter counted out ten one-hundred dollar bills. When they met at the same time and place the next afternoon, Mayfield turned over a set of fictitious records the hospital had trumped up and put out his open palm. But when the sleazy journalist removed the chair that was propped up against the door to keep out unwanted visitors, he was placed under arrest by the detectives waiting expectantly on the other side. Warrants were also issued for the arrest of the editor and management personnel back in Florida. And since the tapes showed the reporter calling interstate, the federal authorities were invited to join the case.

The irony of the incident was not lost on anyone who followed the saga of Roman Marchetti, his comatose wife and infant daughter, and their mysterious surrogate. Appearing on several TV sound bites, Ronnie pleaded with the press to let private people live their private lives. Within three days of the sting, the national press retreated from Denver. No one celebrated more joyously than Roman, who was finally able to take his baby girl to their home in Castle Rock.

A Critical Witness

Finding themselves whisked back to the more familiar turf of state court, the two defense teams inaugurated the month of February with a discovery offensive, James having completed her first round of depositions of Sanders and his medical personnel before Christmas. First ones up on the now joint defense list were the witnesses down in Pagosa Springs: Doctor Crenshaw; the Pagosa hospital pathologist; and the two members of the search and rescue team. Meanwhile, Evan assisted Ronnie by interviewing the Swedish Hospital personnel on duty during Juliette's emergency surgery and tubal ligation. Unfortunately, neither the operating nor recovery room nurses had much of substance to add to the case. Cooper's lack of success only fanned the flames of James' resolve to locate the resident who had assisted Sanders through both surgeries.

After weeks without results, the firm's private investigator finally got a lead on the missing surgeon, Doctor Trisha Hill. As James was to learn, Hill had left Denver after she had completed her residency and married a neurosurgeon who was originally from Iowa. Taking her husband's last name, she was now known professionally as Doctor Patricia Trenckmann. The couple had returned to Iowa City, where the husband had joined his father's neurosurgery practice and the wife had set up her own office.

Since Doctor Trenckmann was initially uncooperative in discussing the case with Ronnie over the phone, the Marchettis' attorneys decided the best course of action would be to fly out to the Midwest and take the doctor's deposition by video, in spite of their fear that her testimony could turn out to be highly favorable to the defense. "We can't force her to come here to testify," acknowledged James. "Our subpoena power doesn't extend outside of Colorado. But we can always subpoena her for a deposition where she lives or works and, unless she wants to hire an attorney to fight it, we can get her testimony that way."

"But what are we going to get?" asked Cooper. "If she won't talk to you on the phone about the surgery, doesn't that suggest we might be throwing a few thousand dollars down the drain? I mean, that's what it's gonna cost to fly out there and get a court reporter and videographer and then get it all transcribed and have copies made. It could turn out to help the defense more than us and be a big waste of money to boot."

"True," Mark chimed in, "but it could go the other way too. I don't know why, but I've got a feeling this doctor may be more concerned about her own skin than about Sanders. For all she knows, we still could turn around and make her or the hospital defendants in this thing, too. Right?"

"Well," conceded Evan, "you've got a point there. But she could also just be covering for her buddy Sanders. He did use her a lot as his assistant for about three years. Maybe she looks upon him as a mentor and feels she owes him some loyalty."

"Unless Powell's been holding out on us and has known where Hill's been all this time, which I seriously doubt," Ronnie weighed in, "I'm inclined toward Mark's opinion. If the defense knew where to find her and she was favorable to them, they would've disclosed her location months ago. And I don't think Powell would play loose with the rules. He knows he could get sanctioned big time for pulling the surprise rabbit out of his hat at the last moment. No, I think they felt she couldn't help their case, so they didn't spend the money like we did to hire someone to find her. That would mean she's either going to be a help to our case or, at the worst, not help or hurt anybody. Even though we've got no idea what she's going to say, I think spending the money on this witness is worth the risk."

James was amazed to find direct jet service from Denver to the Cedar Rapids/ Iowa City airport, arriving in the Hawkeye State in the early evening of a cold March day. When she got to the law offices of a local firm that had graciously made their conference room available for the deposition, she met Doctor Hill, now Trenckmann, who was accompanied by her personal counsel, Roger Litton. Ronnie had spoken with Litton on the phone the week before, the day after the Cedar Rapids process server had handed the subpoena to Doctor Trenckmann. James had done her best at that time to assure him that she had no intent of making his client a defendant in the case. "After all, Counselor," James rationalized, "if we thought your client was the negligent party here, we would have brought in Swedish Hospital as her employer months ago."

Litton conceded the point and agreed not to attempt to quash the subpoena in an Iowa court. As a courtesy, James taxed copies of the pertinent sections of Juliette's hospital records to the lawyer's Iowa City office so his client could refresh her memory of the events that took place three-and-a-half years ago. So here was Ronnie, on a $3,000 gamble, prepared to elicit testimony to be used at trial from a witness who gave no promise of cooperation. But then again, for all James knew, Litton might have brought his client around when he related the gist of his conversation with the plaintiffs' attorney.

About ten pounds heavier than she was when she lived in Denver, a luxury which she attributed to her release from the pulse-pounding pressure cooker that typified the life of a resident in a metropolitan hospital, and with the first gray hair or two sprouting from miscellaneous places on her otherwise dark brown head, Trenckmann showed distinct signs of nervousness as the proceeding got under way. Besides James, the witness, the court reporter, and the videographer, Litton had accompanied his client at her request. Megan O'Brien, Powell's junior partner from the Sanders' deposition, had caught the same flight as James to appear for Doctor Sanders, and a young attorney from the HPM&S home office in Chicago made the four-and-a-half-hour drive west to cover the proceedings for Willis.

After going through the witness' background and training, Ronnie took her step by step through the events of the day – starting with the call from Sanders' office, requesting her assistance in the emergency surgery, and ending with her cleanup after the first phase. When James turned to the second scrub before the tubal ligation, the witness tensed noticeably.

"Do you recall having any conversation with Doctor Sanders related to the use of spring clips as the method of sterilization as opposed to some other technique?" Ronnie queried.

"Yes, I do," Trisha replied.

"What do you know about how the choice was made to use clips?"

"While we were scrubbing up for the tubal, I was curious about why clips were being used since the right tube wasn't salvageable, in my - opinion, and the left tube was going to be ligated to prevent future ectopics, so I asked Doctor Sanders if the patient had elected to go with clips."

"And what did Doctor Sanders tell you?"

"He said that the choice to go with clips was his."

"Did he tell you whether he'd discussed the various options with the patient or her husband?"

"I don't specifically recall him saying one way or another."

"Did he say why he'd chosen to go with clips?"

"Yes. He said that clips would afford a greater possibility of reversal if medical advances in the next few years allowed the adhesions which were blocking the patient's tube to be cleared. He said that the patient was a relatively young woman with a definite intent to bear children – this wasn't a woman who had already had her share of children and didn't want to bear any more – and that the couple would thank him at some time in the future." Out of the corner of her eye, Ronnie could see O'Brien scribbling as quickly as her hand could fly across the paper. She thought she detected a slight wince on Megan's face as Trisha made her last comment.

"Were those his exact words – 'the couple would thank him at some time in the future'?" Ronnie asked as a follow-up.

"To the best of my recollection," the witness replied, "that's what he said – or something close to that. He might've said something like 'down the road.'"

"From what Doctor Sanders said to you, what was your understanding about whether the patient and her husband knew you were using spring clips as the method of sterilization?"

"My understanding . . . " she said, pausing to answer the question with precision, "was that the patient did not know which method we were using."

"Does a surgeon who's about to perform a tubal ligation have a duty to discuss the various methods or techniques of that surgery with the patient?"

"Well, that's why I brought up the subject," Trenckmann explained. "I was curious about the choice of clips and I didn't know whether it was incumbent upon the physician to discuss those details of a procedure or not. I was trying to get the benefit of Doctor Sanders' experience."

"Do you have an opinion about whether a surgeon about to perform a tubal ligation should discuss the various techniques with his or her patient?" James restated the question.

"About whether it falls within the standard of care?" the witness clarified.

"Correct," agreed Ronnie.

"My understanding is that a doctor does *not* have a duty to consult with a patient about whether one technique or another is to be done."

"If a tubal ligation is being performed not as a method of birth control but as a measure to potentially save the life of the woman, would the doctor have a duty to consult with the patient about whether one technique or another is to be used?"

"That might change things," Trenckmann admitted. She paused deep in thought. "I don't know," she added shaking her head. "I don't know. I can't say the doctor has a duty to discuss the techniques, but . . . " She stopped short and looked up at James, obviously ready for the next question.

"If those circumstances presented to you, as the surgeon, Doctor Trenckmann, would you discuss the options with your patient?"

"If it happened to me personally?" she again clarified the question. Seeing a reassuring nod from James, she continued. "Yes, I would."

Having mined some unexpected gold in the scrub room, James turned to the operating theater. Trenckmann agreed that the incision Sanders had made for the emergency salpingectomy left both surgeons an adequate view of the patient's fallopian tubes. The patient's bleeding into the area was minimal because most of the bleeders had been tied off or cauterized during the emergency surgery an hour or two before. Both she and Sanders clearly, identified the fimbriated end of the left tube, as the surgical report had said. Then they traced along the tube toward the center of pelvic area, Sanders grasping the tube itself with a pair of soft-tipped forceps. Trenckmann paused.

Ronnie massaged the witness. "So what happened next?"

"I remember that Doctor Sanders grasped the tube just medial to the fimbria and then looked over his shoulder and said something to one of the OR nurses. Just as he looked back, the tube slipped out of his grip, so he grasped it again. Then, as he was sliding the forceps toward the midpoint, the tube slipped out of his grip again. And I remember him getting upset about that and cursing, which was not at all like him, and then he grasped it again."

"The third time he grasped the tube, are you sure it was the tube itself?" James sat forward in her seat, her attention piqued by the details she was receiving.

"No, I'm not," the witness declared reticently.

"Why not?"

Trenckmann cleared her throat. "When he got it the third time, I remember asking him if he was sure he got it. In medical school, we were taught to go back to where we started, which in this case would have been the fimbria, and trace down the tube again. So I was just double-checking."

"Did you have any reason to believe that the tissue he had grasped in those forceps was not the tube itself?"

"I just wasn't sure."

"Then you had some doubt about whether the tissue was the tube?"

"Yes. That's why I asked him. He'd done a lot more of these than I had. He was the surgeon; I was just the assistant and only a resident at that."

"What did he say when you questioned him?"

"The best I recall, he said, 'Of course!'"

"Was he still upset about dropping the tube twice?"

"He seemed to be."

"Was he upset with your question?"

"He didn't say anything, but his tone of voice seemed to indicate that, yes."

"What happened next?"

"He told me to slip the clip implement through the space between the body cavity and the upraised tube."

"Did you do so?"

"Yes."

"Did the thought cross your mind that the tissue he was going to clip was not the actual tube?"

"Yes."

"Did you stop giving suction to the area when you reached for the clip tool?"

"Yes."

"Did blood collect in the body cavity under the upraised tube?"

"Yes."

"Could that amount of blood have obscured your view of the tube lying against the serosal tissue?"

Trenckmann paused and looked over at Litton. He returned the look, his face devoid of expression. The witness put her hand to her mouth and cleared her throat as she turned back to face James. "Yes, it could have," she replied in a soft voice.

"Is it not a fact that striations, folds, and other tissue can resemble the fallopian tube?"

"Yes."

"Is it possible that Doctor Sanders missed the tube when he attached the clips?"

"Yes."

"Have you reviewed the surgical summary and the hospital pathologist's lab report on the tissue removed from Juliette Marchetti's pelvic area?"

"Yes, I have."

"Based upon those reports and upon your recollection of the events that occurred during Missus Marchetti's tubal ligation, is it more probable than not that Doctor Sanders missed the tube when he attached the clips?"

Trenckmann hesitated. "Well . . . I . . . I don't know if I could say that. I don't know if I've . . ." She shook her head. "I don't know. I just can't say."

"Doctor Trenckmann," James persisted, "would you agree that other than error in placement, the only other possibility that would account for the clips being now attached to serosal tissue and not the tube would be migration?"

"Based upon what I see in these reports, yes. That would be the only thing that would account for the clips not being in the right place." She paused and then continued, "other than error in the original placement."

"Doctor, have you reviewed the report of Doctor Benjamin Steinberg regarding his examination of the tissue sample with the attached clips?"

"Yes. I looked at that yesterday, too."

"How do the measurements made by Doctor Steinberg compare to what you would expect had you made similar measurements of spring clips after affixing them to a patient's fallopian tube?"

"From what I see in his report, the clips on the tissue sample appear to have been positioned very similarly to where clips attached by the appropriate instrument would have been – parallel to each other and a precise distance apart."

"Doctor, in your years of experience, have you ever heard of a case in which two foreign objects in the body migrated in tandem, maintaining both the parallelism and the distance at which they were originally inserted?"

"No, I've never heard of such a case. And I've never had a personal experience like that in my practice."

"Doctor, I'll ask you again. Based upon all the reports we've recently discussed and upon your recollection of the events that occurred during Missus Marchetti's tubal ligation, is it more probable than not that Doctor Sanders missed the tube when he attached the clips?"

Trenckmann turned to glance at her lawyer, pausing more for the mental formulation of her answer than for his counsel. Then she turned back to Ronnie, who looked at her expectantly. "In my opinion, yes. It is more probable that Doctor Sanders and I attached the clips to the peritoneal tissue next to the tube and not the tube itself."

"Is that an acceptable performance within the standards of the profession?"

The witness started to speak but stopped mid-word to clear her throat. "No. No, it's not."

A Surprising Admission

Two hours into the interrogation, James' gamble had reaped unanticipated benefits. The reluctant witness had ended up burying the hatchet in Sanders' back with her graphic account of the details of the operation on Juliette, all of which gave a convincing factual basis for the plaintiffs' claims of negligence. Sensing that she had gotten more than she might have hoped for from an untested source, Ronnie terminated her direct examination. After a fifteen minute break, the young lawyer from Willis' Chicago office deferred to Megan O'Brien, who took over the questioning.

The junior partner from Powell, Kaminsky & Rader was, like the witness, an unknown quantity to Ronnie. A dedicated career professional, still unmarried at forty-four, she had been the first woman to make partner at her firm eight years after being hired. Initially a crusader out of law school, she had worked in the public sector for seven years before the lack of pay and the lack of shrinkage in the principal on her law school loan debt got the best of her. Three years now a partner in a successful law firm, she finally had been able to retire the loan debt and assume another – a $175,000 mortgage on a two-story, four-bedroom suburban home on the west end of Denver out Highway 6.

Taking the lead in a deposition for the first time in the case, she started off slowly, allowing the witness herself to undermine the basis for her opinions. Trenckmann admitted that she had never performed a clip insertion before that day – that her familiarity with the procedure came just from her training during her internship. However, she had observed others perform the procedure, maybe two or three times, and she had performed the procedure once in lab on a cadaver. She agreed with O'Brien that she was not an expert on the procedure – either then or now.

Responding to further questioning, she explained that she currently had a small private OB/Gyn practice in Iowa City but admitted that she did not do any surgery as part of that practice. She also conceded that she did not have any expertise in pathology and admitted she was not up to date on the latest literature concerning migration of foreign objects within the human body.

"It's been four years since the tubal ligation was performed, correct?" asked the defense attorney.

"Yes, thereabouts."

"And a lot of changes can take place within the human body within a four-year period, isn't that true, Doctor?"

"Yes, that's true."

"And it's possible, isn't it," insisted O'Brien, "that the clips migrated from their original positioning over the last four years?"

"Well, yes," Trenckmann begrudgingly conceded. "It's possible." She paused to collect her thoughts. "But – "

O'Brien interrupted the witness' thought, changing tack. "When you were a resident at Swedish, you were not married, correct?"

"That's correct."

"You assisted Doctor Sanders on numerous occasions, did you not?"

"Yes, several. I don't know if I'd say numerous. Maybe a dozen. Maybe a few more than that. If that's numerous – "

"And you looked up to Doctor Sanders did you not?"

"Yes. Sure. He was doing what I wanted to do with my medical career – go into private practice and perform surgery."

"In fact you were quite taken with him, were you not?"

Trenckmann stared at her accuser. "I'm not sure what you mean by that. If it's what I think you mean, the answer is no. I had no feelings for Doctor Sanders that were other than strictly professional."

"Isn't it a fact that your testimony today is your way of getting back at Doctor Sanders for his rebuff of your romantic interest in him?"

"Absolutely not," Trenckmann insisted, glaring at O'Brien with a fierceness that would have rivaled a lioness on the hunt. "I never had any such interest in Paul."

"But you did socialize with him on more than one occasion when you were only a resident at Swedish, didn't you?"

"Sure, but it was never anything more than having lunch or supper together in the hospital cafeteria after surgery."

"So you're denying that you ever went to dinner with him outside of the hospital?" O'Brien pressed on.

Trenckmann's face showed a trace of surprise then a slight blush. "No. I'm not denying that, but I don't remember going out to dinner with him. Maybe we did. I just don't recall."

"Isn't it a fact, Doctor Hill, I mean Doctor Trenckmann, that you had dinner out with Doctor Sanders on more than one occasion?"

"You obviously know something that I don't," the witness shot back defiantly. "I told you before, I don't recall going out of the hospital to have dinner with Doctor Sanders, but I'm not denying that it could have happened – and it could have happened more than once. That's all."

"Do you recall a dinner at the Brown Palace Hotel downtown?"

Trenckmann's face turned a deeper shade of red. "Yes. That rings a bell."

"Do you recall another evening at a French cuisine restaurant on Broadway?"

The witness paused, scratching her temple. "Yes. That sounds familiar too."

"Isn't it a fact that those two social occasions with Doctor Sanders were your idea, not his?"

"I honestly don't recall." She looked to the side at her attorney, then down at the table. Before O'Brien could voice the next question, Trenckmann voiced an explanation. "But you've got to understand, I was a lowly resident. I was trying to get on the good side of all the surgeons I met at Swedish, hoping that they'd call on me to assist them. That way, I could get the experience and training I wanted. But that's *all* it was. I wasn't trying to hit on them, for God's sake."

"But you knew Paul Sanders was married, did you not?"

"Yes. I'm quite sure I was aware of that."

"You knew he had a family – three children – didn't you?"

"I believe I knew he had kids, but I don't recall anything about how many or – "

"And in spite of that knowledge, you, a single woman, invited a married doctor to have dinner out with you?"

"But you're coloring it a shade that isn't right," Trenckmann insisted. "You're trying to make it seem as though my interest was romantic and it wasn't. If I spent time outside of the OR with a surgeon, it was to help further my career."

"So you deny categorically that your testimony today is influenced by any motive of retaliation against Doctor Paul Sanders? Is that what you're saying, Doctor?"

"Yes, that's what I'm saying."

"And you're denying you had a romantic interest in Doctor Sanders and he rebuffed your advances because he was a devoted family man, is that right?"

"Yes. I absolutely deny that. It's just not true." The witness started to continue, then hesitated, obviously pondering her next statement.

"I believe you testified earlier," said O'Brien, flipping back to the first page of her notes, "that your husband, Doctor Joseph Trenckmann, is a neurosurgeon, correct?"

"That's right."

"Where did you meet him?"

"In Denver."

"Could you be more specific?"

"At Swedish."

"When did you meet?"

"During my last year of residency."

"That would have been after Missus Marchetti's surgery, would it not?"

"Yes, I believe so," she answered. Pulling over the stack of Juliette's medical records, she found a date of admission on the cover sheet. "Sure. At least a year later."

"How did you meet?"

"I'm not sure I understand the question."

"Okay, Doctor. Let me try it this way. Isn't it true that you first met your future husband in the operating room?"

"Yes."

"He needed someone to assist him in an emergency surgery one night when he was on call and you were on the floor, correct?"

"Yes, that's right."

"And he was the surgeon and you were the assistant, right?"

"Right."

"And that's the same position you had with Doctor Sanders – he was the surgeon and you were the assistant?"

"Yes."

"And you subsequently became romantically involved with Doctor Joseph Trenckmann while you were acting, on occasion, as his assistant surgeon, did you not?" James winced as the trap sprang shut. No matter how virtuous Trisha Hill Trenckmann proclaimed to be, the defense had punctured her credibility with her own words. Ronnie had to admit it was a masterful ploy by her adversary. Not fatal, but damaging.

"Yes, but – "

"Thank you, Doctor Trenckmann. That's all I have." O'Brien turned to look at James. "Your witness, Counselor."

On redirect examination, James patched up some holes deliberately left by the defense attorney. After putting the witness' romantic relationship with her future husband into a proper perspective, Ronnie went back to the comments Trenckmann appeared to be about to make when her questioner cut her off. "You were answering a question put to you by Miss O'Brien about the possibility that the spring clips Doctor Sanders inserted had migrated in the four years since the operation, and you indicated that migration was possible. Do you recall that answer?"

"Yes."

"Had you completed your answer to that question before defense counsel asked the next question."

"No, I hadn't."

"What else were you going to say?"

"Well, I have to admit that I'm not up on the literature about migration of foreign objects within the human body, but I don't believe that the two spring clips Sanders and I affixed moved from where we attached them. I'm not a mathematician either, but if the likelihood that a clip like that, which was still snapped in place and secure, could move would be, say, one in a hundred or even one in a thousand, the likelihood that the pair of them could move exactly the same distance and direction and remain the same distance and angle apart would have to be something like one in a million. With what I remember about the actual surgery, I'd say that the odds would be a thousand times better that we just missed. I'm sorry to say it and I feel really bad that the patient had another ectopic pregnancy, but that's the truth. We just missed the tube."

Two weeks after she returned to Denver, Roman visited the firm's offices for a progress report. Ronnie had sent him a copy of Trenckmann's transcript the day it arrived in her offices, which the client ravenously read that same evening. "I was telling Juliette the other day," Roman said as they walked down the hall to her office, "you did a masterful job of drawing that testimony out of her. I was quite surprised when I read some of the things she said. I thought we might be wasting our time with a witness who didn't want to fully cooperate."

"So was I," she agreed. "So was I."

"So how'd you do it?" the client queried as they entered Ronnie's office and closed the door behind them.

"I don't know that I had any magical formula," she conceded. "In fact I was quite surprised that she was so candid too." She hesitated as she took a seat on the couch. "Remember what I said months ago when we talked about whether Crenshaw would be as up front with a jury as he was with you? Same thing. It's like the thin blue line mentality when the police are challenged and draw in their ranks. I've had a lot more experience with that situation than with doctors, but it's the same thing – sort of a thin white line, with hospital coats instead of police blues.

"Some of it's professional integrity. They don't want to believe that their well-trained cohorts can be careless. Some of it's akin to pack mentality in the animal world – surround and defend their kind from attack. Some of it's financial – they fear their med mal insurance rates will go up if another case of medical negligence is proven.

"They think their rates are too high now and that it's unfair and that's why they get their insurance companies to lobby legislatures incessantly to push some of the most extreme tort reform proposals. But the reason their rates are so high is because when a doctor screws up, it's usually a big mistake. They take people's lives in their hands and if their otherwise usually sure hand slips during a delicate surgery, the patient could end up like Juliette. Well, as you know from what that health plan has been shelling out for the last few months, its costing very big money to *care* for her. And who should bear those costs? The person whose carelessness was responsible for the injury or the victim? So they're not paying too much. They're just in a high-risk profession."

"Yeah, I see what you mean," said Roman.

"You know, the ironic thing about it – studies show that the primary reason that judgments against the medical profession have gotten so costly is the medical profession itself."

"How so?"

"Well, it used to be when a doctor slipped up, say, during surgery and did something that endangered the life of the patient, the patient would die as a result. Now, modem medicine has a way of keeping their victims alive. And who gets paid for looking after them? The medical profession!

"A huge share of those multimillion-dollar awards that make the headlines goes to pay for the medical machinery and professional care an injured patient wouldn't even have gotten forty, fifty, or sixty years ago. Doctors screw up and damn near kill their patients and then bitch like crazy because their medical malpractice insurance has to pay so much money to support the work of their medical colleagues in keeping the victim alive. Ironic, no?"

"God, you're getting to sound like a real personal injury lawyer," commented Roman, tongue in cheek.

"Oh, no!" Ronnie exclaimed as she threw her hands up in mock horror. "It was bad enough when I left the D.A.'s Office and suddenly I felt this public loathing for doing criminal defense work. You know, being responsible for letting all the criminals like O.J. walk free." She burst out laughing as she reflected on her current professional state. "Now I've become an ambulance chaser too."

Uncooperative Witnesses

While James had managed the medical malpractice discovery, Cooper had assumed the duty of preparing all the written discovery to the defendant Union Health Management. Their top priority was to identify, among other things, all those persons responsible for devising and interpreting the guideline which directed its participating physicians not to test for pregnancy plan enrollees who had been sterilized. According to the managed care company's answers, the persons identified as the principal authors of that particular provision were two of its employees – Eleanor Montgomery, a vice president, and Franklin Marshall, an economist. But what was left unsaid was of greater interest to Ronnie and Evan. Union Health failed to identify the doctor, nurse, or claims representative with whom Sanders had discussed the case the day of Juliette's last-minute appointment, asserting that their office had no records of any such conversation.

Also, outlined in the company's answers were the reasons for the no-test directive which precipitated Sanders' telephone call. "Actuarial studies have shown that the costs of thousands of tests have not been justified by the negligible risk that a sterilized woman would actually turn out to be pregnant," the answer to interrogatory number fourteen read. "A primary object of our health plan is to trim unnecessary medical costs, thereby, keeping the costs of health insurance as low as possible for its participants. Based upon the most relevant and best available statistical data, the employees and officers of Union Health Management, Inc., prepare guidelines to assist physicians in selecting the most cost effective and efficient cost of treatment. Tests and treatments that have been shown over time to be economically inefficient or needless are discouraged."

As soon as the plaintiffs' lawyers had analyzed the written responses and made a cursory review of the more than 600 pages of documents produced, Ronnie called Willis to schedule the depositions of the Union Health personnel identified. One week of hemming and hawing by Willis turned into two. Finally James got fed up and fired off two deposition notices to her dilatory adversary, setting the depositions of Montgomery and Marshall for the company headquarters in Chicago two weeks later.

"That bastard better not be playing around," she threatened during an early morning planning powwow with Cooper. "There's no excuse for him not giving me the courtesy of keeping in touch. If his people have scheduling problems, fine. We'll adjust. But he could at least give me a call to let me know he's working on it. Instead, I've left five, six messages, and he hasn't returned one of my calls."

Ronnie's suspicions were confirmed when, the next day, a bicycle courier delivered a package of pleadings from Willis' office. She found Evan in the library and plopped the stack of motions down on the table. He looked up at her somber expression, then glanced at the pile of paperwork. "Willis?" he surmised.

"Yes," she muttered the word with a taste of spite. Then she sank down into one of the gray leather swivel chairs.

"Let me guess," he added, carefully surveying the size of the stack. "We've probably got a challenge to the claim for vicarious liability. Motion to dismiss, right?"

"Right."

"Probably another motion to dismiss or some kind of challenge to the baby's position as a plaintiff. Probably in the nature of questioning her standing – saying she's not a real party in interest, not entitled to sue because she isn't really Juliette's child."

"Right again."

"And for good measure, to slow things down some more, probably a motion for a protective order to prevent us from taking the depositions of any of his client's employees, at least until these motions are heard."

James glanced over at him with a puzzled look on her face. "Had you already seen these?" she asked.

"No," Evan replied. "But those first two are where we're slightly vulnerable, so we've gotta assume Willis is going to try to draw some blood. And they'll always throw in a protective order to mess up the discovery schedule."

"Is he going to have any luck?" she queried.

"I seriously doubt it on the standing question. But the HMO probably figures if they can knock off the baby's potential quarter million in noneconomic damages with only few thousand in legal fees, it's a risk worth taking," Cooper rationalized. "As to the vicarious liability question, we'll see." He smiled reassuringly at Ronnie, then began to pour over each pleading, jotting his thoughts on a nearby legal pad. His partner took the cue and left the master to his craft.

Fortunately for the plaintiffs, Judge Williams put the defense motions on a fast track, setting oral argument on all three for a month after their filing. Never one to be on the defensive, Ronnie had fired off a salvo of her own just three days before the hearing – a motion to compel more sufficient answers to her first set of interrogatories. In response to Cooper's meticulous written discovery requests, Sanders had produced his office telephone records for the day the doctor asserted he had called Union Health to question the treatment guidelines. An entry in the log of a six minute, forty-two-second call in the late afternoon confirmed his prior testimony. That the telephone number to which the call was made was that of the Union Health physicians' inquiry line was proven by a whole host of the HMO's own forms and other printed materials. Ronnie was being stonewalled, and she was hopping mad about it.

On a chilly morning in early April, the lawyers appeared in judge Williams' courtroom to resolve matters. After giving the lead attorneys a few minutes to summarize points and authorities on each motion, Williams issued her rulings. "I'll take them in the order in which they were filed with the court," she said. "First, as to Defendant Union Health Management's motion for partial summary judgment on the claim of vicarious liability, I'm going to deny that motion. Usually, the contract between a managed care company and one of its provider doctors is dispositive on the issue of the physician's status as an independent contractor. However, in this case, Doctor Sanders' testimony presents a fact question of control that needs to be more fully developed. So I'm also denying the motion for a protective order. Miss James, you may schedule the depositions of Missus Montgomery and Mister Marshall at the parties' convenience."

"As to the motion to dismiss the claim of Roman Marchetti as guardian and next friend of Juliet Abbott Marchetti, a minor, that is also denied. While I have to admit that the timing of Missus Marchetti's injuries and the baby's birth presents novel questions, I must take as determinative the order of a sister court declaring Mister and Missus Marchetti to be the lawful parents of the child. Since I have neither the authority nor the inclination to effectively vacate a decision by that court, I suggest that you pursue this argument in another venue, Mister Willis. Exactly how you're going to get the standing to challenge that order declaring parenthood I'll leave to you." James glanced over at Cooper, whose sober facial expression was artfully disguising his mental rapture.

"Now, is there anything else we need to clear up this morning?" the judge asked, surveying the faces before her.

"Your Honor," James spoke up, "if I may. We filed a motion to compel a few days ago. I don't know if the court has had time to review it, but –"

"Your Honor," Willis interrupted. "We'll be responding to that motion in due course. Of course, we just received it and have hardly had time to look it over, what with preparing for our hearing today. We'll be filing our response within the fifteen days we're allowed under the rules, and perhaps then the court would be in a better position to rule."

"I'm familiar with your motion, Miss James, and I was prepared to discuss it today, but Mister Willis is entitled to his time to respond. However, I will caution you," Judge Williams said, casting a stern eye toward Willis, "and this applies to all of the attorneys and parties – not just Union Health Management and its counsel – that I have developed a reputation for being quite liberal when it comes to handing out sanctions for discovery abuse. All of you know the rules – wide-open discovery in civil matters. No holding back. No gamesmanship. I've got a saying in my court: 'If you seek to delay, your client will pay!'" Her singsong rhythm brought slight smiles to the somber crowd, with the notable exception of Sylvester Willis.

"On this matter," the judge resumed, "I've only read through Miss James' motion and looked at her evidence. But she's got the sworn testimony of Doctor Sanders that he spoke with a Union Health Management representative on the day in question. She's got a telephone bill that shows a call more than six minutes long. And the number dialed was the same office number that appears on documents that Union Health itself has produced in this matter." She looked over the top of her reading glasses at the HMO's attorney. "So give your client fair warning, Mister Willis. I'll wait the twelve or thirteen more days you're entitled to for your response, but those may be days of discovery time and trial preparation that you'll never get back. We've got a trial date, ladies and gentlemen, and we're staying on track. Do I make myself clear?" Seeing affirmation written across the faces of all those present, she excused them and called the next matter on her docket.

Chicago in late April presented both of its faces to Ronnie. Thursday started off warm and sunny. The tulips along Michigan Avenue were in full bloom and small white sailboats dotted the lake. But Friday brought to life Chicago's reputation as the Windy City. A storm swept down from the north across Lake Michigan shortly after midnight, dumping a three-inch coat of slushy snow on downtown during the wee hours of the morning. Whatever the weather, the mood inside the HPM&S offices through the course of her visit was consistently chilly.

She arrived on the early-morning flight to take the depositions of four Union Health employees – Montgomery, the vice president; Marshall, the economist; Sue Ann Langtree, a claims manager; and Peter Wolaski, the representative who most likely had spoken with Sanders. The latter two had finally been identified by Willis shortly after Judge Williams' warning. After catching a cab at O'Hare, which whisked her to the downtown high rise like she was on an emergency mission, James started off at the top with the V.P. who had given final approval to the volume of written treatment guidelines. An attractive woman in her late thirties, of medium stature, with light brown hair cut short and permed into large looping curls, Montgomery wore a two-piece light gray plaid business suit and an off-white silk blouse. With Union Health since her graduation from Ohio State, she had risen meteorically through the rank and file of claims adjusters to management. An officer since 1993, she was in charge of "the formulation and implementation of prospective utilization review guidelines and procedures." Along with her team of researchers, both medical and economic, she had drafted, finalized, and released the set of guidelines in question.

Under aggressive cross examination by James, the witness admitted that the wording in the guidelines could be subject to differing interpretations. She further acknowledged that she had not received any training in the medical arts and sciences through a recognized institution of higher learning. However, she disputed James' assertion that she did not have any medical training at all, pointing to her many years of experience in handling medical claims and the numerous seminars sponsored by various insurance companies and associations that she had attended.

"So all of your training in the medical field has come under the auspices of this insurance company, right?" Ronnie confirmed.

"Right," the witness agreed, "under doctors or other medical experts retained by the insurance company."

"But never through a medical school?"

"No, never through a medical school."

James studied Montgomery reflectively for a few seconds. The momentary quietude caused Willis and the other attorneys to look up at their adversary. Ronnie's next question oozed out, coating the atmosphere with a thick paste of surprise. "You have an OB/Gyn you go to, don't you, Miss Montgomery?"

"Yes . . . of course," the witness replied. Her visage evinced that she had not expected such a personal question.

"If you went in to visit your doctor for a female problem, would you be more comfortable entrusting your care to your physician," James posed pointedly, "or to a person trained in medicine by an insurance company?"

Montgomery glanced over at Willis for some psychological succor as she shifted uneasily in her seat. After a pregnant pause, her eyes shifted back to Ronnie. "My own physician," she replied meekly.

By the time the two-hour deposition was over, about half-past noon, Ronnie was ready to chew on something more palatable than an insurance company executive. Along with an old law school classmate who was practicing immigration law in the area, she enjoyed a taste of some of Chicago's famous barbeque as the two women reminisced about their days in Provo at Utah Law and their ensuing careers. By two o'clock, Ronnie was back in the Michigan Avenue offices, waiting for the statistician to arrive.

When Marshall walked into the conference room, it was as if he had just walked out of the pages of a comic book. He was slight in stature, with a muss of curly brown hair, black-rimmed eyeglasses with thick lenses, and a wisp of a mustache. His tan plaid sportcoat clashed violently with his dark gray slacks and burgundy-flowered bow tie. *God*, Ronnie thought as she rose to greet him, *I'll bet he's got a pocket protector under that jacket*. Her suspicions were confirmed within minutes when he slid his hand under his left lapel to pull out a pen, exposing his shirt pocket to the lawyer's inquisitive glance.

Looking forward to an afternoon and early evening touring the Magnificent Mile, Ronnie wasted little time with the witness covering his background and lack of formal medical training within the first thirty minutes. What it all came down to, she was to discover, was that the statistics showed fewer than one in 220,000 incidents of pregnancy in women who had been sterilized by a physician. Marshall admitted that he had derived only the statistical data from the medical literature and was not aware of any case-factual specifics. Deciding that she would be better to save her more aggressive questioning for trial Ronnie wrapped up the bean counter's examination by three o'clock.

Her shopping trip took a direction other than the one she had planned after her dinner companion advised her of the latest weather report during drinks at a nearby watering hole. Already the wind had picked up force and changed direction, blowing a steady, frigid wind in from the north. Not anticipating such a dramatic change in weather, Ronnie had left her trusted Sorel snow boots at home. So, aside from a new blouse and a couple of accessories from Brooks Brothers, her prize apparel trophy turned out to be a pair of rubber galoshes she picked up at the last minute to cover her black patent leather pumps. The next morning, she made the six-block walk from the downtown Marriott through the brown slush to the law offices – cold but dry. She had instructed Willis the afternoon before that she wanted to speak with Peter Wolaski next, since his deposition was likely to be longer than that of his superior.

When Ronnie arrived shortly after nine, she found everyone present and ready to get started. Wolaski was younger than she had anticipated, maybe twenty-four or twenty-five, tops. Attractive, with a thin build on his six-foot-one frame, he had received an associate's degree from a local business college, worked as a claims adjuster for a large auto insurance company, and then moved into claims handling at Union Health two years before.

Suspiciously to Ronnie, he drew blanks when it came to his conversation with Doctor Sanders. The company had been able to digest their computerized telephone logs and determine that the call had come through to Wolaski's station, but the young man claimed no independent memory of the call. Furthermore, his file failed to show any log of notes taken during that span of time. Ronnie drove her points home.

"Isn't it the policy of Union Health that its representatives make notes of their conversations with patients and doctors?" she queried as she handed him the appropriate pages from Union Health's own manuals.

Looking over the documents, Wolaski conceded the truth of her assertion. "Yes, ma'am."

"Was it your routine practice to enter notes into your computer as conversations were taking place?"

"Yes, ma'am. Or shortly after."

"Are you aware of any other cases in which you've failed to comply with both company policy and your own practice?" Ronnie inquired curiously.

"Objection," interposed Willis. "Assumes facts not in evidence. I believe he's testified that he doesn't recall talking to Sanders, so he can't state that he's failed to record notes of a conversation he's not sure he ever had."

"Okay, Counselor, I'll back up a step," replied James. Tapping her pen against her chin, she framed the proper predicate. "Do you deny speaking with Doctor Sanders on the day in question?"

"Objection," Willis jumped in. "Asked and answered."

"No, it hasn't been asked and answered," shot back Ronnie. "He's said he doesn't recall the conversation. Now I'm asking him if he denies that it took place." Turning to the witness, she pressed on. "Please answer the question, Mister Wolaski."

"I don't know."

"Don't know what?" James shot back.

"Don't know the answer to the question," Wolaski said innocently.

Reaching for a set of documents Cooper had obtained by subpoena of the phone records for the Union Health line Sanders had called, she flipped through to the desired sheet. Pulling out copies for the court reporter and the other attorneys, she handed the marked exhibit to the witness. "Are you familiar with the Union Health telephone records that show that a telephone call from Sanders' number in Denver was put through to your station at the time his records indicate he made a call to your company?"

"Objection," Willis stated. "Assumes facts not in evidence." Ronnie ignored him.

Wolaski glanced down at the paper, perused it quickly, and then looked up at James. "I've heard talk about that, yes. And I've seen some papers indicating that."

"Having reviewed those documents then, do you deny having spoken to Doctor Sanders on the day in question?"

"No – "

"Objection," Willis interrupted, but his timing was a split second behind the employee's rapid reply. "Asked and answered. Move it along, Counselor."

Turning to the court reporter, Ronnie requested a read-back of the last question and answer. When the court reporter's stenographic tape indicated that Wolaski's answer had made it into the record, Ronnie smiled. She had what her opponent was so desperately trying to avoid, a free rein to develop a one-sided view of the conversation. Sanders' rendition. Now Wolaski could not testify about any details of the call without impeaching himself, and he could not deny Sanders' version of the conversation either.

The final witness, Sue Ann Langtree, proved to be an equally difficult nut to crack. With no independent recollection of her conversation with Wolaski about Sanders' call, "I don't know" became her stock answer. More polished as a witness than her subordinate, she paused artfully for a second or two before attempting to answer Ronnie's questions, giving Willis sufficient time to state his objections and drop a hint or two about what she should say and what she should not. Since she was an experienced claims manager, her level of expertise exposed her to numerous hypothetical situations, her responses to which subsequently provided the plaintiffs' team with small bits of ammunition for trial.

"They've got to bring either Wolaski or Langtree to the trial," James confided to Mark by phone during a break in Langtree's deposition.

"Of course they do," asserted Frey. "Otherwise, Sanders'll give his version of the conversation, which'll be as slanted in his favor as he can possibly make it, and Union Health won't have any way to counter it." He hesitated, then changed direction ever so slightly. "So you've seen the witnesses and evaluated their demeanor. What's your take on this?"

"Frankly," she replied, "I think they're covering the whole thing up. And in the long run, that'll be good for us. It's inconceivable that Wolaski would fail to make notes about his conversation with Sanders. If we wanted to spend the money, we could probably get permission from the court to get a computer geek to figure out if there's a record or two missing – like someone hit the delete button after we served them with papers." She paused as her mind whirred with deductive activity. "I'll bet the real truth of it is that neither one of these last two witnesses talked to any of the medical professionals on staff about the matter."

"Maybe the doctors had all gone home for the day," Mark suggested. "After all, it was after five Chicago time."

"Maybe," replied Ronnie. "But however it happened, someone here just shot out a medical decision without giving it a second thought, and now it's backfired on them. It was probably that Langtree woman. She's an iron maiden if I've ever seen one."

"Tough to prove," commented Frey.

"Sure, if you demand hard proof," Ronnie retorted. "But all we need is a seed of doubt to be able to make a good argument to the jury. Since Sanders can conclusively prove that he was on the line with somebody here for more than six minutes, it's the only reasonable explanation. He talked to someone who also wasn't trained in medicine, and that person told Sanders what to do with his patient. It'll be clear to the jury when we explain it to them."

"So are you going to press on with this witness," asked Mark, "and see if you can find a crack in that armor?"

"No, I don't think so," explained Ronnie. "I'm thinking of wrapping it up with Langtree shortly. It's noon now and I don't see any reason to break for lunch and then come back. I've got one more series of questions and I think I'll let it go at that. Maybe catch an early plane out of here."

"I thought you were gonna stay the weekend, see Chicago for the first time."

"Nah," she stated, catching a glimpse of her galoshes in the comer of the conference room. "The weather in this toddlin' town really sucks!"

A Shocking Maneuver

The vibrancy of a beautiful early May day in Denver was infectious. Frey, Cooper, and James sat around the large conference table bubbling with optimism about the Marchetti case. "I think we're making really great progress, Ronnie," Mark said. "These depositions from Chicago do very little to help Union Health - very little at all."

"I agree," echoed Cooper. "It all seems to be falling in line quite nicely."

"And no record of Sanders' phone call?" Frey added sarcastically. "Who are they kidding? Do they think the jury is going to be made up of a bunch of idiots?"

"And the way you caught that woman with the question about who she'd trust more with her own medical care," added Cooper. "Sheer genius."

"Thanks, Evan," Ronnie replied, "but not so sure it was so much a stroke of mental genius as much as it was just an emotional reaction. As I was questioning her and listening to her answers - observing her demeanor and all - I had this image of her in one of those long white doctors' coats coming in the door of my doctor's examining room and telling me what was what. So I figured she's probably got an OB/Gyn too. Wonder how she'd feel if the tables were turned? So it just came out."

"Well, however it came out," Frey said, "I'll bet it wasn't something she'd been prepared for by Willis and his cronies."

Ronnie chuckled. "From her initial reaction, I'd say not."

"So what's next on the agenda," Mark queried.

"Looks like all we've got left are just the economists for both sides," James explained. "We're trying to work out a few dates through the early summer that don't interfere with everyone's vacation plans. No one seems to want to sacrifice a minute of their personal time. After that, I guess we'll just coast and start organizing all of this." She swept her hand across the conference table, stacked with a growing pile of deposition transcripts.

"Coast, huh?" Evan's face screwed up into an expression of minor disquiet. "Problem is, we've still got seven months till we go to trial. Call me paranoid, but as poorly as things seem to be going for the defense, I'm just wondering if they've got some kind of trick up their sleeve."

The legal maneuver not anticipated by the trio came in the form of a three-page motion and a nine-page supporting brief, with an additional twenty-four pages of attached exhibits. Minutes after scanning through it, Ronnie stormed down toward the library, bursting through the partially closed door. Evan, who had buried himself deep into some much-needed research on a securities fraud case, was all but hidden behind foot-high piles of reporters, treatises, and digests splayed out in an arc in front of him. Ronnie's brusk entrance almost caused Cooper to jump out of his seat, so startled he was. Though he seemed to find great humor in his own overreaction, his colleague only stood there grim-faced. She tossed the handful of papers at him.

"What's this?" Cooper asked.

"You won't believe it," Ronnie replied, seething with irritation. As Evan glanced through the motion, Ronnie continued to fume. "Remember that doctor the defense hired to conduct an independent medical examination of Juliette a few weeks back?"

"Yeah. Doctor Craig something-or-other, wasn't it?"

"Actually, it's Doctor something-or-other Craig," she corrected. "Well, guess what!" She did not even pause long enough for an answer. "He says she's dead!"

"Who? What?" Evan eyed her, his visage showing his confusion. "What are you talking about?" He tried to unclutter his mind of the myriad facts of the dozens of cases he had just spent the last two hours studying.

"Craig claims that Juliette is clinically dead," James responded sardonically. "And that she has been since shortly before he examined her. So our good buddy Willis is asking the court to restrict our economic losses for lost earnings and future medical costs. Can he do that?" She stood there in a defiant posture, her arms crossed, her toes tapping nervously on the carpet.

"As I recall," Evan replied, "that's the law in Colorado." He turned through the stapled pages, put his finger on something, reached for one of the volumes of the Colorado Revised Statutes with his other hand, and leafed through it. When he found what he wanted, he sat back up and leaned the book against the stacks in front of him, holding the pages open with his right hand. "Here it is: '. . . and, in tort actions based upon personal injury, the damages recoverable after the death of the person in whose favor such action has accrued shall be limited to loss of earnings and expenses sustained or incurred *prior to death* and shall not include damages for pain, suffering, or disfigurement, nor prospective profits or earnings *after date of death.*'"

"So that means what?" Ronnie inquired.

"It means that if she'd actually died on the trail, her family, survivors, dependents – whatever – couldn't recover any damages for her loss of earnings from her career over the next twenty or so years. Any damages Roman would try to claim due to the income Juliette would have contributed to the family unit would be disallowed. And no royalties from future writings based on her research. And, of course, it means any amount we could get in punitive damages would have to come down accordingly. Generally, a plaintiff can't get punis in Colorado in any more than a one-to-one ratio with the actual damages."

"So how do you read what they're asking the court to do," Ronnie inquired as she pulled out a chair and eased herself down into it.

Evan skimmed through the remaining pages of the brief while James sat placidly. "Basically," he conceded as he glanced over his glasses at his cohort, "it's like you said: declare her dead. That way, the defendants won't have to pay a couple of million dollars in future lost earnings . . . among other things."

"I understand that, but what are they trying to get the court to do about Juliette?" Ronnie asked with a deep tone of concern to her voice. "It seems like they're asking the judge to order someone to pull the plug."

"I guess in a legal sense, at least, they are," Evan said resignedly.

"What do you mean 'in a legal sense'?" Ronnie followed up.

"I don't think they can get the court to actually order Roman to cut her life support," Evan replied. "I don't believe they'd have standing to do that."

"That'd have to be someone like maybe Juliette's parents, right?" Ronnie interrupted.

"Yeah. Someone with standing to challenge his decisions as her legal guardian and all," Evan answered.

"Well, no worries on that count," Ronnie asserted confidently. "I know the whole Abbott family is solidly behind Roman's efforts to keep her alive. Someone is over at the care facility almost every day, helping with all that physical therapy and sensory stimulation the doctors have been putting her through. I'm sure they're hoping for a miracle too."

"But to answer your previous question about what I meant by 'in a legal sense,'" Cooper continued, "I think there's something else behind this." He drummed the lead of his pencil on the tabletop. "I'll bet the defense is calculating that if the court believes that Juliette's chances of revival are minimal and declares her legally dead, at least as far as this lawsuit is concerned Roman won't be financially able to continue to maintain her in that long-term facility. Then he'll be forced, economically at least, to discontinue her life support"

"Those bastards!" Ronnie muttered. "That's not fair!" She paused as she pondered the significance of Evan's analysis. Inflecting an emotional tone, she added: "Forcing him to make a decision like that in this way would be devastating."

"And keep in mind who's currently paying those bills to maintain Juliette," Evan reminded her. "And who'd have to pay all those future medical costs."

Ronnie looked over at him, searching his eves for the answer she was supposed to know. Then it hit her. "Union Health!" she exclaimed. "Of course!"

"So instead of the eight to ten million we've projected," Cooper added, "with this state's restrictions on noneconomic damages for Roman and the baby, we'll be lucky to get close to *one* million."

"So what you said a minute ago about the one-to-one ratio," James reflected, "if they cut down those big ticket compensatory damages – no future medical costs, no future lost earnings – that'll significantly limit how much we can get in punitive damages."

"You got it," Copper concurred. "When you look at the big picture, winning this motion could be worth six to eight million to them." The two attorneys sat there silently, contemplating the enormous significance of the legal task now cast before them.

* * *

"The Hell they will!" Roman bellowed as he exploded out of his seat on Ronnie's office sofa. "No one's pulling any plug on Jules. No one! It's not gonna happen. No way!"

James rose slowly and followed her client over to the picture window. "I know how you must feel Roman. This has been quite a shock to all of us too."

Roman stared out at the plaza a hundred feet below. Ronnie gave him time to let the news sink in. Finally, he spoke: "Can they really do this?" His voice was tinged with pain, exposing his vulnerability.

James put her hand on his left shoulder and answered him with softness and strength. "Yes, they can. And if they get this from the trial court, you can be sure Union Health will soon send you a letter indicating that they will stop paying for Juliette's care. Then you'd have to sue the health plan in a separate case to force them to pay. From what we now know about ERISA, that'd be an action for a determination of rights under the policy, and you'd have to bring that one in federal court. And they're banking on the probability that any judge who hears *that* case will just follow the ruling they hope to get out of *this* court."

Roman turned his head and eyed his lead attorney. "But she's *not* dead!" he entreated. "I know it as sure as I'm standing here. I know it seems as though she's had some setbacks lately, but she's not dead!"

Ronnie smiled consolingly at her client, admiring his display of faith and resolve. But her professional rationality soon returned. "Unfortunately, Judge Williams is not going to consider your feelings in this matter. It's going to come down to a war of the experts, that Doctor Craig they hired versus, I guess, Doctor Mayer. Isn't he the one who's in charge of Juliette's care?"

Roman started to answer with a brief "uh-huh," but the sound seemed to get plugged up halfway between his vocal chords and this mouth. His head bobbed in agreement as he swallowed hard to force the emotions of the moment back down inside. "There's got to be a way," he finally said. "There's *got* to."

"We're not conceding this, Roman," Ronnie reassured him as she gave his shoulder another squeeze. "Not by a long shot. But I want you to understand that this is going to be an uphill battle. And I want you to be prepared for the possibilities. That's all."

"I know, Ronnie," Roman replied. He reached back and patted her hand on his shoulder. "If we lose this and they stop paying for her care, I'll find a way. We're not giving up on Jules."

"Do you realize how much that could cost?" James queried. "If I recall some of our damages figures accurately, her hospital costs and all are running close to $500 per day." She studied his face for a reaction. Seeing none, she continued. "I know you're dedicated to her, and I assume your business is going well, but be careful. You don't want to end up sacrificing your daughter's future." They both stood at the window in silence for several minutes, watching the hundreds of people below scurrying about all over the Civic Center Plaza.

Roman broke the somber quietude. "I know. I know. But that's not the main thing. All these months I've been hoping that if Jules could just wake up, even for a short while, I know just by seeing the baby that she'd find the strength to pull through. I *know* it."

"That would be so wonderful if she could," Ronnie assented. "But it's been over eight months now, and there hasn't been any sign of that."

"But it does happen! That's what Doctor Mayer said," Roman countered, interrupting his counselor's thought.

"That's true," Ronnie conceded. They both stood in silence for a few minutes staring out the window.

"The baby hasn't even met her mother yet," Roman added. His voice bore a tone of resignation. "I've been too afraid to take her there – afraid of what it might do to her. I don't want her to have that kind of image of her mother burned in her memory forever."

"I know, Roman," James interjected. "I know."

"This is all just too much," he added shaking his head. "I'm not sure how much you know, but things haven't been going too well for Jules lately. I know Mayer is concerned, but he tries to be optimistic about her chances. And now this. Why couldn't they just wait until the trial?"

"They could have," James acknowledged, "at least from a legal standpoint. The HMO could have sent you a letter reserving its rights under the plan to recoup costs it might have overpaid. And Willis could have brought this up in his motion in limine, which lawyers usually file just a couple of weeks before trial. But we all know what this is about. It's about putting pressure on you, about trying to weaken your resolve."

"They're doing a good job," the client admitted. "I'm not sure how much more of this I can take. Every day at the hospital – seeing Jules there, never moving, never even reacting to my presence. Just the constant wheezing of that respirator. The smell of alcohol from all the daily body rubs. The touch of her skin, cool and clammy. And then I go home to that beautiful child, who's so full of warmth and life and energy." He shook his head slowly. "Sometimes I feel like I'm being drawn and quartered."

"Maybe it's time to let go Roman," Ronnie suggested as she took a half-step forward, brushing up close against him at the window, "to let Juliette's spirit go free. What was it you said once? 'To soar on wings of light.'"

Roman's breathing halted, his lungs empty, then started again spasmodically as a wave of intense emotion swept through his body. His head dropped down, chin on chest, as a deep breath pushed up from his solar plexus and rumbled out as a low, mournful hum. Ronnie stroked his back comfortingly. Then he turned and embraced his attorney, burying his face against her hair.

What Is Death?

The hearing turned out to be exactly what Ronnie had forecast: a war of experts. Three days after the plaintiffs filed their response to the defense motion, judge Williams telephoned the three lead attorneys for a conference call. After a twenty-four-hour scramble by the lawyers to check all the schedules of their prospective witnesses, a hearing date was set for the first Friday in June. But in spite of the best efforts of both sides to present a number of witnesses, including Roman, Juliette's nurses and therapist, and her sister, the judge exercised her judicial authority and cut the list down to the two James had predicted.

Doctor Herman Craig was a man just over six feet tall, with short red hair, thinning on the forehead and temples, and bespectacled green eyes. He was the head of the trauma unit at a Boulder hospital and former adjunct professor of trauma medicine at the University of Colorado School of Medicine. Educated at the University of Oregon, where he received both his B.S. and M.D., he had moved to Colorado in 1989 after a distinguished ten-year hospital career in Medford. At the age of fifty-seven, he had made so many determinations of death that he had lost count. His best estimate was that the body count was approaching a thousand.

Willis led Craig through his prefatory definition of death determination and its history, from the groundbreaking medical research of the late fifties, to the establishment of the Harvard criteria, to the 1981 Presidential Commission and subsequent promulgation of the Uniform Determination of Death Act. Then the witness summarized Juliette's medical history, from her collapse on the trail until his own recent examination. He detailed how he had been initially contacted by the questioning defense attorney five months prior, how he had reviewed the patient's chart to that date, how he had received supplements to those medical records weekly, and how he had contacted the defense when he perceived that Juliette's medical status had taken a downturn.

"What did you recommend at that time?" Willis inquired.

"I advised you that I thought I should examine the patient in person," Craig explained.

"What tests did you perform on Missus Marchetti, Doctor Craig?" Willis inquired.

"All in all, we performed seven tests on the subject," Craig replied. "The first one was the pupillary reflex test. That's where a strong source of light is directed to each pupil sequentially. We're looking for change in pupil size. If there's a pupillary reaction, then a determination of brain death would not be appropriate."

"What was the result in this case?" Willis continued.

"There was an absence of reaction in the pupils," Craig explained, "no contraction."

"What was the next test you performed?" Willis asked.

Craig glanced down at his notes. "That was the oculocephalic reflex test," he said. "In that test, we move the patient's head quickly from side to side. If there's any movement of the eyes within their orbits, that excludes brain death. This is sometimes referred to as the 'doll's eyes' test. I think you can figure out why."

Willis looked over at the judge who was regarding the witness intently. "What were the results of that test Doctor?"

"That test also was negative," Craig explained. "No response."

"What was the third test?"

"That was the oculovestibular reflex test," the witness answered. "In that test, the head is elevated to an angle of approximately thirty degrees. Then ice water is irrigated into each ear sequentially. If there's any movement of the eyes toward the irrigated ear, that would exclude brain death."

"And was there any such movement in Missus Marchetti's case," Willis asked.

"No. None," the doctor stated.

"And the fourth of the tests Doctor?" the defense attorney continued.

"That's the corneal reflex test," Craig replied as he flipped over a page of notes in his folder. "Now in that test, each cornea is grazed lightly with cotton or soft tissue. Any movement of the eyelid rules out brain death." Before Willis could fire off the usual followup question, Craig added: "In this patient, there was no reaction."

"What was the fifth test?" Willis inquired.

"The gag reflex test," the witness replied. "That one can be performed in two ways. We use a tongue depressor and touch the back of the pharynx. Or we can extend it in a bit further and move into the endotracheal tube. If there is any movement of the uvula or if the patient gags, then brain death is excluded."

"And in this case . . . ?"

"The result was negative," Craig declared abruptly, not waiting for the attorney to complete his question. "No movement of the uvula and no responsive gagging."

"The sixth test then, Doctor."

"That's the cough reflex test," the witness responded as he stood and pointed to the anatomical chart to his right. "We pass a suction catheter through the endotracheal tube into the tracheobronchial tree. Coughing by the subject is negative for brain death."

"And the final test Doctor?" the lawyer inquired.

"If all of the first six tests are negative for brain stem activity," Craig replied, "we perform the apnea reflex test. That has several parts. First, we obtain a baseline arterial carbon dioxide level. Next, we give the patient pure oxygen for a period of ten minutes. Then we disconnect the patient's ventilator and oxygenate down the endotracheal tube at eight to twelve liters per minute of oxygen." Again he motioned to the chart as he described the process. He glanced over at the judge who appeared a bit lost. He summarized the procedure a second time. "Basically, we stop or significantly decrease mechanical ventilation while maintaining a continued administration of oxygen for a long enough period of time to increase the arterial carbon dioxide tension above a physiologic threshold," the witness explained. Williams acknowledged her understanding with a subtle nod of her head.

"And what were the results of this final test?" Willis asked as he studied Williams for any reaction.

"Negative again," Craig said as he slowly shook his head. "There was no evidence of respiratory effort during thirty seconds of apnea. No reaction."

"Did you perform this series of tests just the one time?" Willis queried.

"No," the witness responded. "We returned later that afternoon and repeated the same series of tests."

"With what results?"

"The same," Craig nodded. "All negative, no reactions."

"What else did you rely upon in making your evaluation," Willis inquired.

"We also reviewed the patient's latest electroencephalograph, an EEG," the doctor explained as he turned to face the judge. "A patient without brain function will have electrocerebral silence, or what's commonly called flat line. Of course, there are those rare cases where electrocerebral silence is present even though there is still detectable brain stem activity. So we don't rely on the EEG alone, but only to support a clinical examination that has documented the absence of all brain and brain stem function." Again, he caught Willis with his mouth open, anticipating the next question before it could be asked. "In this case, the subject's EEG was flat lined."

"And based upon the results of all these tests," the attorney queried as he rounded third and headed for home, "did you reach a conclusion about whether Juliette Marchetti is medically alive or dead?"

"Yes, I did," the witness responded. "Based upon consistent negative results, I have determined that the subject has sustained irreversible cessation of all functions of the entire brain, including the brain stem." He glanced over at the judge, who was listening intently to his words as she made her notes.

"And has your determination of death been made in accordance with accepted medical standards?" Willis asked.

"Yes, it has," Craig replied.

"No further questions at this time, Your Honor," Willis stated as he closed his notebook and stepped away from the podium.

Cooper slowly rose from the table, gathered his materials, and strode over to the rostrum. After hours studying the sparse number of cases reported nationwide which dealt with determination of death issues, preparing the key responsive brief, reviewing the latest medical literature, and consulting with the plaintiffs' experts, he had focused in on a very limited number of issues. Assailing Craig's credentials, the plaintiffs' team had decided, would be as worthless as a defense attack on those of Doctor Mayer. The best approach, they decided, would be to create a climate of uncertainty in the mind of the jurist on the bench who had to make the weighty decision. After all, the focus of Cooper's brief had been to argue that there was a fact question as to whether Juliette Marchetti was legally deceased. That small glimmer of hope, he reasoned created a fact question which needed to be presented to the jury at trial and precluded a rush to a judicial decision.

"Now isn't it true, Doctor Craig, that the Harvard criteria call for a twenty-four-hour interval between the series of tests you performed?"

"That's true," admitted the witness, "but I don't —"

Cooper interrupted Craig. "And the Minnesota standards call for an interval of at least twelve hours, correct?"

"Yes, that's true."

"In fact, there's a whole host of different standards, isn't there?" Cooper inquired as he gestured outward and upward with his arms. "Dozens, perhaps?"

"That's probably true," the doctor conceded. "I've never counted them."

"So when you say you've made your determination of death under accepted medical standards," Evan reasoned, hoping he was driving his point home, "you're speaking of that one set of particular standards under which you operate, not a universally accepted set, correct?"

"I guess you could say it that way," Craig acknowledged, pausing to collect his thoughts. Cooper did not let him amplify.

"Now let's talk about the EEG," the cross examiner continued. "You didn't perform an EEG on Juliette that day, did you?"

"No, we didn't," the witness admitted.

"In fact, the results you reviewed were from a test conducted by Doctor Mayer over a week before, correct?"

"Yes, but . . ." Cooper interrupted.

"And you didn't . . ." Evan continued.

"Objection, Your Honor," Willis said as he rose to his feet. "This isn't an inquisition. Mr. Cooper should allow this expert to complete his thought."

"Sustained," Williams ruled. "Doctor, please finish your answer."

"Well," added Craig, "I was just going to say that there was no reason to perform that test anew. The results from the previous EEG were completely satisfactory under accepted medical standards."

"But you could have performed a new EEG on Juliette, right?" Cooper asked insinuatingly.

"We could have, I guess," Craig admitted, "but it wasn't necessary."

"Not necessary?" Cooper decried. "You're deciding issues of life and death and you just figured it wasn't necessary?"

"Objection, Your Honor," Willis boomed as he rose. "Argumentative."

"Sustained," said the judge. "Next question, Mister Cooper."

"But it's true, isn't it, that EEGs are sometimes unreliable?" Cooper asked.

"Infrequently," Craig acknowledged.

"Infrequently," Evan repeated, musing on the response. "Isn't that just another way of saying sometimes?"

The witness glanced over at Willis, expecting an objection. Hearing none, he allowed the similitude. "Yes, I guess it is."

Having scored a small point, the plaintiffs' attorney changed tack. "You also didn't perform any additional confirmatory blood flow studies, did you?"

"No, we didn't," the witness conceded.

"And for the same reason," Cooper reasoned, "not necessary in your opinion?"

"That's correct," the doctor replied. "A blood flow study isn't necessary under our protocol."

Saving his best nuggets of criticism for the plaintiffs' own expert, Evan withdrew and headed back for his table.

"Any redirect Mister Willis," Judge Williams inquired.

"No, Your Honor," the stubby attorney said as he half rose from his seat.

Williams turned to Cooper who was just pulling his chair away from the table. "We'll hear from the plaintiffs' expert then," she instructed.

Cooper shoved the chair back up under the table, turned and nodded to Mayer, then returned to the podium as his witness walked up to the witness stand. Slowly Evan took the doctor through the qualifying preliminaries. Educated at Johns Hopkins Medical School, from which he had graduated Magna Cum Laude in 1962, Carroll Mayer had enjoyed a distinguished career in intensive care medicine. A former Baltimore hospital ICU department chairman and author of numerous articles on the care of patients in comatose and persistent vegetative states, he had been at the forefront of research on and practice of intense multi-sensory, stimulation techniques. In the early 1980s, after concluding his work as a contributor to the report of the 1981 President's Commission for the Study of Ethical Problems in Medical and Biomedical and Behavioral Research, Mayer and three colleagues established their own long term care facility in Minneapolis. In 1990, the partners decided to expand and developed a similar state of the art facility in Denver. Mayer himself relocated to Colorado in early 1991.

In response to a series of questions from Cooper, the witness explained his theory behind his treatment of Juliette which had begun just days after she was returned to the Denver area. "When we can institute vigorous medical treatment during the first two or three weeks and combine that with a course of intense multi-sensory stimulation and concentrated physical activity over a period of weeks or months, we have found that the majority of patients who survive the first week or two will recover. A few others progress only into the prolonged phase of coma, or what's called the persistent vegetative state." By comparison, he claimed, patients who had remained in a coma for more than three months without the extended intense course of therapy had a less than one percent chance of recovery. He went on to explain how Juliette's family had become exhaustively involved from the early stages in the regimen of stimulation and treatment, assisting not only in the rigorous kinesitherapy, but also providing many of the materials personal to the patient used in the multi-sensory stimulation techniques.

Tediously, Evan led the witness through the highlights of eight months of Juliette's charts, explaining her progress, and depreciating her setbacks. Central to his assertions that he was not willing to pronounce his patient dead were the series of regular EEGs he had performed. "You can see here," he offered as he referred to the chart he had prepared summarizing those readings, "the signs of cerebral activity were consistent during the first five months, with little variation. Then we had what I'd call a significant drop at the next reading. But then the activity increased back up to near previous levels at the next reading. It held that way for a month, then started dropping again. In April, it got down to these low levels. But two weeks later there was significant activity again. Then, of course, we got a flat line the last time we did the EEG."

"Based upon that single EEG reading," Cooper asked, "are you willing to concede that Juliette Marchetti is deceased?"

"No, no," the witness replied.

"Why not, Doctor?" Evan queried.

"Several reasons actually," Mayer explained. "First, contrary to what the average layperson might think, a flat EEG does *not* indicate brain stem destruction. Second, Juliette has already defied conventional medical wisdom by living in a coma much longer than the usual two-to-four weeks that medical science accepts as the norm. Third, her records are full of notes by the nurses and therapists as to her skin coloration and texture, muscle tone, and joint flexibility. Her lack of physical deterioration is significantly less than what would have been expected in patient who had been in a coma this long. Fourth, and most important, we recently performed a procedure on her which is called a transcranial Doppler ultrasonography."

"What is that test?" Cooper asked.

"That's a non-invasive technique we can perform right at the patient's bedside that allows determination of cerebral blood flow velocity."

"Why did you perform that test Doctor?"

"Primarily because of the inconsistencies in her EEGS," he explained.

"How does the transcranial Doppler ultrasonography compare to the EEG, Doctor?"

"EEGs evaluate electrical activity from only the surface of the brain," Mayer explained. "But the sonography detects blood flow *within* the brain."

"And what were the results of the TCD I believe it's commonly called?" Evan asked.

"In the event of brain death, the TCD shows a cessation of forward flow and a characteristic oscillating waveform," Mayer explained. "But in the test we performed on Juliette Marchetti, there was a detection of forward flow and the characteristic oscillation was absent."

"Which leads you to conclude what, Doctor Mayer?"

"That there is a significant question as to whether Missus Marchetti is medically dead," Mayer declared resolutely.

Cooper's final plane of attack returned to the issue of appropriate standards. "Doctor Mayer, you heard Doctor Craig testify that his determination of death was made under accepted medical standards," Cooper stated. "Do you have any disagreement with that assertion?"

"Yes," Mayer replied, "I do." He turned to face the judge. "There are numerous guidelines for determining brain death, all published by various authoritative groups. Contrary to what the public might think, when it comes to such an important medical – and legal – decision, there isn't a single set of universally accepted specific diagnostic criteria. I wish there was, but there isn't. To me, that leaves too much room for individual discretion. I don't think it conforms to our right to have medical certainty on such an important issue."

Cooper glanced over at Judge Williams, who was again furiously taking notes. "No more questions, Your Honor," he announced, then moved away to make room for his adversary.

Willis wiped his mouth as he approached the rostrum, a nettling habit he seemed to exhibit only when going on cross examination. "Isn't it a fact, Doctor Mayer," Willis asked, "that the principal differences between the groups who have propounded medical standards for determination of brain death relate to the time intervals between examinations and the choice of confirmatory diagnostic tests and their relative importance?"

"As a very general statement," Mayer replied, "that's correct."

"Now you didn't find any irregularities in the way in which Doctor Craig performed the various tests he described, correct?"

"No," the witness confessed, "I didn't."

"So you don't have any basis to dispute those clinical results, right?"

"No, not with the individual results," Juliette's doctor admitted. "But I do disagree with his composite conclusion."

"I understand that Doctor," Willis said. "Now on this TCD you performed, that blood flow procedure has an acknowledged rate of error, doesn't it?"

"Sure. Any medical procedure does."

"And both false positives and negatives have been reported in the literature, haven't they?"

"Of course. As I said, any medical procedure has its failure rate."

"Let's talk a bit about those EEGs," Willis suggested, changing course. "You'll admit that her EEG results had been declining over a period of last few months, won't you?"

"There's an overall decline, that's true," the witness acknowledged, "but you should not see such inconsistencies in a person who is medically dead. To me, inconsistency is a sign of life."

"Or a sign of human fallibility?"

"I'm not sure I follow you," the doctor declared.

"You've gotten very close to the Marchetti family over the past several months, haven't you, Doctor?" the defense lawyer inquired.

"They've been through an ordeal that has broken many in less time," he declared. "Because of that, I have a great deal of respect and admiration for all of them. If that's what you mean by being close, I guess I have."

"And your hospital is receiving a substantial fee for your services in caring for this lady, aren't you?"

"Just what does that imply," Mayer rapidly retorted, his sense of professional ethics piqued by the sting of the defense attorney's barb.

"I mean you're making a small fortune off caring for someone, dead or alive," Willis shot back, his face reddening.

Cooper shot up out of his seat. "Objection! Badgering! Also argumentative."

The judge glared over at Willis. "Sustained." She took a deep breath, a clear indication that she was ready to wrap it up. "Do you have any other questions of this witness?"

Willis looked up at the judge, then over at Mayer. "No more questions," he declared, then turned to face Williams again. "Your Honor, we'd like to recall Doctor Craig for rebuttal." The judge gave him a quizzical, yet stern, expression. "Just for one or two questions," the HMO's lawyer added.

Williams nodded resignedly and motioned for the defense's expert to take the stand. Once seated, Willis wasted no time in eliciting the responses he wanted. "Doctor Craig, why didn't you perform another test like the transcranial Doppler ultrasonography?"

"Brain death is a clinical diagnosis. All of the various confirmatory tests – the EEG, the TCD, the atropine test, or a four-vessel angiography, or even radionuclide angiography – are not essential to the declaration of brain death. They're primarily only used in selected patients when clinical testing can't be performed reliably. They're not required under accepted medical standards." He paused, then added: "Not under any standards."

Willis flipped through the several pages of notes he had taken during Mayer's questioning, searching for any more of those large stars he had put in the column next to particular notes. Finding none, he addressed the court. "Nothing further, Your Honor."

"Very well, Mister Willis," the judge replied. A quick glance over at Cooper picked up his negative shake of his head. "Then we'll adjourn. I'll try to have my decision ready within a couple of weeks."

As she rose from her seat and stepped down from the bench, Cooper's heart took a dive. *I don't think we got through to her,* he thought. He had argued many a motion in his career and read many a judge by the end of the hearing. And everything his intuitive sense was telling him did not bode well for his clients.

A Breath of Life

An atmosphere of dread filled the courtroom that afternoon on the second Friday in July as the lawyers gathered for the anticipated ruling from Judge Williams. Both sides had spoken confidently to the press after the hearing, but in the privacy of their offices, their remarks were anything but unequivocal. James had done all she could to prepare Roman for the possibility of an unfavorable ruling. And even though he had expressed his desire to attend, she had convinced him that it would be easier on him if he stayed away from the news spectacle that was sure to engulf anyone present at the time of precedent-setting decision. Ironically, the only person fully insulated from the press assault was the judge, who could secret herself in the sanctified seclusion of her chambers and find reporters who approached her in the midst of an active case in contempt.

The creaking of a door hinge sorely in need of a drop or two of oil splintered the silence and stirred the small troupe to attention. Williams' court reporter entered first, carrying her stenography machine before her. The bailiff followed close behind. "All rise!" he called as the jurist stepped up to the bench.

"Be seated," the judge directed as she took her own. She peeked over the edge of the bench at her reporter, watching for the signal that the machinery was all in place. Seeing the confirmatory nod, Williams picked up two sheets of paper that had been lying in front of her. "Good afternoon ladies and gentlemen." She scanned the faces that had become so familiar over the past nine months. Cooper sat on the far right, his stoic demeanor masking his underlying anxiety. Ronnie was next to him, her usual smile a greeting to the jurist. Powell was seated across the aisle at the other table, O'Brien behind him. Willis filled out the front row, another new associate behind him. A smattering of fourth estate representatives were scattered among the gallery seats.

"This is case number 96 CV 1206, Marchetti *et al.* v. Sanders, *et al.*. We are here on a motion made by defendant Union Health Management, Inc. to limit the evidence of damages to be offered at trial by plaintiffs. A hearing on this motion was held on June 26, at which time the court heard testimony and received into evidence documents and other materials relevant to the issues before the court. After careful and lengthy consideration of the evidence, the court is now ready to issue its ruling." She paused, looked away from her prepared text, and addressed the attendees directly.

"I have to state that this is one of the most difficult rulings I have ever been called upon to make. I have reviewed the pleadings in this matter and listened carefully to both experts who testified at the hearing. And I have studied the medical literature both of the doctors provided. And still there are no easy answers." She looked back at her papers.

"We live in a land where the law is supposed to embody the highest ideals of justice our society can envision. Most of the time, the system operates just that way. But now and then, we find flaws in the system – not so much flaws of intent but flaws that reflect our humanness, our fallibility. For there is no way to set up a system of laws that can adapt to every conceivable human circumstance that can befall us. And today, a tiny flaw in our legal system is made to appear as an ever-widening chasm."

James looked up at the judge with a deep sense of disappointment, expecting the worst from the jurist's preface.

"The issue before the Court," Williams continued, "is one of whether evidence of future damages will be allowed. As the moving party, the defense must meet the same standard required for summary judgment or a directed verdict: a clear showing that no genuine issue exists as to any material fact and that it is entitled to judgment on this issue as a matter of law. Of course, this Court is bound to view all of the evidence in the light most favorable to the plaintiffs. But in spite of that heavy burden, based upon all of the evidence presented, the Court finds that no reasonable jury could find by a preponderance of the evidence that Juliette Marchetti is *not* legally dead, as that term is defined by accepted medical standards. Therefore, the Court rules, as a matter of law, that the plaintiffs will not be able to establish a basis for computing an amount of future economic damages."

She directed her next remarks to Cooper. "This Court is aware of the possibility that other courts in this or one of our sister jurisdictions may, at some time in a case related to the present one, or in a similar case, be called upon to apply this ruling to a separate matter. However, I trust that those courts will carefully review the applicable burden of proof required by the issue or issues presented at that time – as I have done in this case – and apply the appropriate standard." She turned and gazed over the courtroom.

"Therefore, absent a clear showing of life activity without mechanical assistance, the Court will grant Union Health's motion and will bar presentation at trial of evidence of damages sustained by Juliette Marchetti after she first lapsed into her present coma. My written opinion will issue forthwith."

Williams reached over and picked up her gavel, tapped it lightly once, and rose from her seat. Two steps to her right she paused – as though she wanted to say something more, maybe something directly to the plaintiffs' lawyers. Reevaluating her impulse, she stepped down from the bench and disappeared through the side door into her chambers.

Roman received the news better than Ronnie had expected. "We're going to ask for an interlocutory appeal on this," she assured him. "It'll delay the trial, but Evan's pretty sure the ruling won't survive the scrutiny of higher courts. Judge Williams is just flat wrong. I know Doctor Craig made out a good case, but there was *some* evidence that Juliette is still alive legally. And that means the issue is supposed to go to a jury." But her words of explanation and encouragement fell on deaf ears. His mind was in another place altogether.

After an hour of fruitless efforts to concentrate on his work, Roman finally surrendered to his mental and emotional strain and took off a few minutes before four o'clock. The highways leading into the foothills were still largely devoid of traffic, resting in anticipation of the commuter rush that was sure to arrive shortly. After meandering aimlessly over the back roads for well over an hour, he found himself heading down the highway that led to Juliette's hospital. He parked his car in the lot and went inside.

His wife was in her bed – the same one she had occupied for nearly nine months, save the regular changes of linens. Her countenance still bore the same expression of lifelessness, her face the same pallor of fleshy gray. The gauntness of her frame – at least fifteen pounds lighter than her normal weight – was hidden beneath the sheets and blankets that kept her warm. But the lines of her face, the ways her cheeks had drawn in, the sharpness of her jaw line, were noticeable to all who had known her before she fell into the coma.

The CD player across from the foot of her bed played some of her favorite music. The soft ballads of Carly Simon, Mary Chapin Carpenter, and Tracy Chapman provided at least some pleasurable alternative to the rhythmic wheezing of the bellows on the respirator in the corner of the room. Once in a great while, the mechanical ticking of the plunger would fall into synch with the beat of a song – like the blinkers on cars stopped at the same light would sometimes do – making it seem as though even lifeless machines were trying to communicate with their stationary roommate.

Roman pulled out the chair from its space against the wall and took his customary position by Juliette's bed. As he had done almost daily for months on end, he stroked her left arm, then picked up her hand and squeezed it. Sometimes he would fiddle with her wedding band, twirling it round and round on the bony finger; other times he would caress her palm and massage her fingers out to the tips. Her nails were smooth and freshly polished – the result of one of the many special services he had arranged to have done regularly for her. Of course, these luxuries – the weekly manicure and pedicure, the occasional hair stylists – were not paid for by any insurance company. But when he knew she was going to have visitors, he made a special point of having her primped.

He sat in the chair for hours. Occasionally his lips would move and soft words of love would utter. At other times, the depth of the silence communicated more than any vocalizations could ever express. Nurses and attendants appeared briefly, observed the scene in the room, and vanished just as quickly. The news had filtered down to the staff, by way of a courtesy call from Ronnie to Doctor Mayer, that the ruling had been unfavorable. So they elected to keep their distance from Roman. There would be time enough in the days ahead to speak their minds and offer up their thoughts and prayers.

When the first shadows of the late summer afternoon began to fall across the windows, darkening the unlit room, Roman stirred from his Rodinesque position. Rising from the chair, he leaned over the bed and kissed his beloved on the cheek. He lifted the covers and slipped her arm back under them. Then he turned and walked sedately out of the room.

By the time Roman arrived home that evening, Missus Hagan had already put Juliet to bed. He reheated with a zap in the microwave the meal the housekeeper had left and sat in silence at the dining table as he ate. The only audible sounds came from the television in the elder lady's room. After scraping and rinsing his plate and utensils at the kitchen sink, he perfunctorily flipped through the small stack of mail Missus Hagan had laid on the corner of his desk, his mind oblivious to the contents of the envelopes. Understandably, his mind was elsewhere.

He walked over to his daughter's room and slowly pushed open the partially closed door. By the dim illumination of a small nightlight, Roman could make out the form of the baby lying in her crib, her tiny body covered with a small cotton sheet and the Alpaca blanket family friends had brought back from a quaint Peruvian mountain village. He stood at the threshold for several minutes, his arms folded across his chest, just listening to the sounds of the house. An occasional commercial barely blared from the housekeeper's quarters; the air conditioner compressor kicked on, thunking and whirring in its usual way; an errant windblown branch scraped on the roof; the crickets outside the nearby window chirped to lure a mate for the evening. He entered and stepped quietly over to the side of the crib, the thick gray wool pile absorbing any sounds his feet were making. As he bent over to give his daughter a kiss, he saw that her eyes were wide open, watching his every move.

He leaned over the rail and smiled at her. "Hi honey," he cooed. He reached out and caressed her cheek. Her eyes blinked but remained fixed on her father. He pulled the covers off of her and picked her up, cuddling her warmly in his arms.

"You should be asleep by now sweetie," he said softly. He wandered about the room with her, gently bobbing her up and down as he had done so many nights before to help her get to sleep. But even after ten minutes of somnolent strolling, her eyes were still wide open.

Roman carried the child over to the oak rocker that he and Juliette had found in one of the many antique stores on lower Broadway a week after Sally's pregnancy was confirmed. Its old joints creaked as he lowered himself onto the cushioned seat. He shifted Juliette from his right shoulder and cradled her in both arms. "I think it's time you meet your mother," he said to the wide-eyed baby. "I've tried to spare you all these months. But maybe it's time. And who knows? Maybe you never really needed to be spared." Prying his loafers off, be dug his socked feet into the plush carpet. "It just seems like everyone wants me to make a decision about her now and I just have no idea what I'm going to do. I don't know what's right . . . for her, or for you."

The squeaky old chair rocked back and forth sedately as Roman rolled his feet from heel to toe against the floor. But still the child remained wide-eyed. "I know I seem to talk about her all the time. Who knows? Maybe you know more than I do about your mother. Maybe somehow you've understood all along, since before you were even born." He slipped one arm from under her and stroked her forehead and wisps of light brown hair. "I often wonder what you know or what you see. I certainly can't tell what you're thinking right now, or even if there are thoughts going through your mind." He smiled at her, chuckled softly to himself from the joy she gave him, and continued to rock the old chair. "I just hope when the time comes, you'll understand."

The soporific motion of the antique rocker turned out to be more effective in delivering Roman to the edge of slumber than the baby. But without the stimuli of her father's resonating voice, warm smile, and radiating eyes, Juliet quickly followed suit. And while the two of them slept in that position through the night, he dreamed of his wife, dreams so intense and so real they came back flooding back into his consciousness in a sudden flash as Missus Hagan woke him the next morning.

Roman spent Saturday tending to Juliet as the housekeeper took the morning and early afternoon to do some much needed shopping and visiting with old friends. By the time she returned, the baby had drifted off for her long afternoon nap. After grabbing an early supper, Roman slipped on his hiking boots, hopped in his vehicle, and drove west into the foothills. Winding around on roads cut through forests of ponderosa pine and juniper, he pulled off to the side of the road to hike a nearby trail which led up toward a weather-worn geologic formation aptly named Elephant Rock.

Though his intention was to take a leisurely late afternoon trek for the exercise, and to clear his mind, the excursion took a dramatic turn halfway down the trail as he hit the first steep incline. Under the heat of the mid-July sun, sweat began to pour down his brow, trickling into his eyes. He stopped midway up the climb, whipped the bandana out of his back pocket, folded it over twice, and tied it around his head. Another quarter of the way up, his thighs began to burn as he struggled for deeper breaths. Coming to a flat area, he crossed the meadow at a brisk pace, trying to shake off the surfacing feelings of trepidation that had seemed to be accompanying the signs of physical exertion. He broke into a trot as he neared a bend in the trail, as though the pounding of his boots on the dry dust would shake off the mood that had attached itself to his psyche and his body.

Approaching the next steep hill, he slowed down to his brisk walking pace, adjusted the fanny pack containing his water bottle, and leaned into the slope of the narrow footpath. Step by step he climbed, but with each foot of elevation gained, another pound of weight seemed to cling to his trim frame. As he approached what he believed to be another crest, the trail zagged sharply back to the right, revealing another climb of greater length. Forging on, he kept pushing himself – step by step, pound by pound. Memories of Juliette danced in and out of his mind – momentarily at first, then more frequently. He sensed her presence, not as a spirit, but as a psychic weight. She was on his back, bleeding to death, her head bobbing lifelessly on his shoulder. He could feel her arms draped over his shoulders and her legs wrapped around his waist, growing cold. Like that dreadful last day at Rainbow, his heart pounded in his chest, thumping and pumping like a fleshy piston. Perspiration from his brow and scalp soaked the cotton band until drops oozed down into the comers of his eyelids, burning the inner sensitive tissue with his own salty sweat. His breaths wheezed in and out of his lungs in erratic gasps. And he heard his mind repeating that maddening mantra – *right . . . left . . . right . . . left*. Over and over again, one step after the other – *right . . . left . . . right . . . left*.

As he struggled toward the final crest of the hill, a deafening clap of thunder shook him to his core. The lightning strike had been so close that every bone in body vibrated from the shock of the sound waves. Previously oblivious to all that surrounded him, he could suddenly see over his left shoulder a dark, menacing rain cloud rapidly blowing in from the southwest. He stopped dead in his tracks, then turned to face the quickening storm. Wild gusts of wind blew forcefully against his chest, then whipped around his body. His muscles grew cold and rigid from the rapid evaporation of his sweat-soaked clothes. A shiver started from his calves and worked its way up his entire body until his neck and head trembled.

The first giant drops of rain splattered on his face, hitting him with their force of size and speed. The wind whistled past his ears. He stood there like a statue, beckoning the assault. And come it did. The cold rain first fell in sheets, then as gravel-sized hail. The tiny chunks of ice pelted his head, stinging his scalp and scratching the tender skin of his face. Trickles of blood were quickly washed away by the torrent from the heavens.

For minutes he stood there, not a muscle moving, his arms stretched straight out to his sides. This was his war, his personal battle with those forces greater than he. And if it meant he had to become a willing sacrifice to the storm gods, then so be it. He would not turn and run for shelter. He would not quit. He would stand on the peak and face whatever fate threw at him.

As the dark gray mass blew on over the hill and the rain lightened to a soft mist, Roman dropped his arms to his sides. His clothes were drenched. His nose, ears, and fingertips were numb from the cold blast. Small drops of blood oozed from the abrasions on his cheeks and chin. He breathed deeply, filling his lungs to capacity, then opened his eyes. Rays of the summer sun peeked out from behind the passing cloud, kissing his skin with warmth.

He peeled off his bandana and wrung it out, then surveyed the trail, now covered with white pellets of melting ice, its once smooth, dusty surface riddled with running rivulets. He stepped over to the grassy edge of the path, turned, and glanced up toward the prominent rock about twenty yards away. Carefully treading through the small puddles and over the wet, slippery rocks, he worked his way up to the summit. With each movement, he felt a lightness return to his step. Gone were the oppressive memories of his struggle those many months ago. Gone was the guilt which weighed him down. Gone was the internal conversation that would not stop.

Walking around the boulders that jutted from ridge line, his eye was drawn to the monochromatic sheet of gray, that hung from the sky, showering the valley below. He found his way up to a comfortable resting spot in the formation of rocks and sat down, leaning his back against the face of a boulder. He closed his eyes and took a deep breath. Sounds of chirping birds buzzing insects and scents of fresh rain and mountain wild flowers flooded his senses. A light breeze grazed his skin. Drops of sweet rainwater rolled down his face from his scalp to the corners of his mouth, seeping into the crevice between his lips. And as he opened his eyes and gazed out to the east, he watched the iridescent double rainbow slowly take form as it stretched across the full width of the green valley below.

Saturday's sudden shower was only the precursor to the monsoonal flow from an early Pacific hurricane that blew its moisture all the way up through the Southwest, where it hovered for the next few days, coloring the usually blue skies of the sunny eastern slope a solemn gray. After a series of telephone calls on Sunday and Monday and a stream of visitors by the house and the hospital, Roman dressed Juliet in one of her pretty new outfits, strapped her into the car seat, and drove over to the hospital.

By the time he pulled into the parking lot shortly after four o'clock, all of those persons he had called were waiting in the reception area. Juliette's brother and sister had picked up the elder Abbotts at the airport. Roman's parents and brother had driven down from the Denver suburbs. Ronnie had picked up Sally at the Tech Center on her way from downtown. Doctor Mayer and Juliette's regular day nurse greeted Roman and the baby as they entered through the front doors.

The assemblage walked somberly down the hall to Juliette's quarter. Holding his daughter tightly, Roman walked over to the bed. He stood quietly for a moment at the bedside as the rest of the family and friends formed a crescent around him. Then he spoke softly. "Jules, this is your daughter. This is Juliet." He turned his face to his daughter. "Honey, this is your mommy." Juliet looked down at the figure in the bed, then back at her father, her head movements jerking in the way that babies her age did. *Does she understand any of this?* Roman wondered.

He bent over and put the baby down on the edge of the bed. Juliet looked up at her father, then over at her mother's immobile body. Roman reached over to grab the nearby chair and pulled it up to the edge of the bed. His left hand slipped up behind Juliet's back and held her steady. His right hand reached through the railing and touched Juliette's arm. For a few minutes he just rubbed up and down the length of her forearm, his eyes darting from mother to daughter, looking for any signs of anxiety or tension. The baby watched him quizzically occasionally glancing over at the strange woman who never moved. Then she reached out and touched Juliette's left hand. Imitating her father, she rubbed it lightly, watching her father's face carefully for a telltale sign of approval or displeasure. Roman smiled as he watched Juliet play curiously with the gold wedding band on her mother's third finger.

Doctor Mayer's whispered words broke the silence. "Do you need some time alone with her Roman?"

Roman glanced over his shoulder at Mayer, then around the room to Juliette's family and friends. "No Doctor. We've all said our goodbyes." He turned his head back around and gazed lovingly at Juliette's expressionless face. A moment later, he rose from his chair and leaned over to kiss her cheek. Then he picked up the baby and nodded to the physician.

Mayer walked around to the right side of the bed, surveyed the machinery by her bedside, made a few notations on his patient's chart, and slipped it under his arm.

"Are we ready?" he asked Roman.

"Yes. Go ahead." Roman took a deep breath and clutched his daughter a bit tighter.

The physician turned and put his finger on the respirator switch. With a flip, the steady click and whoosh of the machine fell silent. Mayer motioned to his nurse who stepped around Roman and the baby up to the left side of the bed. Carefully she removed the two large strands of tape from the mouthpiece of the breathing tube. As the nurse steadied Juliette's head with both hands, the doctor withdrew the tube from her throat and mouth. As it was extruded, the patient coughed, startling those gathered around.

"It's an involuntary reflex," Mayer explained as he rolled up the tube and hung it over the hook on the side of the machine.

With the respirator quiet, the soft beep of the heart monitor resonated through the room. When Juliette had coughed, the rate had accelerated quickly, spiking at near 120 beats per minute, then rapidly decelerated to the intubated rate. But within a few seconds, the rate began to fall off steadily. All eyes in the room fixed on the orange digital numbers . . . *70* . . . *68* . . . *65*.

Roman felt his daughter's gaze. He looked over at Juliet as she glanced down at her mother. Then she looked back at her father. One hand extended and pointed down toward the bed. "Ma-ma," the baby girl uttered. The monitor signaled its illuminated display . . . *63* . . . *60*.

Roman's face accurately expressed his astonishment at his daughter's words, among the first discernable ones she had spoken. The monitor blinked its data: *58* . . . *57*. Juliet looked down at the bed again, then back at her father, her hand still extended in Juliette's direction. Roman shifted the child in his arms and put her down beside Juliette. *57*. The baby gazed upon her mother's face, then down at the shiny golden wedding band. Smiling softly, Juliet began to play with the ring, her lips inaudibly murmuring "Ma-ma." *57. . . 60 . . . 63*.

Mayer looked over at Roman. "I don't know how," the doctor confessed, "but she's hanging on."

Juliet looked up at her father, smiling.

A Fork in the Road

Like a runaway locomotive, another glorious Colorado summer had sped past all too quickly. After the media glitz and glimmer of the furious controversy of June and July, the pace of the remaining discovery all but bogged as one or another of the attorneys took an extensive summer vacation, causing massive scheduling problems. But as the lawyers completed the last round of the depositions of the opposition's economists in mid-September, everyone began looking toward December.

Fewer than two months remained until the trial date when James, Cooper, and Frey went into full battle preparation. The main conference room had been designated as the war room and devoted to the case. To the untrained eye, the entire room appeared littered with depositions, exhibits, documents, and display boards. But to the plaintiffs' attorneys, it was a model of organization.

Each evening, Ronnie kicked off her pumps, curled up on her office couch, and highlighted another deposition, eighteen in all. As she found testimony she considered significant for trial purposes, she tagged the page with a pink Post-It note. If the material suggested a particular question or a line of interrogation, she reached for the Dictaphone and put her thoughts on tape. Ellen, her secretary, was a master at not only timely transcribing but also organizing her boss' mental memos in outline form. Over lunch, James reviewed each set of draft questions and either dictated additional thoughts or made her changes directly through their networked office computers.

Cooper tackled the documents and other non-testimonial evidence, distinguishing those he recommended for use as exhibits. Many were sent out to the nearby copy shop to be blown up to poster size and mounted on foam core boards. When one returned, Evan would attach a cheat sheet to the back of the board, on which he would note the legal objections and exceptions that might interfere with the exhibit's orderly introduction into evidence. If he could not be found in the war room in the evenings, he would be in the library, preparing proposed jury instructions or searching for the one additional case interpreting the evidentiary rules that permitted the admission of the document or testimony they would need.

Frey, ever the master of criminal defense, played the devil's advocate for his colleagues, challenging both testimonial and demonstrative evidence. He also took on the responsibility of preparing a mock defense, anticipating what Powell and Willis might or should do given the evidence available. Even though he admittedly could not hold a candle to Cooper when it came to research, he found himself in the library on numerous occasions, jousting with his colleague for the volume of the Colorado Revised Statutes that contained the annotations of cases for the rules of evidence.

Although it was by no means exclusive, Cooper had always exercised a certain modicum of territoriality over the library. In the short span of years the three lawyers had worked together, both Mark and Ronnie had mastered the art of approaching their colleague with a question on a point of law and then watching him take the lead in doing the research. Of course, Evan was so proficient at the legal treasure hunt and so enjoyed mining for points of jurisprudential gold that a bystander would have had a hard time determining who was the king and who was the servant.

The symbolism of the quest permeated the atmosphere when the hourly employees left the castle to the royalty. And when volume 12 of C.R.S. became the coveted possession, the trophy, the Holy Grail of the law of evidence, mock sword fights would break out between Frey and Cooper, with pens or pencils substituting for the trusty blades of the knights of yore. Even Ronnie (a.k.a. Guinevere) would join in the spectacle, standing by the library door, waving an available scarf, handkerchief, or, if desperate, a facial tissue for the victor to retrieve.

It was in the midst of this jovial atmosphere that the telephone rang late one Wednesday evening. Since James was less involved with the horseplay, she took a step inside the library door and grabbed the phone from the nearby stand.

"Frey, Cooper and James," she announced.

"Oh. I didn't expect anyone to still be there," a male voice stammered. "Uh, is Ronnie James in?"

"Speaking," she said.

"Oh, hi, Ronnie. I thought it was your voice. This is Curtis Powell. I was expecting to just get your voice mail, but since you're there, I wanted to suggest that we get together in the next few days to see if there might be a way to get this case settled."

Ronnie waved excitedly at her associates, trying to get them to hold the noise down just a bit. "Yeah, Curtis. Sure. Tomorrow too soon?"

"No, actually. If it can be later on in the afternoon, that'd be good."

"Sure. How about three o'clock?"

"Three it is. We'll come over there, okay?"

"We?"

"Megan and I."

"You bringing a claimsperson?"

"No. Not yet," Powell replied. "I think maybe the lawyers should just talk first and see whether a full-blown settlement effort is warranted."

"Okay," James agreed. "Sounds fine. We won't have our client here then."

"Yeah, sure. I understand. See you tomorrow." By the time Ronnie set the phone back down in its cradle, Mark and Evan had returned their trusty swords to the table and were looking eagerly at their colleague.

"I assume you got the gist of it," she explained. "Just a preliminary meeting to see if a settlement effort is worth the try. Three tomorrow here, if you're interested." Both of the men headed into their offices to check their calendars.

O'Brien and Powell showed up right on time Thursday afternoon and were greeted by Ronnie. After the cordial offers of coffee or soft drinks, they joined Mark and Evan in the small conference room. James wasted little time cutting to the chase. "Our position is quite simple," she explained. "Our demand is for your client's full limits under the law, one million dollars. We can easily prove damages four or five times that amount. You've seen our preliminary calculations, and you've deposed our economist. Willis' little attempt to limit those damages boomeranged on him. Juliette is still legally alive and not even Doctor Craig is willing to state that a person in a persistent vegetative state is brain dead. You've seen enough jury verdicts in cases like this to know we're not being unreasonable. The only thing that's negotiable at this point is the payout. We're perfectly willing to listen to your annuity proposals."

"As I told you over the phone, Ronnie," Powell explained, "we're not here with any settlement authority from the carrier. I just wanted us to get together to talk about the case, get a few things out in the open, and see what we attorneys could do to settle this. Now don't get me wrong. I don't know if settlement is even possible. When you back somebody up against the wall and say 'gimme everything you got,' you don't leave a whole lot of room for negotiation. But we're here to talk about the case and see if there's anything we can do. That's all I can promise."

"Fair enough," replied Ronnie. "Let's talk about the case. First, let's look at the tube specimen that was removed during Juliette's surgery. Very solid piece of evidence. Your people have had all the time they need to inspect it, and I don't hear anyone offering a credible explanation for it being in the wrong place other than human error by your client."

"Well," Powell hemmed as he cleared his throat. Ronnie's attack had been directed right at his defense's jugular vein. "It's a strong piece of evidence. I'll give you that. But it doesn't conclusively prove that Sanders was negligent."

"Standing alone, maybe not," James concurred, "but we've got some powerful testimony from Patricia Trenckmann too."

"I certainly wouldn't go so far as to characterize her deposition as 'powerful,'" Powell countered with a slight smirk.

"You can say what you will, Curtis," Mark asserted forcefully, "but Trenckmann's video testimony will be very damaging to your client. She portrays Doctor Sanders as arrogant and full of himself. And though Megan scored some points with the fact that Trenckmann married a surgeon she worked next to, like she did with Sanders, that personal attack on her integrity will backfire with a jury."

"We certainly don't buy that assessment," countered O'Brien. "Of course, you haven't heard Doctor Sanders' side of the story about their personal relationship."

"No, we haven't," Evan interjected, "but if that's the only card you've got to play, you're better off folding."

"Let's get away from the character assassination side of things and get back to the substantive evidence," suggested Ronnie. "Even if both experts cancel each other out, you just don't have any credible evidence that those clips migrated in tandem during the intervening years to a point just a few millimeters away. What the jury's going to get out of that argument is that your client is desperate for any kind of explanation – no matter how unlikely. Trenckmann said it best. The odds are a thousand to one that human error is a more plausible explanation for the fact that the clips didn't close off the tube than migration."

After over an hour of bantering back and forth, O'Brien excused herself for a restroom break. The other attorneys took the opportunity to do Megan came back into the reception area, Powell was thumbing through the latest issue of *Time* magazine. With a motion of her hand, she summoned her colleague to the comer by the front door.

In a hushed voice, she questioned the efficacious expenditure of their time. "I know we talked about this on the way over here, about just wanting to assess their resolve and see if negotiations were worthwhile, but I don't get the sense we're really getting anywhere. They want the policy limits. They're emphatic about it. They know they've got a great case of liability and their damages easily exceed the limits. So what I'm wondering is, why are we feeling them out for possible negotiation? What's there to negotiate if they're standing on their demand? You've recommended paying the limits before and the insurance companies have done it. So what's really going on here? Why are we billing time for something that's not going much of anywhere?"

"Look, Megan," Powell replied, glancing toward the receptionist's desk to make sure the opposition was not passing within earshot, "settling this thing is much more complicated than most of the med mal cases you've handled to date. I don't know if you're aware of it, but Union Medical Protective Association is a wholly owned subsidiary of Great Union Insurance & Indemnity, which also wholly owns Union Health Management. At least according to Willis, his Union Health people have no intention of settling. They think the best circuit to reverse the tide of *Dukes*, *PacifiCare*, and *Rice* is the Tenth and that Colorado, with our reputation for conservative jury awards, may be the best place to win at trial . . . if they get pushed that far."

"Okay, fine. But what does that have to do with us settling the claim against Doctor Sanders? Union Medical pays the limits of his malpractice policy and walks away, with a bargain, probably twenty to thirty percent of what a jury would award as full damages. And they save the costs of the trial."

"The feeling I get," Powell expounded, "is that the insurance companies don't want our client to settle because they're afraid he'll get on his high horse with them about insurance people interfering in the physician-patient relationship. You know, there are a lot of doctors who are steamed about the way HMOs make treatment decisions based upon a bean counter's cost-benefit analysis or a claims manager's whim instead of on a trained doctor's good judgment and the wishes of the patient and his or her loved ones."

"You're talking about some of the things he said in his deposition?" she asked.

"That . . . and some other things."

"Like what?"

"Like the new contract Union Health sent him."

"I don't follow you. I don't know anything about his contracts," she confessed.

Powell glanced around again for unwanted ears. "Ever since that *Rice* decision came out in the Seventh Circuit, Union Health has had their Chicago lawyers rewriting the agreements that the HMO has with its contracting physicians, adding confidentiality clauses to keep the doctors from complaining about managed care decisions."

"I'm not sure I'm with you on this," she advised.

"A couple of weeks after Sanders got sued," Powell explained, "he got a letter from Union Health stating that he would soon be receiving a new participating physician agreement. It struck him as a bit odd since the last contract he'd signed was for three years and it still had a year or so to go. So when he got the new agreement, he sent it over to his CPA for a financial analysis. And when the projections came back better than his current arrangement, he signed it and sent it back.

"Then, a week or so later, he was reading through it one evening and he saw some things that concerned him. So he sent it over to the lawyer who handles his business affairs for a review. And his attorney pointed out all the changes to him - especially the provisions requiring confidentiality."

"Is that what all the breaks during his deposition were about?" Megan asked.

"Partly, yes," Powell acknowledged. "He'd just given me a copy the week before he was to testify and he wanted me to advise him whenever the issue came up."

"So what's the import of these confidentiality provisions?" O'Brien inquired.

"By signing it, he essentially agreed not to do or say anything that might undermine the confidence of plan participants, employers, or the general public in Union Health or the quality of its services."

"That's more wide sweeping than a court gag order!"

"Exactly," echoed Powell. "And quite troubling in its implications – especially if any kind of litigation ensues. Small problems," he added facetiously, "like intimidation of witnesses, suborning perjury, obstruction of justice – just to name a few."

"You said something earlier about this confidentiality requirement coming out of Chicago after the *Rice* case?"

"Well, I didn't intend to make it seem it was just Union Health," Powell went on. "Many of the major companies started doing the same thing after *Dukes* and the other cases opened the window that the complete preemption doctrine had shut. They thought it was a simple way to plug up the leak in the dike, but it's ended up creating all kinds of problems. First, it offends the personal dignity of most health care professionals to be pressured to agree to something like that in writing. Second, there are some real problems with physicians' informed consent requirements."

"You mean, if a doctor and the managed care people disagree about treatment, the doctor might be reluctant to discuss the alternative procedures that the HMO has refused to pay for with his or her patient?"

"That's one example," Powell agreed. "There are a few others. Could be a doctor would be reluctant to even discuss alternative diagnoses and treatments with the patient because it might cast the health plan in a bad light."

"So Great Union and Union Health Management are pressuring Union Medical Protective to keep our client in line," O'Brien reasoned. "And Union Health could dump him as a participating physician if he breaches the confidentiality provisions of the contract."

"Something like that or so it appears."

"But I thought the main reason Sanders wanted to settle was because the media has gotten hold of this case – at first because of the baby and then this brain death thing – and he doesn't want his practice and questions of his competence to be the centerpiece of a highly publicized trial."

"That's right," confirmed Powell. "That's what he's made clear to me in no uncertain terms. He's concerned – and rightly so – this his practice will be severely damaged. He used to have a lock on the south side of Denver with Union Health, but it's signed up three more OB/Gyns during the last couple of year with all the growth down in Douglas County and all over the south side, and he's had quite a number of regulars move over to other physicians since the news broke. Of course, they might've switched because of convenience, but he doesn't think so."

"So what do we do? We've got a client who wants to settle and an insurance company that refuses to do so." She chuckled ironically. "Isn't that the reverse of what usually happens?"

"Yeah, it is, now that you mention it. More often than not, it's the doctors who are screaming for their day in court and demanding public exoneration when the insurance company suddenly decides to pay up and get rid of the claim. Of course, many doctors have settlement approval authority written right into their policies. So this is a little different."

"So, like I said, what do we do?"

"Well," Powell replied, scratching the top of his head, "we're in a delicate position, to say the least. The way things are developing, our firm could well end up caught in the middle oi a serious conflict of interest between the medical malpractice carrier and its insured. Of course, we're both well aware that our duty is to Doctor Sanders, not to his insurance company. On the other hand, the insurance company assigns us the cases and pays our bills." He hesitated, looked off to the side, and shook his head. It's a tightrope, no doubt."

The defense attorneys' privacy was broken by Evan, who whizzed past them out the front door and down to the restroom. "We'll pick this up later," Powell advised his cohort as they walked back toward the private offices.

Stopping off for a cup of coffee outside the conference room, the four attorneys waited a couple of minutes for Cooper to return. Powell got the conversation back on track. "I know it doesn't seem like we've gotten much of anywhere tonight," he said, "but I feel good about the time we've spent. I'm hopeful we can resolve the case or at least our portion of it without having to go to trial, but I have to discuss it with my client and the claims person."

"We're hopeful of that too," Ronnie assured him. "But if we're going to put a settlement together, it ought to be done quickly. Our trial date will be on us sooner than we think. Doctor Sanders must know that we've been fending off the press for months now, but once the trial starts, a lot of what's been sealed by gag orders becomes public."

Megan nodded. "He's aware of that."

"If I may just interpose another thought or two," Frey spoke up. Having garnered everyone's attention, he measured his words carefully. "Ever since we brought in Union Health as a defendant, the scope of this case has changed. And I'm not just talking about deeper pockets and more money." He hesitated, looking Powell straight in the eye. "Our claim against your client has always been one of simple negligence. Doctors aren't gods. They're human like everybody else. And they make mistakes. But their intentions are usually good.

"On the other hand, Union Health's part in this goes beyond the pale of simple negligence. We think we can prove that what they did was reckless. Your doctor calls in and expects to talk to a colleague, someone with equal or greater medical experience. But what does he get? People with little or no training in positions where they make decisions about what is and what isn't appropriate medical care. That's reckless to me. And they make those decisions based on cost-benefit analyses – or their own limited experiences. They don't consult a team of specialists. They don't set up contingencies. They just rule the roost and strut around the henhouse of health care like the cock of the walk – "

"Look, Mark . . ." Powell interrupted.

"I'm sorry, Curtis," Frey replied. "Excuse the sermon. We'll save it for our closing argument to the jury. But I'm trying to make a point, and that is: your client's negligence was simple error. You pay us the limits; our client can live with that. He hasn't forgotten what Sanders did for Juliette that first time. But Union Health is a different matter altogether. We're damn serious about our claim for punitive damages against them, and we don't intend to let up."

"But what does this have to do with Doctor Sanders?" Powell inquired.

"So what I'm saying is," Mark spelled out, "that if your client agrees to settle, we'll expect his full cooperation on Union Health's interference with his professional medical judgment. He's already testified in his depo that he would have checked for pregnancy, no matter how slim the odds, because of the risk to Juliette. But Union Health had sent him treatment guidelines, and somebody there directed him to follow them when he called about it, and he sure as Hell knew he had to comply or they'd pull his business. So make sure that point is discussed with your doctor. Any settlement will include a provision related to his fullest possible cooperation. Understand?"

"I understand perfectly, Mark," Powell resigned. "Perfectly."

Shattered Hopes

All the pretrial discovery had been completed; all the pretrial motions had been filed, argued, and decided. And the trial date was drawing nearer day by day, now less than five weeks away. Powell and O'Brien had set up a meeting with Jay Frick, the claims person handling the Sanders file for Union Medical Protective. An experienced claims handler, Frick had worked a dozen years with another medical malpractice insurance carrier before taking a position as Union Medical's Denver office claims manager. He had a reputation as a savvy negotiator, his finely honed skills having saved his company probably a million dollars over the last ten years.

Powell's defense firm offices occupied the forty-fifth and forty-sixth floors of the RepublicBank Tower in downtown Denver. Lavishly trimmed in red mahogany paneling and brass fixtures, each partner's office and conference room had a spectacular view of the Rockies to the west. The lowly associate attorneys had to content themselves with high-rise views of the less stunning eastern plains.

A punctual Frick was ushered into one of the small conference rooms by Powell's secretary. Less than a minute later, Powell and O'Brien joined him, closing the door behind her. After a couple of minutes exchanging the usual pleasantries, Powell got down to the purpose of the conference.

"The reason I asked you to come by today," he explained, "was not only to discuss where the discovery stands but also to see if there's we can do to effect a settlement. I've talked at some length to our client and, to be quite frank with you, Doctor Sanders doesn't want this thing to go to trial. There's already been way too much media attention here in Denver. Of course, malpractice suits happen all the time, so that's not the problem. Luckily, most of the attention hasn't focused on Sanders. It's been on the circumstances of the mother's injuries and the unusual circumstances of her daughter's birth. Then there was all that negative publicity with Willis' motion on brain death.

And when the husband shut off her life support and she didn't die like everyone was sure she would, it made the lady into something of a folk hero with the local press. And while Sanders hasn't really been the focus of much of that, it keeps him in the public eye in a way that's very negative to him. And if this goes to trial, our doctor is going to catch more than his share of the fallout."

"I can't believe she's still alive," Frick remarked, referring to Juliette.

"Well, technically she's in a persistent vegetative state," O'Brien offered. "Not all that much alive, but definitely not dead by any legal standards."

All Frick could muster in response was a disgruntled "Humph."

Powell steered the conversation back to his client's needs. "Anyway, our doctor's pretty concerned about it and he wants to try to get this thing settled before it gets worse. I assume you've read Doctor Trenckmann's deposition, and I can't say that there's a lot going for us with the medical evidence. Sure, we've got our expert to back up Sanders' conduct, but a jury's going to pay a lot more attention to an assistant surgeon who doesn't have much to say in support of her superior. Meg did the best job anyone could've done to dent Trenckmann's credibility, but there's not much damage there, not really. And that could all backfire on us too, just like the legal determination death thing did."

Frick shifted in his chair, becoming uneasy with the tone of the briefing. "I thought we were going with the migration theory on the clips," he commented.

Powell and O'Brien exchanged glances. Powell spoke up. "It's the only explanation we've got for the position of the clips, but that doesn't mean it's a good one. Trenckmann hit the nail right on the head when she said the odds that it was human error were a hundred or a thousand times better than migration. Sure, there are a couple of articles in the literature about movement of foreign objects after affixation, but our expert is going to have to concede that there are hundreds or thousand more cases of doctors just plain screwing up."

"So have the plaintiffs softened their demand?" asked Frick. "Last I recall, you'd said they wanted the policy limits, but it was never a formal demand."

"No," answered Powell. "They still haven't put anything in writing, but they're not going to drop below the limits. After all they said in that informal meeting a couple of weeks ago, I can guarantee that.

We've looked at their elements of damages and they easily top our limits under tort reform – considering the pain and suffering the woman went through over the last two days of her life and the mental anguish of her husband, carrying her out of the back country like that. All that story checks out. They're going to have the jury passing around the Kleenex box the whole time Marchetti's on the stand."

"Not to mention the economic losses," added O'Brien. "Missus Marchetti was thirty-six years old at the time of her injuries, had a work life expectancy of another thirty years, give or take a few, and was pulling down about $75,000 a year as a research scientist. Figure in cost of living and merit raises and then reduce it to present value and it still exceeds two million on its own. Their economist is also prepared to support another half million of economic damages from lost royalties expected on the decedent's research and writing. And I'm sure you're familiar enough with the costs your company is paying out for her medical care. Then we've got the daughter who'll grow up probably never knowing her mother in any way other than just as a body lying lifeless in that bed."

"We're just hitting the highlights," Powell continued. "It'll all be itemized in the trial memorandum we'll be sending over to you sometime next week or so. But the point is, even if we trim their damages down to the bare bones, we're still way past the policy limits."

"So what you're recommending is just paying the limits?" Frick asked.

"That's our recommendation," agreed Powell. "It's been two years since we advised any med mal carrier to pay off on a doctor's policy, but in our opinion paying the limits is justified when you consider all the various elements of damages the plaintiffs can put on the board." He could tell that the claims manager was having a hard time swallowing their dose of reality. To make it a bit more palatable, he backtracked a bit.

"Look, Jay. You've been around this business long enough to know the score. We've got two things we can do to defend against any lawsuit – attack the liability or attack the damages. We're telling you in plain and simple terms that the migration theory won't hold water. It's the best we've got, but it's not a good defense to the liability question."

"Then come up with something else," Frick suggested. "That's what we pay you the big money for." The office atmosphere was thickening with tension.

"We can't manufacture a defense just like that," replied Powell with a sharp snap of his fingers and a sharper tone to his voice. He leaned forward, his arms resting on the granite table top. "That's not what we do. We've got to have some evidence to support it, and the bald truth of the matter is we don't have any. There was nothing wrong with the clips. They were still intact when the tissue was removed. There is no question about it. Both our experts examined the specimen independently. And they both reached the same conclusion. And there wasn't any kind of problem with the instrument our doctor used to affix them either. And I could go on and on." He eased back into his chair. He hated to appear confrontational with the claims people he worked with from day to day.

"And on proximate cause," Powell continued, "the best we could do would be to lay some of the blame for the severity of her injuries onto both her and her husband for taking off up into the mountains when she wasn't feeling well or on Union Health's personnel for refusing to go along with the pregnancy test that would've diagnosed her condition. And if we even try to dump on the victim or her husband, with what we know about his efforts to save her, we'll alienate everyone on the jury. The woman almost bled to death because she had an undiagnosed ectopic pregnancy. And whether it's because of the failed sterilization or the failure to do a pregnancy test, both charges fall at the feet of your insured."

"As for the damages," O'Brien interjected, "the economist that we're sharing with Willis is prepared to argue all day about cost of living and merit adjustments and their side's present value reductions. And she's got a good basis for challenging those projected royalties as purely speculative. But even if the jury accepts our figures for economic damages, we're only down from $3.2 million to $1.7 million. And when you add in the future medical costs and then the noneconomics for pain and suffering, loss of consortium, and the others, well . . ." She shrugged her shoulders.

"For us to end up with an award under the policy limits," Powell added, "the best we can hope for is that the jury lays a large share of the comparative negligence on the HMO's shoulders. But the down side is that Union Health isn't subject to the same damages limitations as doctors are."

Frick's ears appeared to perk up. "Not sure I'm tracking you on that one," he queried.

Powell glanced over at O'Brien and nodded. She illustrated the point. "Let's say the jury awards five million dollars in damages. Sanders doesn't have to pay more than a million of that, under any circumstances. And if the jury finds him ninety percent negligent, comparatively speaking, that means Union Health has only a ten percent liability. So they'd pay $500,000 and you'd pay a million. But if the jury finds fifty-fifty comparative negligence, then you still pay your million, but the HMO would have to pay two and a half million. And, of course, that doesn't take into account any punitive damages that might be assessed against Union Health if the plaintiffs are able to prevail on that part of their claim."

"I think I get your point on the figures," Frick said. A few moments of silence passed as the three reconsidered what had been said and what needed to be added. The Union Medical man gave Powell a hard look, then O'Brien. "Got a phone I can use?" he inquired.

"Sure," said Powell pointing toward the phone set on the credenza in the corner. Gesturing to his colleague, he added, "We're going to step down the hall for a cup of coffee. Want some?" Frick shook his head and Powell closed the door behind them.

The two defense attorneys stood around the coffeepot, reflecting on the future. "So what do you think?" asked Megan. "Is he going to recommend payment of the limits?"

Powell arched his eyebrows. "Don't know. Frick's gotten where he is today by being tight with his company's money. You don't advance to a management position by giving it away. But in this case I think he's justified. It's not a question of a plaintiff making a demand for damages he can't substantiate. There's more than enough here to go around. At least if they settle now, they cut their losses."

"Yeah," agreed O'Brien with a touch of sarcasm, "but that's mostly our legal fees."

"Well, that and expert fees," added Powell. "Those'll damn near match our bill." Pausing to refill his mug, he shifted the focus a degree or two. "It's not like there aren't some reasonable grounds for appeal here."

"But do you really think we'd prevail at the appellate level?"

"Probably not," conceded Powell, shaking his head slowly. "But as far as the insurance company is concerned, it's a whole lot better than a double or nothing chance. They pay an additional five or ten thousand dollars to brief and argue the case for the chance that they don't have to pay a million dollars."

"I see what you mean," replied O'Brien. Catching a glimpse of Frick heading toward the lounge, she alerted her senior partner.

"Sure you don't want some coffee?" Powell asked as Frick entered the room, holding the half-full pot aloft.

"No thanks," the claims manager responded, holding up his hand.

"Shall we get back to work?" Powell suggested, gesturing toward the door.

As they gathered again in the conference room, Powell could not help but notice that his usually amiable claimsperson was a bit on edge. The reason soon became apparent.

"I've got orders to take this case to trial," he announced bluntly.

"Over our recommendations?" Powell replied incredulously.

"Yep," answered Frick. "The company doesn't want to settle."

"But you told them that their insured does, right?" inquired O'Brien. "We got that across to you loud and clear, didn't we?"

"Yeah. I understood that," replied Frick. "And I told them, but it's not his right to say if we settle or how much we pay. That's what he surrendered to our company when he signed on to the insurance policy."

"We're not challenging your right to make settlement decisions under the policy," Powell reassured the claims person. "And that's not what Sanders is doing. He's saying that he doesn't have a defense to this claim and that the publicity from this trial can cost him much more than an increase in premiums."

"Well, that's not our problem," Frick shot back, getting a little snippy.

"Well, it may very well be *your* problem," Powell retorted, trying his best to restrain his temper. "You realize that it's possible that Sanders could drag the company into court for bad faith settlement practices if you expose him unnecessarily to the risk of a loss of business."

"I doubt that he'd do that," Frick replied defiantly. "He knows a move like that would cost him big time."

"I wouldn't be too sure about that. But if Sanders did prevail in a bad faith claim, the judgment will cost your company *big time,*" Powell argued, throwing Frick's words back at him.

"Now hold on, Curtis," the claims manager said as he popped up out of his chair. "Your firm's been handling our business for a long time now and you certainly get your fair share of it, but I hope you're not advising Doctor Sanders to come after us, because if you are . . ."

Powell raised his hand to quiet the accusation and passively leaned back in his chair. "No. No. No. We're not advising, Sanders on anything with respect to his contractual relationship with his insurer. That'd be a clear conflict of interest, and you damn well know it. But you also know that he's our client. Our legal and ethical duties are owed to the insured, not the insurance company. He's the client, not Union Med. The fact that you sold him an insurance policy that obligates you to pay for his legal defense doesn't change that."

Frick waved his hands in the air. His voice whined. "I know who the client is and all that stuff – "

"It's not just *stuff* Jay," Powell asserted in a booming voice as he too rose to his feet. "It's our professional code. It's the law. It's what we do; it's what we follow. *Sanders* is my client and my obligations run to him. I've got no obligations to Union Med other than those that flow through Sanders' insurance contract with you. He's agreed to let you make the settlement decisions, and you have to be informed of the status of the case to be able to make such decisions competently. That's what the policy says. But he's still the only one who's our client, not the insurance company."

"Just don't forget who butters your bread," Frick replied snidely.

Powell took a couple of steps toward Frick and then poked him lightly but meaningfully in the chest. "Listen to me carefully, Jay. Don't threaten our firm with a loss of business. If you do, you're inviting another lawsuit, this one by our firm. What you're suggesting could be construed by the criminal courts as extortion." He paused to let his words sink in. Then he backed off and sat on the edge of the conference table.

"You damn well know we've always done our best to save every dollar we could for every insurance carrier who's retained us," Powell added, his tone of voice ratcheted down a notch or two. "But our first duty is to our client. His best interests have to come first." He took a deep breath and paused while Frick evidenced his self-control by easing down into his chair.

"Look-it, Jay. Sanders doesn't want to go to trial," the senior attorney pleaded earnestly. "We've assessed the liability here and nine out of ten says he loses. No, make that ninety-nine out of a hundred. And we've evaluated the damages and they exceed the limits of the policy." As hard as he tried to keep calm, his volume and forcefulness escalated, exposing his irritation. "If you refuse to settle for the limits and expose him to the bad publicity that's sure to follow, and you're doing all this because your parent company owns Union Health, you stand the risk of having your certificate of authority to do business in this state pulled by the insurance commissioner. You might even be investigated by a Colorado legislative committee. So I'm telling it like it is." His tone of voice reflected his urgency and his building frustration. "You'd better get on the damn phone or fax or e-mail, or if need be hop a plane to Chicago, and talk some sense into your executives and come up with some money in this case, or you're going to end up paying in more ways than one."

Frick's face was ashen by the time Powell finished his diatribe. But instead of debating the point any further, he merely rose from his seat, picked up his valise, and left the room.

O'Brien's look of dead seriousness was slowly replaced by a bemused smile. "I can't believe what I just heard!"

"I kind of went off the deep end," Powell conceded sheepishly.

"No. No. Everything you said was right," Megan affirmed. "It's just I never thought you'd say something like that . . . at least not to someone in management."

"I guess it's been building up for a while," Powell reasoned, "like maybe for the past few . . . decades." His face broke into a smile as he the realization came to him. "Maybe it's time I put it straight to those sons of bitches and told them the way it really is. I've been at this more than thirty years now, almost all of my career in insurance defense, and I've taken enough of their bullshit. When it's time to settle, it's time to settle."

"Do you really think he'd follow through with that threat and take away some business over this?"

"To tell you the truth, I really don't give a damn if they do pull their business." His attitude was defiant. Motioning toward the open door, he patted his younger colleague on the shoulder. "We'll convert this firm overnight into a plaintiff's practice and drive the sons of bitches right into the poorhouse."

Opening Salvos

It was a ten-minute walk in the bitter cold of an early December morning from the Frey, Cooper & James offices in One Civic Center across the vast, open expanse of the plaza to the City & County Building, which housed the Second Judicial District courtrooms. But to Roman Marchetti it seemed like forever. It was his appointed time for that ever-elusive fifteen minutes of fame, but it was not a fate he really relished. As he had come to see it over the fourteen months since the lawsuit was brought, it was a time for him to tell the story of his Juliette and, perhaps, to find for her that peace he intuitively sensed her spirit desired.

The third-floor courtroom of Judge Beth Williams was one of the smaller ones, fortunately for the principals concerned. With three parties, a multitude of attorneys and paralegals, corporate representatives, witnesses, experts, and family members, virtually every seat in the house was filled, save the few reserved for the press. The representatives of the fourth estate – their ravenous appetites for the dramatic story reinvigorated by the saga of the heroine clinging desperately to life itself – were greatly perturbed by the judge's decision to lot off the remaining seats on a daily basis. "Move to a larger courtroom," they pleaded. "At least put in a closed-circuit television camera with audio and feed it into a separate press room." "The public has a right to see what goes on in our courts." But the threats made by high-profile media attorneys from the east and west coasts to seek an order of mandamus from the appellate courts, forcing Judge Williams to accommodate them, fell on deaf ears. She had gotten quite enough of the flavor of it all the previous summer.

Court TV had already made its bid and lost, leaving town in a huff after assigning one of its least experienced reporters to do daily updates from the courthouse steps. The big networks also saw their starlike visions of major air time fade with the coming dawn. But the local stations and newspapers continued to fight for the scraps like a pack of starving pit bulls, each reporter or journalist hoping the piece of the story they uncovered could be an opportunity to move up to the big time.

Set off in a corner at the end of one wing, the courtroom had no grand vaulted ceilings or gold leaf trim, no ornate carving or fancy millwork on the bench and doorways, no chandeliers or ten-foot windows. Overall, it was rather lackluster in appearance, with just a modest amount of oak paneling surrounding the judge's bench. The only bold colors came from the U.S. and Colorado flags on either side of the judge's chair.

While the court did not go very far out of its way to accommodate the press, the clerks were able to rearrange the counsel tables and add a third. It was a tight squeeze, the judge apologized as they organized the courtroom after the pretrial conference, but "maybe the closeness will help us all get to know each other just a little bit better." Her tone bore a tinge of sarcasm, but her message was dead serious.

Precisely at eight-thirty, Judge Williams entered her courtroom and gaveled the proceedings to order. Starting with an unusually large pool of sixty prospective jurors at the urging of Willis, who had been granted leave to submit a two-page jury questionnaire the week before, their number was eventually whittled down to twenty acceptable candidates. With each of the three parties exercising four peremptory challenges, the civil jury of six, with one alternate, was seated shortly after the noon hour. "I still say we could've taken the first six people who walked into that courtroom," commented Ronnie during lunch with her client and associates back in the firm's war room, "and had just as good a chance as we've got now."

"Spoken like a true prosecutor," Mark opined with a smile. "Only remember," he cautioned, "you're a civil prosecutor here, not a criminal one. There might be some big differences."

Monday afternoon's opening statements by the three lead attorneys ran almost two hours, so it was not until after the mid-afternoon break that Ronnie began to present her evidence. Following a strategy carefully, devised in concert with her partners, she opened by pulling hard on the jury's heartstrings. The first witness to the stand was Vernon Philips, the man in the search and rescue team from Pagosa Springs who had answered Roman's desperate cell phone plea for help. Starting with a copy of the 9-1-1 tape, which he had heard in the dispatcher's office when it came in, she took him to the scene he happened upon about half a mile up the Rainbow Trail and the subsequent events. As the lawyers had expected, there was not a dry eye among the jurors when Philips' concluded his direct testimony. Having already taken his deposition, both Powell and Willis had determined that nothing good could come of cross examination.

Accordingly, they both asked a few harmless questions on details of no great significance and passed the witness.

Ronnie next called Doctor John Crenshaw. After he recapped his distinguished background, she led him through the events of that fateful Tuesday afternoon, concluding with his surgical findings. After having the surgical summary and pathologist's report admitted into evidence, Ronnie showed Crenshaw the vial containing the pieces of the fallopian tube that he had removed from Juliette's pelvic area. But instead of entering the tissue and attached clips into evidence, she placed the container on the corner of the plaintiffs' counsel table, within easy view of the jury. She and her associates had discussed whether the tissue should be admitted into evidence but elected not to do so because of its morbid nature. Instead, they chose to make the existence of the vial obvious to the jury without delving into the macabre.

After authenticating the evidence, Crenshaw described what he had examined in the hospital laboratory, reading the pertinent portion of his report and the separate report of the hospital pathologist, upon which Crenshaw had relied. "In your opinion, Doctor Crenshaw," Ronnie asked, "were the clips properly placed on the left fallopian tube?"

"Objection," stated Powell as he rose from his chair. "Competence. Doctor Crenshaw is not an OB/Gyn. Nor does he routinely perform sterilization procedures of the kind Missus Marchetti received."

"Your Honor," replied Ronnie, sensing that the court would sustain the objection. "If I may lay a predicate?" With a nod from the judge, she continued. "In your experience as a general surgeon on call with the various hospitals you have previously told us about, have you performed emergency surgeries on the reproductive organs of women, as you did with Missus Marchetti?"

"Yes, many times," Crenshaw answered.

"Have you ever performed surgery on or about the fallopian tubes?"

"Yes, several times."

"Prior to performing the surgery on Juliette Marchetti, had you ever examined body tissue of a woman who had undergone a tubal ligation?"

"Oh, sure. Yes."

"Were any of those tubal ligations that you observed done with spring clips?"

"Yes, some were."

"Can you give the court an estimate of how many times you have observed the placement of clips within the female anatomy or on tissue specimens?"

"Probably about a dozen, I'd say."

Turning to the bench, Ronnie tendered the witness as competent to render an opinion on the proper placement of spring clips for the purposes of sterilization. "*Voir dire* the witness on his qualifications, Mister Powell?" the judge inquired.

"No, Your Honor," came the meek response.

"Objection overruled," declared Judge Williams.

Ronnie turned back to Crenshaw and repeated the pivotal question. "In your opinion, were the spring clips properly placed on the left fallopian tube?"

"No," Crenshaw stated, "They were not."

On cross examination, Powell got the witness to concede that his experience with sterilization procedures was much more limited than that of a gynecologist who practiced in that specialty. Crenshaw also admitted that many changes can take place within the human body after the affixation of foreign bodies like clips. But most important to the defense, the physician had to acknowledge that the tissue samples he had to work with were a far cry from what would have appeared in the body of a woman whose fallopian tube had not severely hemorrhaged. Willis again exercised his better discretion and passed on further cross.

When it came back to Ronnie for redirect, she patched up the small holes her opponent had forced open. "Doctor Crenshaw, if you had seen a thousand spring clip placements instead of the dozen you testified to, would your opinion on whether the clips inside of Juliette Marchetti had been properly placed be any different?"

"No, it would not."

"And finally, Doctor, do the facts that Juliette's left fallopian tube had severely ruptured and that you had only fragments of tissue to examine leave any doubt in your mind that the clips were not properly attached to the fallopian tube?"

"No. No doubt at all," the witness said confidently. "What was salvageable clearly showed an affixation to the serosal tissue adjoining the tube, but the clips were not occluding the tube itself. There was no tubal tissue within the clip. None at all."

The plaintiffs' next witness was their medical expert, Doctor Benjamin Steinberg, professor emeritus at the University of Colorado Medical School. Now seventy-two years old, he strode to the witness stand with the spunk and vigor of a man twenty years younger. Cropped fuzzy white hair covered most of his head, with the exception of a monk's bald spot in the back. Standing about five-foot-seven and lean from ten years on the treadmill since suffering a mild heart attack, he was nattily attired in a subtle tan sports coat with leather patches on the elbows. As he took his oath and stated his name, his distinctive New York accent was obvious.

Qualifying her expert, Ronnie laid out his professional background. He had attended New York University Medical School, graduating in 1951. After completing his residency at Manhattan General Hospital in OB/Gyn surgery, he opened a private practice, which he pursued for the next thirty-two years. He had moved his practice to Denver in 1964, and, six years later, took on additional duties as an assistant professor of clinical medicine at CU, where he taught obstetrics and obstetrical surgery for twenty-two years. Among other subjects, his courses included instruction in tubal ligation procedures. In 1992, he retired to a position as professor emeritus. "All that means," he joked, "is that you still have to do everything you did before. You just get to do it a lot slower."

He had been board-certified in OB/Gyn since the 1960s and was a member of a number of professional associations. He had published twenty-four articles and had been a frequent lecturer at continuing medical education programs all over the United States. After having his curriculum vitae entered into evidence, Ronnie tendered her witness to the court as expert in obstetrics and gynecology and related surgeries just as the five o'clock hour approached.

Court resumed Tuesday morning with Steinberg back up on the stand. With well-planned questioning and the assistance of numerous anatomical illustrations, the professor explained the basic reproductive process and the infrequent occurrence of ectopic pregnancies. Reviewing Juliette's 1993 medical records from Doctor Sanders' office and Swedish Hospital, Steinberg explained why the hysterosalpingogram showed she had been at a high degree of risk for a repeat ectopic if she got pregnant again. He concurred that Sanders conformed to the standard of care in advising the tubal ligation, but the witness disagreed with the choice of spring clips as the preferred procedure. Whatever method was favored by the surgeon, he added, the physician should have discussed the options with the patient and her husband, more so because the risk of injury was at issue, not merely family planning.

Steinberg further testified that he had reviewed Crenshaw's surgical records and the Pagosa hospital pathologist's report and that he had conducted his own examination of the tubal tissues. To remind the jury of the vial's presence, James brought it forward for the witness to identify, then returned it to its former position. Based upon that information, Steinberg had concluded that Sanders had missed the tube when he affixed the spring clips. Anticipating the defense's explanation, James asked him about movement of the spring clips within the body after their affixation.

"There's a one in a million chance that the position of the spring clips was due to migration," he asserted. "Oh sure, the literature contains histories of foreign objects, especially staples and such, that migrated from the tissue to which they were initially affixed, but most of those cases can be explained by change in tissue size. The body grows. People gain weight. People lose weight. Things like that. But I didn't see any evidence of significant change in this patient's tubes. For example, her body weight at that office visit on the Friday before her death was only two pounds more than the body weight noted at the time of her first visit to Sanders' office more than four years before. That's why clips are generally a good bet to stay there permanently," the veteran doctor reasoned. "After all, if there was any significant chance they'd migrate, spring clips wouldn't be considered a reliable birth control method, now would they?"

After letting the import of the rhetorical question sink into the jurors' minds, Ronnie continued to pursue her line of attack on the anticipated defense. "Doctor, are there any other reasons you believe that migration of the clips was not within the realm of reasonable medical probability?"

"Probably the most important reason has to do with the clips themselves," the professor replied. "On top of all that theoretical stuff, when I was examining the tubal tissue, I took a good hard look at the clips. The first thing I did was measure the space between the clips as they now appear on the tissue specimen and measure their angles relative to each other."

"What was the result of those measurements?" Ronnie jumped in.

"Oh, all those measurements were within expected tolerances."

"What does that mean, Doctor," James asked to clarify his choice of terms, "'within expected tolerances'?"

"When spring clips are affixed, the surgeon uses an applicator that attaches them both at the same time. You don't attach one and then the other. They both go in at once. So there's a specific distance between them that's set by the instrument, and, of course, they're parallel too."

"So what did your measurements indicate?"

"Well, first, let me also add that I examined the lock or snap on each clip and there was no evidence that they came open, moved, and then re-clipped. Now the other point is that the spring clips were still the distance apart that I would have expected the applicator to have set them. And they were roughly parallel given the condition of the tissue to which they were attached."

"And what did you conclude from all that?" asked Ronnie.

"Oh, okay. Sure. It was this: the idea that the two spring clips would move in perfect tandem in the body is wholly without merit. We in medical science rarely admit to impossibility – because we've seen things that we thought were impossible actually happen. But if I were to try to find something that might approach that definition of impossibility, I'd say that tandem migration of these clips would be very close."

"Based upon your review of the materials in this case, do you have an opinion on how the clips got to be in the position you observed them to be in?"

"Yes. In my opinion, the surgeon misidentified the tube, mistook an adjacent strand of serosal tissue for the tube itself, and then affixed the clips onto the wrong tissue."

"What would be the result, for purposes of sterilization or birth control, if the spring clips were not on the tube?"

"Well, then there'd be no occlusion or blockage of the tube and the sperm and egg could meet in the tube. And, boom, they've made a baby."

"Professor Steinberg," said Ronnie, using the formal title to bring importance to the next series of questions, "if a surgeon misplaces a pair of spring clips so that they fail to occlude the fallopian tube, would this constitute medical negligence?"

"Yes. In my opinion it would."

"Would that surgeon have failed to conform to the standard of care?"

"Yes. Yes, the surgeon would have. And in this case the surgeon would have been especially negligent since he was doing a mini-laparotomy, an incision down through the abdominal wall, and had the reproductive organs fully exposed – eyeball to tube, as it were. That's quite different from how most tubals are done now, with a laparoscope."

"Would you explain laparoscopy to the jury, Doctor," Ronnie requested.

"Oh, sure," Steinberg agreed as he twisted the swivel chair a few degrees to his right. "A laparoscope is a little tube with a miniature camera lens on the end that gets inserted through a tiny incision in the woman's umbilicus or navel." One of the female jurors flinched at his description, unconsciously laying both hands across her stomach. "It's a little more difficult to identify the tube with a scope than by looking at the exposed tube with the naked eye, you see. But, of course, even surgeons who perform the procedure with a scope are held to the standard of properly identifying the tube."

Having covered the tubal ligation as productively as she felt she could, Ronnie switched topics. Steinberg testified that he had also reviewed all of Juliette's records from the fertility clinic and from Doctor Sanders' office for the three years between the first ectopic and the second, paying special attention to her last visit to Sanders. In the professor's opinion, a reasonably prudent physician should have performed a pregnancy test on a patient presenting with the complaints that Juliette had voiced and the signs and symptoms she exhibited, especially if that patient had a history of a prior ectopic.

Sterilizations were not foolproof, he insisted. The literature even contained case histories of women whose tubal ligations had been performed properly getting pregnant. Some studies reported a failure rate with spring clips oi zero-point-three percent, while other, less reliable studies gave a failure rate as high as two percent. So, he concluded, the possibility that the sterilization had failed was recognized by the medical community.

Furthermore, Steinberg reasoned, the patient had told the doctor that she was going to be in the back country without access to medical care for the next few days. A pregnancy test could have been performed and results easily obtained before her scheduled departure. Then the physician could have notified her of the perceived risk and had her put off the trip for more comprehensive testing and observation. In Steinberg's opinion, it was medical malpractice for a doctor to let economic or other considerations get in the way of his professional judgment to decide what was best for the health of his patient.

On cross examination by Powell, the plaintiffs' medical expert admitted that he had not performed surgery in more than ten years. His professional experience now, he conceded, was limited largely to teaching and administrative work, although he still had a few active patients through his part-time position as an OB/Gyn at a local woman's clinic. However, he resolutely denied that he was out of touch with current standards. "I still have to teach them!" he insisted. With equal force and conviction, he denied that he had not kept up with the latest in techniques. "I have to teach those too, you know." But he did have to admit that he had not actually performed many of the procedures outside of the classroom during the last ten years.

Steinberg also acknowledged that he had performed only about a dozen tubal ligations using spring clips. Of the hundreds and hundreds of other tubal ligations he had done, he favored use of the Pomeroy method with removal of part of the tube, but he had also performed both bipolar and unipolar cauterization of the tubes, and he had used the Falope Rings, silicone bands which were wrapped snugly around a loop in the midpoint of the tube. He had to confess that he might not be as much an expert on spring clips as some doctors who had done hundreds of that particular procedure, but he strenuously defended his point that the error lay in misidentification of the tube, not a question which demanded hours of practical experience with actual use of the clip-affixing instrument. And, he concluded, he would stack his hands-on experience in identifying a fallopian tube up against anybody else's.

Willis concentrated his challenge on Steinberg's level of experience in dealing with health management organizations, their policies and procedures, and their current role in the health care system. The witness had experienced only limited contact with managed care during his last few years of private practice and was not currently involved with an HMO in his present part-time position with a federally and privately funded women's center. Accordingly, he conceded that he held a measure of distrust of something with which he was not familiar. Wrapping up, Willis tried one last round of attack. "Doctor Steinberg, have you ever advised a patient to undergo a certain kind of treatment or test and the patient refused?"

"Sure. It's happened."

"And has anything unfavorable ever occurred to one of your patients who refused?"

"I don't know. But off the top of my head like this, I'd have to say yes."

"And to the best of your recollection, have some of those patients made that decision to refuse based on religious grounds?"

"Yes."

"Or for financial reasons?"

"Yes."

"Maybe because they believe the risk is too remote?"

"Yes. That could be one reason."

"Or maybe they've just refused for other personal reasons?"

"Yes, they have."

"And sometimes persons other than the patients make those decisions for them, do they not?"

"Yes, quite often."

"Spouses, parents, children?"

"Yes, that's true."

"So it's not unheard of for persons other than the patients to refuse certain medical procedures, is it?"

"No, it's not." With that concession from the professor, Willis passed the witness and returned to his table.

James was quick to point out what was left unsaid during the last series of questions. "Those persons who've made health care decisions for the patients, in your experience were those persons close to the patients?"

"Oh, yes."

"Family members?"

"Yes."

"Loved ones."

"Yes."

"Husbands or wives, children, parents?"

"Yes. Yes."

"What about an insurance company claimsperson a thousand miles away?"

Steinberg shook his head and emitted a soft laugh. "No. No. Can't say as I've ever had anything like that."

Having concluded with her medical expert, Ronnie returned to her list of fact witnesses. The decision to call Sally had been carefully debated, but it was the witness herself who had made the final decision the week before trial. Knowing that her closely guarded anonymity – effectively protected by Judge Williams' gag order and a discovery agreement among the parties that her name would not have to be included on the publicly filed witness lists – would be blown by the appearance, she stood resolute as she faced the trio of Roman's lawyers in the firm's war room. "Juliette is the big sister I never had. Not testifying would be like not letting me visit her. I'll accept the consequences. We'll deal with it," she concluded as she squeezed her husband's hand.

"Your Honor, plaintiffs call Sally Rifkin."

The courtroom was abuzz as they waited for the attractive young redhead to take the witness stand. All along the back rows, whispering voices of the members of the press could be discerned above the general murmur of the gallery at the mention a name not heretofore disclosed. "Who is she?"

"Her name's not on my list."

"Mine either."

"Is this the surrogate?"

A Friend and A Lover

Sally's account of Juliette was poignant, full of memories of her comatose friend, her "big sister." Ronnie took her witness methodically through their relationship – from boss to confidant to the surrogacy contract. Sally moved the jurors emotionally with her anecdotes of warmth and affection. To those who watched and heard her, it was as though she was more than a physical surrogate. Through Sally's testimony, James was able to impart the depth of love that Juliette would have given to her baby, key evidence for the child's loss of companionship damages.

After struggling through her first two attempts, Sally was finally able to recount the story of the last time she spoke with Juliette, when her boss left the office an hour earlier than her usual time on Friday afternoon, complaining of what she thought was a mild case of food poisoning. Since Juliette was finally getting away with her husband on their long-awaited backpacking trip and Sally would not be seeing her best friend for at least a week, that day's goodbye was it little more protracted and emotional than their usual end-of-week parting.

"Now you take care of our baby while I'm gone," Juliette had said as she held Sally's hands, "and you take care of yourself too. Okay? Is there anything you re going to need?"

"No," Sally had replied as she dropped her hands to her stomach. "We're all taken care of."

Then, in an afterthought, Juliette grabbed a scrap of paper from Sally's desk and wrote something down. Turning back to Sally, she handed her the slip. "And, oh, by the way, here's Roman's cell phone number. You probably already have it in your Rolodex, but just in case, put this one in your purse. I know you're still weeks away from our due date, but if anything out of the ordinary happens, and I mean anything, you call us, okay?"

Sally had nodded her assent, stashed the phone number, and given Juliette a long, warm embrace. Then Juliette had knelt down on the floor, put her hands on either side of Sally's stomach, and placed her cheek up against the front.

"I'm going away for a while, my darling baby," she had said, "but I'll see you really soon. I love you very much." She held her cheek there for a few seconds while they both felt the baby move in Sally's womb, Juliette smiling more broadly with each quiver. Then she rose, gave Sally a peck on the cheek, and left the office.

On that note, Ronnie closed her direct examination. Knowing that nothing could be gained from further questioning such a sympathetic witness, Powell and Willis both waived cross examination. As Sally stepped off the witness stand, James announced, "Your Honor, we call Roman Marchetti."

Roman rose from his position between Ronnie and Evan, buttoned his jacket, and took a few steps toward the witness chair. Sally stopped to greet him, grasping both of his hands affectionately and whispering words of strength and encouragement. After stepping up to the stand and taking the oath, he glanced across the courtroom as he took his seat. Each face etched an indelible impression in his memory – a frozen photograph for his mind's eye.

With care and precision, Ronnie evoked the couple's chronological history, from their puppy love romance in eighth grade to their unanticipated revival of love at the high school reunion. He retraced Juliette's years without him, summarizing her educational achievements and her professional accomplishments. Ronnie then turned the witness' attention to the events of October 1993, when he received a telephone call from Sanders' office, telling him that his wife had been taken to Swedish Hospital for emergency surgery. Painstakingly, Roman described their meetings with Doctor Sanders and their discussions about ectopic pregnancy, tubal damage, the risk of future ectopics, and the decision to undergo a tubal ligation of the remaining tube.

"At any time during these discussions with Doctor Sanders, was the surgical method to be employed brought up."

"No. Never."

"When was the first time you heard the words 'spring clips' used in reference a sterilization procedure?" Ronnie asked.

"Not until that afternoon in . . . Pagosa," the witness replied, clearing the emotion from his throat.

"Do you recall ever talking to Doctor Sanders about reversibility of the sterilization procedure?"

"No. We never talked about that. I didn't know . . ." His voice trailed off.

James paused while her client struggled to regain his composure. "Do you recall ever talking to Doctor Sanders about the possibility of repair of the remaining fallopian tube at some time in the future?"

"No. I didn't know that could be done. The way he talked about it, it seemed quite final. The remaining tube had numerous adhesions, scar tissue from something, and there wasn't anything that could be done. That's the way I recall it."

As difficult as it was for Roman, he also had to tell the jury about Juliette's last days, beginning with the Thai food and ending with her collapse on the trail. The testimony was slow and arduous, but Ronnie was masterfully prepared to introduce bits and pieces of documentary evidence at emotionally charged points to give not only the witness and the jurors but also herself time to gather strength for the next series of questions.

As they approached the noon hour, Roman related the events of Tuesday morning, starting with the scream of agony that had awakened them both. He spoke of Juliette's courage and strength with a radiating pride. But when he finished his tale of her struggle with those last words she had whispered into his ear, the courtroom became as quiet as a crypt. In a soft voice, Judge Williams broke the silence with an order to recess for lunch.

The midday meal was already laid out for them in the small conference room when Roman and his legal team entered the office. As they finished their sandwiches, Frey turned to his client and imparted a few words of advice on what to expect later in the afternoon. "Don't let Powell or Willis intimidate you," he directed as he munched on the last of tortilla chips. "If either one of them pushes you, you push back, understand?" Roman nodded as Mark pressed the point. "If need be, you feel free to give them just what they give you. Don't be intimidated."

When court resumed at a quarter past one, Ronnie carefully guided Roman through Juliette's efforts to become a mother, starting with the first ectopic pregnancy, the four failed in vitro implantations, the adoption application, and, finally, the gestational surrogacy. Each story was an emotional battle for him, especially Juliette's miscarriage of the only successful IV implantation. His wife had been devastated by that loss, he explained, taking weeks to pull herself out of a state of depression. But her inner strength finally brought her back, and he had never seen her so happy when the first attempt to impregnate Sally with the Marchettis' preserved embryos succeeded. He buttressed Sally's prior testimony about Juliette's active role in the surrogate pregnancy, the childbirth classes, the social outings with the Rifkins, and that special look in his wife's eyes as she watched the Rifkin children play in her backyard. They had talked late into the night after that July Fourth barbecue as she described the thoughts her mind envisioned of her own child examining spring tulips in the back garden, or running through the lawn sprinkler on a hot summer day, or diving into a pile of autumn leaves, or making a snowman with the first big winter storm.

Then it came time to talk about his child, Juliet, now just over one-year-old. With photographs and words of pride and praise, he related the story of the legal process he and Juliette went through to be declared the legal parents of a child not yet born. Ronnie elicited the details of the surrogate process, introducing copies of the medical records from Mountain Fertility Specialists, showing the chain of custody of Roman's sperm and Juliette's egg and the DNA test results from the Marchettis' blood and the baby's amniotic fluid, which had been previously submitted to the family court judge as conclusive evidence of their parentage. He concluded his story with a touching description of her birth and a brief summary of her first year of life.

"How often do you take Juliet to visit her mother?" James asked.

"Usually about twice a week," Roman replied.

"How do you spend the time during those visits?" James continued.

"All depends," Roman explained. "A lot of the time, I'll hold my daughter in my lap or let her sit on the bed next to her mother and read to her. I'll take books that have stories of mothers and their babies in them – mother ducks and baby ducklings, or mother hens and baby chicks, or whatever. And when we get to those parts about the mother and her babies, I tell her about how much her mother loves her and how she will hug and kiss her when she wakes up." The emotional tide finally overwhelmed him, and he broke down on the stand. Williams spared the witness further disconcertion by declaring a short recess. As court resumed, Ronnie turned her recollected client over to a defense eager to score some points with a jury heavily under the emotional influence of a well-structured plaintiffs' case.

Powell tiptoed lightly when questioning the victim's husband knowing that he could turn the entire jury against his client if he pushed a sympathetic witness too hard. As he had done during the deposition, the attorney focused on the events of the day of Juliette's surgery.

"It would be fair to say that you were under a great deal of emotional strain that day at the hospital, would it not?"

"Yes. Absolutely."

"And we realize you're not a medical doctor and don't have any professional training in medicine, but it was your understanding, was it not, that your wife nearly died that day?"

"Yes. That's my understanding."

"But she didn't because Doctor Sanders recognized the problem and performed an emergency surgery, correct?"

"Yes."

"He saved her life, didn't he?"

"Yes, he did." Roman glanced over at the physician and gave him a firm look of appreciation, an acknowledgment not lost on either the jurors or the attorneys.

"You'll agree with me, won't you, Mister Marchetti, that there was a lot going on at the hospital that day . . . as far as your wife was concerned?"

"Yes. I'm sure there was."

"Your wife was in a great deal of pain when she came in to see Doctor Sanders, wasn't she?"

"That's what I understood to be the case, yes."

"And after Doctor Sanders opened her up and got the bleeding stopped and stabilized her condition, you and your wife were suddenly faced with making another major decision , this time one that affected your future reproductive history, right?"

"Yes."

"And that decision pertained to whether she should have something done to the tube that hadn't ruptured, correct?"

"Yes."

"Now, during the time the two of you discussed her medical condition with Doctor Sanders, your wife was still under the influence of the anesthetic, wasn't she?"

"Yes."

"So would you agree with me that her mind wasn't a hundred percent clear?"

"Yes. That's probably right."

"And that put a lot of weight on your shoulders, didn't it?"

"Yes, it did."

"And given the stress of the moment and the importance of what you and she had to decide, you can't really be positive that Doctor Sanders didn't discuss the various methods of sterilization with the two of you, can you?"

"No, that's not correct," Roman answered forcefully. "I don't agree with that. Yes, I was under a lot of stress and I was hearing things I wasn't familiar with, like the medical terms and all that, but I know what I heard and I know what I didn't hear. And, with all due respect," Roman looked directly at the defendant, "your client did *not* discuss spring clips or various methods of doing the sterilization with us. I know that. I'm *sure* of that."

Frey, who was sitting directly behind the plaintiffs' counsel table in the front row of the gallery, smiled and shifted comfortably, crossing his legs and arms. *Give 'em Hell* , he thought. *Just like I told you . . . stand up to them.*

By the time Willis took up the attack, the clock was nearing the magical hour of five o'clock. Having been reminded of that fact by the judge, the attorney reordered his planned cross examination, hoping to impress the jury with a strong defense point at the close of the day. Focusing in on the money angle, his strategy was to make the jury believe that the greed of the plaintiff was the reason behind his lawsuit against the insurance company.

"You testified earlier that you brought this lawsuit against Union Health Management, your wife's health insurance company, so that her story could be told, isn't that right, Mister Marchetti?"

"Yes, that's what I said."

"The principle of the thing?" Willis said in a tone singed with cynicism.

"If you want to call it that," Roman countered, unperturbed by the insinuation.

"And you feel you've been wronged by the people who managed her health plan, isn't that right?"

"Yes, I do. She was wronged . . . Juliette."

"So you feel your wife was wronged, but you weren't. Is that what you're saying?"

"My wife was treated negligently by your clients, Mister Willis." Roman shot back assertively, "and she suffered a great deal because of that, and now every day she lies motionless in a hospital bed. Sometimes, her eyes are open, but she can't even see her own beautiful daughter. Sometimes she makes sounds, but she can't talk to her daughter. Sometimes she cries, but she can't even feel her own baby. And since that day on the mountain, I've suffered too. And so has my daughter, who may very well have to grow up without ever knowing her mother in any other way. So we've all been wronged, sir . . . my wife, my daughter, and myself."

Willis could feel the momentum slipping away as the witness asserted control. He grasped for his focal point. "And you're here today for the principle of justice, is that right?"

"That's correct . . . to tell her . . ."

Willis cut him off. "May I approach the witness, Your Honor?" the attorney requested. Seeing a nod from the judge, he picked up a piece of paper from the table and traversed the courtroom. "That's not the entire truth, though, is it, Mister Marchetti? You're suing the defendants here for a lot of money, aren't you, sir?"

"Yes, we are."

"Eight million dollars, isn't that right?" he insisted he prepared to offer the piece of paper to the witness.

"I believe that's the amount, yes."

"That's a lot of money . . . eight million dollars . . . isn't it?"

"Yes, it is."

No longer needing to confront the plaintiff with one of the documents Ronnie had filed stating that amount, Willis rested his hand and the paper on the backside of his hip. Leaning slightly, he placed his other hand on the front rail of the jury box for support, as though seeking both a physical and a psychological affinity with the jurors. Then he raised his voice, speaking in accusing tones. "That's really what this case is about, isn't it, Mister Marchetti? Money? Eight million dollars?"

Roman glared at the lawyer with a fire in his eyes that would have seared the heart of a normal man. But Sylvester Willis was not a normal man; he was an insurance defense attorney. Thinking he had the star witness on the ropes, Willis continued to press doggedly, edging even closer to the jury box. "This really isn't about the principle of the thing, is it, Mister Marchetti? It's about eight million dollars, isn't it?" Ronnie started to rise and object for badgering, but Evan reached out quickly across the empty chair and caught her arm. His sign of reassurance dispelled her concern.

Roman's jaw flexed rigidly, then loosened as an image of Juliette's smiling face flashed in his mind's eye. His facial expression softened and a twinkle came to his eye. He looked up at his accuser and spoke directly to him in a voice filled with tender sincerity. "If you had known Juliette before this happened to her, Mister Willis . . ." He choked on his words. "To me, having my wife back, healthy and full of life like she used to be, that'd be worth eight million dollars." For a second, the eyes of the combatants locked. Roman broke the silence with a question of his own. "I see you're wearing a wedding band there, Mister Willis," he said, motioning to the attorney's left hand still clenching the rail, just a few feet from the jurors. "How much is your wife worth to you?"

The Sudden Stranger

She was the last to leave the courtroom that afternoon. Frey had needed to slip out for an office appointment, and Evan had scooted down a floor to a five o'clock hearing as soon as Judge Williams recessed. Both defense teams had packed up and headed out within five minutes after the judge had stepped down from the bench. Roman left the courthouse flanked by members of his family and his in-laws.

As Ronnie hauled the two large cases full of trial essentials out of the courtroom, she was joined by the man who had been waiting patiently in the hall since court adjourned. Standing about five-foot-ten-inches, with a dark complexion, full head of coal, black hair, and neatly trimmed mustache, he wore an exquisitely tailored double-breasted suit which advertised his worldly successes.

"Miss James?" he inquired, obviously knowing who she was. "I'm Joseph Medrano." He offered his hand, forcing her to choose between setting down a case and stopping to shake it or heading on down the hall. She chose the latter, with not even the slightest break in her stride.

"If you have a minute, I have something of great importance I'd like to discuss with you," he added as he fell a step or two behind her.

Disquieting thoughts crossed Ronnie's mind. *Oh, God. Another reporter! Maybe a Hollywood producer wanting to make a movie about my clients. Shit! I'm too busy for this.*

"If I can help you with one of those cases," he offered.

"Look, Mister . . . " She drew a blank on the name he had just recited. The rhythmic clickety-click of her heels on the polished stone floor reverberated off the walls.

"Medrano," he repeated. "Joseph Medrano."

"Mister Medrano," she continued, huffing and puffing a bit more from the exasperation brought on by another bird of prey hovering about her shoulder than from the weights hanging from them. "I'm in trial right now, and I really don't have time to talk about movie or book deals. Whatever you're selling will just have to wait until this trial is over."

"I don't think it can," he replied critically. "I'm an attorney." He had to speak in short sentences as her pace was becoming an exertion even for him, unladen though he was. "I've been retained by Doctor Sanders to pursue a claim against Union Medical Protective."

James stopped dead in her tracks. "Now that I have your attention," he chortled between wheezes, "may I help you with one of those briefcases?"

"What do you mean you've been hired by Doctor Sanders?" she asked. "What about Powell?" Still unsure about this dapper Latino, she gripped both handles securely. "And what you do mean 'against' Union Medical? They're his insurance company. They're responsible for part of this fiasco."

"As I said, I've been retained by Doctor Sanders outside of his medical malpractice insurance contract," Medrano repeated. "Mister Powell and Miss O'Brien know that I'm involved, but attorney-client confidentiality prevents them from disclosing it to anyone, especially people at Sanders' insurance company."

As the strain weighed on her shoulders and arms, she plopped down the cases. "Okay," she conceded, with a wisp of a smirk on her lips, "you've got my attention."

"I specialize in plaintiffs' bad faith cases against their insurers. My practice is currently located in San Francisco, but I worked for Masters, Rodgers & Tuttle here in Denver for my first seven years." James recognized the name of the largest insurance defense firm in town. "That's where I met Powell. We started there the same year."

"You said you represent Doctor Sanders?" James inquired, intrigued by the implications.

"I'd rather not discuss that here," he said, glancing around the courthouse hall. Although it was quite empty by that time, people were still wandering out of one office or another every minute or so heading home for the day. "Now, if I can help you with one of those cases, I'd be happy to discuss the substance of why I'm here when we get to your office."

"Sure," she said as she slung the shoulder bag for her laptop over to the side less fatigued. "You can have 'em both. It's better that way," she cracked, grinning slyly, "for the balance. You know?"

On their way out of the courthouse and across the Civic Center Plaza to her office tower, Medrano continued to brief Ronnie on his personal background. "Then a headhunter coaxed me to join a bigger firm out in the bay area. Since I was from southern California originally, it was a homecoming of sorts. But I've continued to maintain my Colorado bar license.

"Anyway, after ten more years doing mostly insurance defense work, I got sick of the games they play and of kissing up to them, so I went solo." He explained that he'd started with a general plaintiff's personal injury practice, but after two or three years he found himself specializing in bringing insured's claims against their insurance companies. "I've been exceptionally lucky to get clients who dealt with incredibly stupid claims agents," he laughed. For the last eleven years or so, he went on, he had been limiting his practice to bad faith claims. He handled cases all over the country and had notches in his gun handle for sizable jury awards in seven different states.

Finally stepping off the elevator in front of her twelfth floor office, Ronnie arrived with her guest just as her secretary was leaving. "Anybody else in there?" she inquired, nodding toward the front door.

"Mister Frey is in his office and Mister Cooper is in the library," Ellen replied as she caught the same elevator car down.

Ronnie directed Medrano to the large conference room, where they disposed of the briefcases, then invited him into her private office. Without the physical burden of lugging the trial materials, she had used the time to size up this stranger. Although in his late fifties, he was quite fit for his age, hardly missing a breath or a beat as they covered the considerable distance between courthouse and office at her usual hurried pace. His looks were noticeably Latin, with deep-set dark brown eyes, thick eyebrows, and high cheekbones. "Okay. Now that we're away from prying eyes and casual eavesdroppers, what's this all about?"

"I'll get right to the point. I have authority from Doctor Sanders to offer you a settlement in this matter," he explained, hesitating for a moment as the words sunk in, "but the deal has to be struck before you play Doctor Trenckmann's video deposition or call Sanders as a witness. If either of those things happens, any deal I'm authorized to make is off."

"That certainly doesn't give me much time," James demurred. "I was planning to get to at least one of those two tomorrow."

"I apologize for the timing," Medrano said in his own defense, "but that's just part of the uncertain nature of litigation."

"I understand," said Ronnie. "Go on."

"The deal is this. Sanders will execute and deliver a promissory note in favor of your clients in the amount of his policy limits. The note will be secured by a second on his office building and equipment." Medrano handed Ronnie a financial statement attested to by a certified public accountant, which showed the current first mortgage on the real estate and the security interest on the medical office equipment and other chattels. "You can see that the unsecured interests alone total two-point-five million dollars, which is way more than enough to cover his policy limits.

"Additionally, my client will assign to the plaintiffs a half-interest in any bad faith cause of action he may have against Union Medical, his carrier. If he recovers from them, by way of settlement or judgment, your clients will receive half. However, Doctor Sanders will retain all control over settlement decisions. He'll also execute an affidavit stating his earnest intent to prosecute his bad faith action against Union Med with due diligence. If he fails to do so, you'll be entitled to recover liquidated damages of an additional half million, which will also be secured by the same property through a separate instrument.

"You'll agree to put off collecting any monies from him until his dispute with Union Med is resolved. If you have to challenge his due diligence through prosecution of a claim against him and a court rules in your favor, you can levy against the original one million then too. He'll agree to attorneys' fees and costs being awarded to the prevailing party in any dispute under the settlement agreement. We assume you'll agree to confidentiality provisions and his disclaimer of non-admission of liability." Medrano shrugged his shoulders. "That's the crux of it."

James found herself in a most uncomfortable position for a lawyer truly at a loss for something to say. She stared down at her notes, but she saw only squiggly lines of blue ink on yellow paper. Her mind was so fuzzy she could not even translate her own scrawl into intelligible words. After a minute or so of silence feigning intense contemplation, she bailed out. "I'm going to have to discuss this with my partners. Since they're both here, why don't I see if I can get them to join us?" With an acknowledgment from Medrano, she disappeared down the hall.

Both attorneys were where Ellen had said they would be, Mark flipping through a file at his desk and Evan researching cases on the Westlaw computer. The expression on Ronnie's face as she asked each of them to join her down the hall was more than enough to stimulate their curiosity about the stranger in her office. After introductions and an exchange of pleasantries, James went through the terms of the startling settlement offer. Cooper sat there stunned, his mouth agape, but Frey just grinned. He had heard of Medrano and knew of his reputation. He had even expected something like this at the last minute, but he could not have predicted it would come from such a heavy hitter.

Medrano continued where James left off. "Doctor Sanders is caught in the middle and being squeezed and he doesn't like it. That's why he hired me. I'm here to protect this doctor's reputation and his livelihood, which his own insurance company doesn't seem to really give a damn about. We hope you'll look at this thing sensibly. There can be no benefit to your clients to destroy Sanders' practice. He's a good doctor with hundreds of satisfied patients. He's been in private practice for more than fifteen years now, and he's never been sued for malpractice before. And that's saying something for an OB/Gyn." Mark and Ronnie nodded in assent. "The worst you can say, and that's if you can prove it to the jury, is that he just made a small mistake, but one that had terrible consequences. But that's the risk doctors take when they deal with life-or-death matters."

As Medrano carried on, Ronnie kicked off her shoes, leaned back in her swivel chair, and propped her legs up on the corner of her desk. Focusing his hearing on Medrano, Mark watched his associate out of the corner of his eye as she seemed to drift off. After scanning the financial statement and passing it on to Cooper, Mark asked Medrano to step outside and give the three attorneys a couple of minutes. Pointing out the door to the office's kitchen area and inviting their visitor to help himself to a cold drink out of the refrigerator, Frey closed James' office door.

"Ronnie," he said comfortingly, "why don't you go on home? You're beat and you've got to save up what you've got for trial tomorrow. "This deal looks promising, but we can't pin all our hopes on it. And besides, you were expecting to call Sanders tomorrow afternoon, weren't you?"

"Uh-huh," she mumbled as she slid her legs off the desk.

"You can't handle everything. Leave this to me and Cooper. Evan will brief you in the morning. Okay?"

"Yeah," she conceded, more relieved than disappointed by the gesture. *Mark's right,* she realized. *I have important witnesses to prepare for tomorrow. And even if the case against Sanders does settle, I still have to go on with the trial against Union Health.* After making arrangements to meet Cooper for an early breakfast at Shelby's Restaurant, she grabbed the notes she needed for the evening from the briefcases in the conference room and slipped out the front door.

With the run of the office, Frey and Cooper invited Medrano to join them in the back office, which had been set up as an informal conference room, more akin to an executive lounge, replete with a wet bar and private restroom. Relaxing on the plush velour sofa, Frey and Medrano turned to face each other while Cooper fixed a round of drinks. For the next hour, the trio discussed the fine points of the settlement offer as well as details important to the plaintiffs not addressed in the draft document. Although he assumed that Medrano's connection to Powell had brought the Frisco attorney into the matter and that Sanders' malpractice defense attorney had fully briefed his West Coast comrade on the plaintiffs' demands, Mark related the highlights of his conversation with Powell of several weeks before. He reiterated that Sanders would have to fully cooperate with the plaintiffs in railing against the evils of health management organizations setting policies that affect a physician's right to exercise his or her best judgment.

Medrano listened carefully while he sipped his drink. When Mark concluded, Medrano addressed his concerns. "Of course, since these are settlement negotiations, anything I tell you about Doctor Sanders' feelings would not be admissible in court."

"Of course," Frey reassured him.

"Good. Then I can assure you that Doctor Sanders will be a cooperative witness. I've discussed this matter with him and have been authorized to tell you that he, like many other practicing physicians, would dearly love to get out from under the thumb of the second-guessers at these HMOs. If his testimony against the way Union Health handled its decision that day can play a small part in remedying the problems that both physicians and their patients are having, he's highly enthusiastic about it."

Cooper had his reservations. "We understand how he might feel about overseers from an insurance company hundreds or thousands of miles away interfering with his professional judgment and dictating medical treatment, but we're talking about your client's meal ticket here. We've covered this during discovery. Sanders gets about seventy-five percent of his business directly through Union Health Management. If he gets up on the stand and attacks their policies and their personnel, he's going to make an instant appearance on their shit list, and he'll probably be blackballed by the rest of the industry too."

"That's why he hired me," boasted Medrano, pointing his extended thumb back toward his chest. "I'm his insurance policy that such things won't happen."

"How so?" inquired Cooper.

"Mister Medrano – " Frey started to address the question.

"Joe," the newcomer insisted. "Just Joe."

"Okay." Mark acknowledged. A little simper – half wit, half liquor – formed on his lips as an image of his mock sword fights with Evan popped into his mind. "Joe the Just here . . ." The three of them laughed heartily at Frey's play on Medrano's words.

Picking up immediately on Mark's theme of chivalry, Evan contributed to the round of witticism, tapping Medrano on each shoulder with a pen. "From this day forward, you shall be known as – Just Joe from Frisco." More laughs led to another round of drinks.

"As I was going to say," continued Mark when the conversation turned back to business, "Just Joe here will sue the pants off Union Health if they mess with his client. And I'd imagine you figure you could get enough damages in that case to cover anything Sanders would lose from his practice over the next ten or twenty years, right?"

"Right," was the response. "And those economic losses could be staggering."

"So you really think your client will stick his neck out?" asked Cooper, needing additional reassurance.

"He's like a lot of doctors today," Joe explained. "He thinks things have to be changed, either federally or on the state level, to keep insurance companies and their bureaucrats and statisticians from dictating to doctors what is and what isn't sound medical treatment. All in all, I'd say he's getting quite political about it all. I know you're going out on a limb with this proposal, seeing as how you don't have all of his sworn testimony in hand, so the best I can do is assure you that you'd find my client to be a very good witness in your claim against Union Health Management. And we all know that's where the big bucks are in this case, what with limitations on tort damages against physicians."

Mark rose from his chair and walked over to the window, looking aimlessly into the dark December sky, hands on his hips. After a minute of reflection, he slowly spun around and addressed Medrano. "I'd be prepared to recommend this settlement to our client," he announced, "but with one addition." Joe's eyebrows arched with inquisitiveness. "What's your take on why Union Med doesn't just pay its limits and let your doctor get out of this trial?"

Medrano shrugged his shoulders. "I've only been in this thing for a few days, so I really can't say at this point. Could be any number of things. Why? What are you getting at?"

Mark drummed his fingers against the side of his empty glass. "Union Med is owned by Great Union, isn't?"

"Yeah," replied Medrano. "And so is Union Health." He studied Frey's face. Then a little light went on. "So you're thinking Great Union might be strong-arming their med mal carrier – to keep them from paying off Sanders' limits?"

"That way," added Mark, "they can keep him in line, keep him from bad-mouthing Union Health during the trial."

"So you're thinking Sanders may also have a tortious interference claim against the parent company?"

"Per-xactly," replied Frey. "Union Med has an insurance contract with Sanders. That insurance policy says the company has to pay off claims against Sanders when there is no valid defense. But if Great Union is pressuring the med mal carrier to ignore its contractual obligations to Sanders to protect Union Health, then the parent company's interfering with Sanders' rights and benefits under the contract. And to me, that's tortious interference with a contract."

"Like the *Pennzoil versus Texaco* case from some years back?" inquired Evan.

"Well," added Medrano, "except for the nine billion dollars in damages, you could say that."

"So what I'm thinking . . ." Mark started to add before he was interrupted.

"I'm a step ahead of you now," Joe interjected. "You want the assignment provisions in our settlement agreement to be broadly worded to include a piece of any other claims Sanders may have against Great Union?"

"And you might as well throw in Union Health," added Frey. "Make it a triple play."

"Now it's starting to come together," Medrano muttered as he pondered his prior meetings with his client.

"What's that?" Frey asked.

Medrano glanced at his two companions, then spoke with some measure of hesitation. "We agreed earlier that this negotiation session is confidential, that you can't use statements, admissions, or any information divulged here and now if you haven't already acquired them through some other source, right?"

"Right," Cooper and Frey concurred in the same voice.

Joe gave each face a hard, serious look. "Sanders has a provision in his contract with the HMO that's been bugging the Hell out of him. It gives Union Health grounds to declare the agreement in default and seek damages from him if he disparages the company, its policies, or decisions."

"So the HMO really *has* been putting the squeeze on Sanders," Cooper deduced.

"That they have," Medrano acceded.

"My daddy used to have a saying," Mark reflected, thinking back to his father's storied career as a criminal defense lawyer in Atlanta. "If you've got a lot of squeezin' to do, be sure to bring along a pound or two of sugar. The fruit jes' may turn out to be a bunch of lemons."

As Mark and Joe finished their drinks, Cooper went outside to his secretary's desk, turned on her computer, opened the optical character recognition program, and ran Medrano's draft agreement through the scanner, saving it to a floppy disk. Returning to the lounge, he booted up the PC in the corner and began to insert changes as the attorneys continued their negotiations. When the grandfather clock in the reception area struck eight tones, Frey rose from the couch and stretched.

"Gentlemen, I expect that we're going to be here for a little while longer this evening. And what with all the fun we've been having, I think we've overlooked supper. So if everyone is agreeable to Chinese, I'm going to call a little place a couple of blocks away that delivers. Shrimp and chicken dishes okay?" Seeing no dissent, he headed into his own office. Joe got up and perched near Evan's shoulder, reviewing the amendments and offering suggestions.

Once he had ordered the food, Frey flipped through his Rolodex. Pulling out two cards, he made quick calls to attorneys he knew in San

Francisco. After concluding the last conversation, he felt confident that Medrano's reputation for honesty and integrity in the course of settlement negotiations was sufficient to allay his and Evan's concerns. Then he called their client. "Have you got the evening free?"

"Yeah," replied Roman, bewildered by the sudden call, "more or less. It's just me, my daughter, and Missus Hagan here."

"Good. Keep it that way. Evan and I are going to be driving down to Castle Rock later on this evening – probably a little after nine or so. We've gotten a settlement offer we think is worth talking about."

A Courtroom Surprise!

The courtroom scene on Wednesday morning presented a study in contrasts. On the defense side, all the HMO attorneys and corporate representatives were milling about, chatting in a relaxed manner. Powell and Sanders were sitting silently away from their counsel table in the chairs against the railing. But on the other side of the aisle, Roman, James, and Cooper were as tense as they could be, as they waited for the fuse to burn its course up to the powder keg. Huddled close together, leaning against their table with their backs to the bench and whispering about the surprising events of the evening before, they did not notice the judge walk into the courtroom and take her familiar position. But when Williams gave her customary tap of the gavel to formalize the beginning of that day's session, Ronnie all but jumped out of her skin.

"Good morning, ladies and gentlemen," the judge greeted those before her with her usual opening inquiry. "Do we have any matters that need to be addressed before I bring in the jury?" Glancing at the throng of lawyers, parties, and parties' representatives assembled around the counsels' tables, she caught a glimpse of James stepping toward the podium.

"Yes, Your Honor. We do have a matter that needs to be addressed." Willis and his entourage, now seated, looked upon their adversary with varying degrees of puzzlement. "The plaintiffs wish to inform the court that they have reached a settlement accord with defendant Sanders."

The instantaneous uproar of a myriad of voices became so loud that Willis could barely be heard as he popped to his feet like a jack-in-the-box, shouting, "Objection! Objection, Your Honor. We know nothing . . ." Frustrated, he broke off, waiting for the judge to restore a semblance of order. Meanwhile, Frick, the Union Medical Protective claims manager, bent over the bar from his front row seat and hissed at Powell, trying to get his attention. But Sanders and Powell just ignored him. No one noticed a tardy Frey slip in through the double doors and take his first row seat behind the Plaintiffs' table.

After Judge Williams had banged her gavel three or four times, the courtroom began to quiet down. She looked over at Willis, his round face now as red as the sunburned side of a peach. Meanwhile, Union Health's corporate representative tugged at the lawyer's coat sleeve, muttering directives inaudible to the rest of the courtroom. "You can't object to a settlement, Mister Willis," Judge Williams said matter-of-factly, as if she were explaining the basics to a first-year law student.

Finally catching the eye of Powell, Willis glared at Sanders' lead defense attorney, who just shrugged his shoulders as a sign of his ignorance. "May I have a moment to confer with my colleague, Mister Powell?" Willis requested.

"Of course," replied the judge, leaning back in her chair, trying to mask her amusement at the scene before her. Respecting the decorum of the tribunal, James waited patiently for the judge to recognize her.

Stepping to the far side of the courtroom, Willis whispered to Powell, "What the Hell 's going on here?"

"I don't know," Powell replied with a most serious expression of innocent ignorance.

"Did you reach a settlement with the plaintiffs?" Willis demanded.

"No," Powell insisted, measuring his words with precision. "I haven't discussed settlement with the plaintiffs' attorneys for weeks now." Willis just gazed at his colleague, befuddled.

"Okay, Curtis," Willis said smugly, touching Powell lightly on the side of the arm. "I'll take care of it from here." As Sanders' attorney turned away, Willis was unable to detect the wisp of a smirk forming on Powell's lips.

"Your Honor, if I may," Willis said as he returned to a standing position behind his chair. "I'm sorry to say . . . I'm afraid there's something funny going on here, and I would hope Your Honor would put a stop to it before someone makes a mockery out of your court."

"Your Honor," a restless Ronnie pleaded, trying to regain the floor, "let me assure you that no one is mocking this court." She had hardly completed her first sentence when Willis interrupted.

"Your Honor, I've just conferred with Doctor Sanders' attorney, and he has told me in no uncertain terms that he doesn't know anything about this purported settlement," explained Willis as he worked up an emotional lather of indignation. "So if the plaintiffs' lawyers have cut some kind of a deal directly with the defendant behind his counsel's back, that's improper, unethical, and probably a whole lot of other things and every one of them should be disbarred. We demand that the court get to the bottom of this."

"Your Honor," James began again, "if Mister Willis would just . . ." Her voice was drowned out by the deep tones of a forceful voice resonating off the back wall of the courtroom.

"Your Honor," boomed the San Francisco attorney as he strode up the aisle toward the bar. "My name is Joseph Medrano. I apologize to the court for being the cause of this confusion, but if Mister Willis would be patient, Miss James will be able to explain this matter to everyone's satisfaction." By the time Medrano reached the gate, the courtroom had fallen as silent as a morgue.

"Thank you, Mister Medrano, for helping me to restore order. I should probably inquire why an attorney of your stature would be present in my court for a case in which you have not entered an appearance," Judge Williams said, glancing over the top of her reading glasses and raising her eyebrows, "but I trust that Miss James will soon enlighten me." As she turned her head toward Ronnie, she caught a glimpse of Frey rising from his familiar spot in the first row and taking a place off Medrano's left shoulder. "Mister Medrano, if you would, please step forward. And Mister Frey, you too." Looking over at Ronnie, she yielded the floor. "Now, Miss James, you have our undivided attention." A quick glance toward Willis at the appropriate word got her message across.

"Thank you, Your Honor," said Ronnie, taking a deep breath. "Mister Medrano is an attorney currently practicing in San Francisco who has been recently retained by Doctor Sanders to attempt to reach a settlement of our claims against him. Let me first assure this court, and both Mister Willis and Mister Powell as well, that our firm has been negotiating exclusively with Mister Medrano. We have not spoken to Doctor Sanders at any time since the filing of our complaint against him, except during his deposition and in the course of other depositions he attended with Mister Powell or, of course, while in this courtroom." She caught sight of Willis exploding to his feet again.

"We have to object, Your Honor," the defense attorney apologized.

"Mister Medrano can't appear in this case. Doctor Sanders already has a lawyer and there's been no motion to substitute counsel. Besides, Mister Medrano hasn't filed an entry of appearance. We encourage the court to dispense with this charade!"

"Your Honor, if I may," Medrano interrupted. Seeing an amused nod from the judge, he continued. "If it's just a question of a formality, I have an entry of appearance right here," he said as he held up a set of papers. "I tried to file it with the clerk fifteen minutes ago, but she said I'd have to file it with Your Honor because the matter was in trial and the file was up in the courtroom. May I approach, Your Honor?"

"You may," the judge replied, motioning to him. Medrano handed her the original entry and then distributed a copy to each lead attorney. After a quick study, the judge passed it on to the Court Clerk and told her to file stamp it. Meanwhile, Williams flipped through a volume of the pleadings on her desk. Her look of amusement replaced by a slight scowl, she glared at Willis.

"We now have the entry of appearance you demanded, Mister Willis, so that objection is overruled. And it is a matter of law that a party can have as many attorneys in a case as he or she can afford to hire. And oh, by the way, how many attorneys in your firm have worked on this case for your client, Mister Willis?"

"I'm not sure I understand your question, Your Honor."

"Well, just glancing at one of your pleadings here, I see the names and registration numbers of four attorneys, including yourself. And I suppose you've had several of the newer associates doing some office work on the case, summarizing the depositions, reviewing the documents, and so forth. So your second objection, that Doctor Sanders already has an attorney, doesn't hold much water. Overruled. Now, Miss James, please continue with your explanation."

"As I said, Your Honor, Mister Medrano has been authorized personally by Doctor Sanders to settle our clients' claims against him. A settlement agreement was signed by those parties and their attorneys early this morning. Therefore, the plaintiffs wish to dismiss all of their claims against Doctor Sanders and proceed only with our case against Union Health. We have amended our witness and exhibit lists, deleting that evidence which related only to our clients' claims against Doctor Sanders, and we wish to tender them to the court at this time. May I approach?"

"You may." While the judge surveyed the amended lists, Ronnie handed out copies. "Thank you for the explanation, Miss James," judge Williams said. "But before I rule on your submission of these amended lists, I am going to retire to my chambers. Let's take a fifteen-minute recess." And with that, she tapped her gavel, rose, and slipped out the side door into her private office.

Those present before the bar drifted to separate areas of the courtroom and huddled in their respective camps – lead attorneys, junior attorneys, clients, and clients' representatives. Willis kept a watch out of the corner of his eye on the other groups as Montgomery, Union Health's designated corporate representative for the trial, vociferously complained to her attorneys, all the while trying to explain via her cell phone the recent happenings to an enraged superior back at the Chicago office. Sanders and Medrano moved over to the jury box and took seats in the back row, slightly elevated above the fray they had created. They talked and joked, and, occasionally, Willis caught a look or gesture that seemed to be directed toward his cluster of bodies. Ronnie, Mark, and Evan leaned up against the rail and chatted amiably with Roman about his daughter's most recent developments.

Upon hearing James' full explanation, Frick had darted out of the courtroom at the first opportunity to call his home office. Powell sat on the edge of his counsel table, speaking casually with O'Brien and the paralegal they had brought to assist them with the documentary evidence. Willis kept an eagle eye on his now-untrustworthy confederate, who, he was beginning to believe, had become part of a neatly contrived conspiracy. An occasional sly smile exchanged between Powell and Medrano cemented Willis' suspicions – at least in the minds of all those in Union Health's camp. Powell's countenance changed dramatically, however, when Frick returned to the courtroom and summoned the attorney to join him outside. But the claims manager was doubly frustrated when Powell pleaded complete ignorance of the deal between Sanders and the Marchettis.

Meanwhile, Willis' team brain stormed their options. "We have little choice," the lead attorney concluded, "but to ask the judge to declare a mistrial."

"On what grounds?" inquired one of Willis' staff.

"On the grounds that a settlement by one party in the middle of the trial unduly prejudices the other defendant," Willis shot back.

"How so?" asked Montgomery.

The jury could tell that the case against Sanders was quite strong, Willis reasoned. "So they're going to think that if the plaintiffs settled with him, it must be because he got scared and caved in."

"So what you're saying," the V.P. interrupted, "is that the jury will conclude that Sanders knew he was liable and didn't want to face the music?"

"Exactly," confirmed Willis. "And those implications will transfer to Union Health Management. This jury will be more likely to be prejudiced against us because our codefendant has all but confessed."

Another one of the Junior attorneys chipped in her two-cents worth. "Additionally, most of the evidence presented so far has related to the claim against Sanders. The plaintiffs have barely scratched the surface in the presentation of their case against us."

"Good point," commented Willis. "So we can argue that declaring a mistrial of their case against us would not be a waste of judicial resources. The court can reset the trial date for, let's say, six months down the road and impanel another jury. We'll start this thing all over again, only this time with just their case against us."

"Well," conceded Montgomery, "that'd seem to be better for all concerned. The plaintiffs have time to pare down their case. The jury wouldn't have to be expected to disregard two days of testimony that's not relevant to much of anything now. And it would certainly be fairer to us."

"And much easier for us to prepare an efficient defense," added the junior attorney.

Their deliberations were interrupted by the bailiff's call. "Please rise!"

As the judge came back in, bodies scrambled in every direction, each trying to find its appropriate position suited to the decorum of a convened courtroom. But Judge Williams tapped her gavel and told the attorneys and their clients to be seated wherever was most convenient. She caught a glimpse of Medrano and Sanders trying to hustle out of the jury box without making a scene and gestured to them to be seated where they were.

"Ladies and gentlemen," she announced, "I've decided to excuse the jury for the day, so these proceedings will stand in recess until tomorrow morning. But unlike the jury, the rest of us are not going to take the day off." She hesitated and gave a serious look to each lawyer in the room. "We're going to work today. And we're going to work hard.

"I want all the attorneys involved in this matter, no matter what your position, however high or low, to take rest of the morning to discuss a complete resolution of this case. We have enough rooms available in the courthouse to accommodate all of the various camps I see here today, all with telephones so you can contact those persons with authority to settle assuming that they're not already present." She glanced over at the jury box. "And that includes you too, Mister Medrano. And Doctor Sanders, since you have two separate sets of attorneys here today, you have the luxury of deciding where you want to be. Or for that matter, you can go back and forth between the two." She forced back a grin at the humor of it all. Looking over the room, she added: "Our bailiff will escort you to a room.

"It's now ten after nine. If you can't reach a resolution by noon, lead counsel will come to my chambers and report that fact to me. Since I'm still presiding over this trial, I won't want any of the details – just whether you have or have not resolved it. You know the drill.

"And if the latter be the case, I suggest you spend the remainder of the day getting ready to continue trying whatever claims may be left tomorrow – presumably with one less defendant and an amended witness and exhibit list."

As she reached for her gavel, Williams caught a glimpse of Willis rising to his feet. "Mister Willis," she declared, acknowledging his intent to plead. "Somehow I thought you might have something to say," she quipped as she leaned back in her chair, placing her hands across her mid-section.

"Your Honor, in the interests of justice, I move at this time for a mistrial of the claims against Union Health Management." He glanced up at the judge and down at his notes as he set forth the reasons outlined in their brainstorming session. The judge sat back up in her chair and listened intently, taking careful notes.

When Willis concluded his argument, Judge Williams looked over at Ronnie. "Response, Miss James?"

"Yes, Your Honor," Ronnie replied. "We are most fervently against a mistrial of this matter. First, I'm sure the court has noticed we have a particularly good jury seated in this matter. We've learned through *voir dire* they're eager to serve and interested in the subject matter of this case. And we've watched them through two days of testimony, some of it quite technical and complicated, and all of them have remained alert and attentive.

"I'm afraid that Mister Willis has underestimated the amount of evidence we've admitted against to this point against his client. Since we have stated a claim of vicarious liability against Union Health for Doctor Sanders' failure to administer a pregnancy test to Missus Marchetti, we would have to present a large part of our expert medical evidence all over again. Additionally, since both defendants have pleaded comparative negligence, the jury is going to have to assess liability not only among the two defendants but between the two incidents of negligence – the failed sterilization and the failed diagnosis. Therefore, having to impanel another jury would be duplicative and wasteful.

"And, I would argue, a new trial would be especially hard on my client, Mister Marchetti, who would have to get back up and relive the tragedy at the heart of this case all over again. A mistrial would not be in the best interest of justice, Your Honor. It's only in the best interest of Union Health Management.

"As a final point, Mister Willis argues that news of the settlement with a codefendant will unduly prejudice his client's defense with the present jury. But Your Honor knows that claims settle in the middle of a trial all the time. And our appellate courts have consistently urged trial court judges to take measures short of a mistrial, such as curative instructions, to offset any supposed prejudice to one defendant that may occur as a result of dismissal of a claim against a codefendant. Union Health has not presented anything other than a spur-of-the-moment argument to evidence prejudice to their defense, and I seriously doubt that Mister Willis will be able to do so. For these reasons, we oppose their motion for a mistrial."

As Ronnie stepped away from the podium, the judge turned her eyes to Powell. "Counselor, do you have anything to add to this issue?"

Powell hesitated for a second and then slowly rose to his feet. He was about to give a brief reply when a curious smile replaced his usual deadpan countenance. "Just think of me as Harpo," he quipped. "I don't say anything. I just stand around and look funny." Everyone but the Union Health team joined in the sudden outburst of laughter.

As the last titter subsided, Judge Williams reasserted her control. "Thank you, Mister Powell, for the needed bit of levity." Turning to Willis, she ruled. "Mister Willis, your motion for a mistrial is denied. I see minimal prejudice to your client by virtue of this apparent last-minute settlement by a codefendant. I assume you were prepared to try this case in its entirety when you gave your opening statement, and I have no reason to believe that the presentation of your defense has been compromised by Doctor Sanders' decision to settle. Now you just have less of a case to worry about. That should make things more efficient, not less.

"I further find that a mistrial would be a waste of judicial resources. I concur with Miss James' assessment that much of the evidence presented to date goes to one or another of the theories the plaintiffs are trying to prove. However, if you feel this jury his been prejudiced, you may prepare a jury instruction appropriate to the happenings here today and I will take it under advisement. We're not going to throw out the baby with the bath water. If a curative or cautionary instruction will suffice, a mistrial is overkill.

"I further find that a mistrial would subject the plaintiff, Mister Marchetti, to an undue hardship. I have listened to him testify about what happened to his wife and I have been moved deeply – as have the members of this jury. I note that during your cross examination you have not attempted to controvert his rendition of those facts, and I do not see any witness on your list who is likely to do so. So, there's no need to put Mister Marchetti through that again. Motion for a mistrial denied." She surveyed the faces of the attorneys.

"Now, if there are no other motions . . . ," she invited, hesitating a few seconds for any response, "I suggest you take me up on my offer to use conference rooms in the courthouse and get to work. I will be available in chambers the rest of the day should the need arise. And it just so happens that I had lunch yesterday with Judge Simonson, and he told me the case he was set to try this week settled after only one witness. So I called him a couple of minutes ago while I was in chambers and briefed him on the present situation. He said he'd be available to help mediate this matter if you want a section 1-17 court settlement conference – assuming, of course, that you'd all agree to waive the notice requirements?"

All nodded, including Willis, who just could not let it go without verbalizing something. "If we'd agree to that, Your Honor."

"Of course, Mister Willis," replied the judge, confused by the meaning of Willis' comment. "You'd waive the notice requirements if you agree to have judge Simonson mediate this matter today. Your presence in this courthouse for the rest of the morning is required by my order, but if you don't want to settle, you don't have to."

As he was trained to do when backed into a comer, Willis tried to cover and jab his way out the only way the lawyer in him knew how – by flapping his yap enough to make his opponents think he was unflappable. "Well, of course, Your Honor, we're always willing to discuss settlement."

But the judge was at the end of her rope with the pudgy defense lawyer. "Mister Willis, your posturing before this court is wasting valuable settlement time. Now, if you have something of substance to put before the court, please do so. If you don't, please take a seat."

"Yes, Your Honor," he replied as he sank into his seat to the hush of the courtroom.

Gunpoint Negotiations

The throng of seven lawyers and three clients spent the remainder of Wednesday morning cooped up in four different conference rooms on the third floor of the courthouse, each one a few doors far enough away to keep Willis' agitated bellowings from booming into quarter. At the request of the HMO's lawyer, Judge Williams had released the subordinate attorneys, whose forced captivity she deemed inessential to a speedy resolution. Willis and his senior associate stayed put, as did Powell, O'Brien, and Medrano from Sanders' camp and James and Cooper from the plaintiffs' side. Frey zipped back to his office to reorder the exhibits for Thursday's testimony to conform with the amended exhibit and witness list Ronnie had submitted. Meanwhile, Willis' two junior associates hit the law library running, searching for any case law which might breathe new life into their argument for a mistrial. Their paralegal grabbed two of her Counterparts and began chopping up their witness and exhibit lists.

The attorneys having taken Williams up on her offer to supply a mediator, Judge Alfred Simonson, a veteran of twenty-five years on the bench as both a county and a district court judge, shuttled from room to room every ten minutes or so, caucusing with each party and their attorneys. In his many years hearing cases, Simonson thought he had seen it all. At least, that was what he *had* thought. Sure, many a case had been settled right out on the courthouse steps. He could recall several cases that had settled after one party or the other got a good look at the jury pool. He even remembered numerous cases that had been resolved while the jury was in the middle of its deliberations. And he could talk for hours about the case he presided over about four months before that had settled after the fifth day of trial, when a critical expert witness caved in under intense cross examination. It seemed the opposing attorney had dug up an obscure article from an Australian psychological journal that the professor had written more than twenty years before, which directly contradicted his current opinions. In the legal vernacular, the witness had cratered – in asteroidal proportions.

But that was then; this was now. He shoved aside the backlog of motions piled high on his desk, each of which had attorney after attorney clamoring for a speedy ruling, and dove headfirst into a case that was not even his. Such was the price of judicial etiquette. He scratched Williams' back now; he would someday soon develop an itch worthy of his present sacrifice.

Fortunately, Simonson had followed the local press coverage of the case with the usual curiosity of a member of the public, and that factual background, combined with his extensive familiarity with the issues of law, was sufficient to prepare him to mediate the matter. But after more than two hours, all of his shuffling about produced nothing more than a pair of tired feet. A few minutes before noon, he released the host of lawyers to report back to Williams' chambers as previously ordered.

Once all the attorneys were present, Williams got her elder colleague on the speaker phone and elicited his opinion that an afternoon session might be worthwhile. His only suggestion, he added, was to allow the second-chair attorneys to leave. With Simonson still on the line, Williams went around the room, requesting assent from each lead attorney to continue. Ronnie said yes. So did Powell. And Medrano. Last, the judge turned an inquiring eye upon Willis.

Union Health's defense attorney found himself in an awkward position. *If I refuse her request,* he thought, *it's likely to piss Her Honor off. One way or another, she'll make me pay for it during the trial.* So, in the end, he agreed too, although maybe a little less enthusiastically than his colleagues.

When the lawyers and their clients returned at a quarter past one, Simonson headed straight for the HMO's conference room. While the attorneys were feeding their faces with twenty-dollar lunches, the aged jurist had been throwing around his considerable judicial weight. He got Williams' court reporter to make a copy of the diskette of Roman's trial testimony which he popped into his own PC and read through on the monitor screen. Then, starting with the deposition of Missus Montgomery, he sped through the transcripts of the four Union Health employees. Lunch in the traditional was dispensed with. He took bites of a turkey and Swiss sandwich each time he passed through his chambers on track from one room to another – finally finishing his modest meal somewhere after three o'clock.

Ronnie used the gaping breaks between judicial visits to phone Mark and Evan back at the office. As an ally, Paul Sanders would be an entirely different witness than the one for which she had prepared. So her partners took her examination script and rewrote it, removing whole sections which covered matters no longer at issue. Fearing that the judge would no longer allow James to cross examine the surgeon as an adverse party, all the leading questions had to be converted to non-leading ones – no mean task on short notice.

After nearly four hours of persistent arm-twisting by the well meaning mediating judge, Simonson lamentably concluded that Union Health's appendages were made out of rubber. Mercifully, he called a halt to the effort, sending the clients home and the remaining lawyers over to Williams' chambers. James explained her frustration to Cooper and Frey when she arrived back at the office. "Union Health never put anything substantial on the table – just the paltry sum of $50,000 as nuisance value. The whole thing was just a great big waste of time."

While displeased with the breakdown of negotiation efforts with the remaining defendant, she was delighted to find a completely new direct examination script for Doctor Sanders on her desk ready for her final touches. Expecting that the doctor would be on the stand all morning, Ronnie would only have the economist, a claims administration expert, and the Union Health employees as witnesses before she rested the plaintiffs' case. As Evan walked her through the revised script for Sanders, Mark rearranged the remaining poster-size exhibits they would use and packed the large carrying case. For the first time in weeks, the FC&J office was empty by seven o'clock.

With three scripts and four depositions tucked under her arm, Ronnie lugged her evening's work into the smallest bedroom of her two-story townhouse, recently converted into a study. Flipping pages with one hand, she shoveled down the leftovers from a chicken and vegetable casserole she had made the previous Sunday, microwaved back to life with a palatable warmth. Exhausted from the events of the day, she caught herself nodding off twice. Finally, as the time approached ten o'clock, she decided to call it a night, setting the alarm for five a.m. and promising to make up the lost time in the early morning hours.

She was just starting to doze off when the sudden jingle of the bell shattered the tranquil darkness. Under most circumstances, she would have let the answering machine pick it up, but the harshness of the ringing so irritated her in her drowsy state that she rolled over and picked the receiver up off the night stand.

"Hello?" she mumbled.

"Ronnie?" a familiar male voice responded. "It's Sly Willis. Hey, I'm sorry to be calling you so late, but, considering all the factors, I thought it would be better than letting it sit until morning."

By the time he finished his introductory comment, James was keenly alert, scooting up in bed, numerous pillows stuffed behind her for back support. She reached over to click on the bedside lamp and took a deep breath to dispel the last wisps of fog from her mind. "So what's going on?" she asked.

"I've been meeting with my clients since we left the courthouse this afternoon, trying to come up with a way to get this matter settled, and I've managed to get them off dead center. So I've got some great news for you."

Having done the homework on her adversary, she knew that the excitement in Willis' tone was only camouflage to hide the depth of his concern. His nickname of Sly, according to several attorneys in town who had butted heads with him regularly, was well earned. But, then again, they had insisted, so was the more disparaging play on his given name, always used behind his back, of Syllie Willie. She assumed the persona on the phone was the former and replied reservedly, "Oh?"

"I'm not gonna beat around the bush, Ronnie," he promised bluntly. "My client is prepared to offer half a million to settle this case." He paused strategically to let the figure sink in. Hearing no timely response, he greased the wheel. "That's a generous offer, Ronnie, considering the questionable status of the law here. Congress is always dickering around to reform ERISA. All it would take would be the slightest change and the courts would close up the gap in this narrow exception that *Dukes* and those other cases have opened. Then you and your clients would be left with virtually nothing." He paused again, inviting a response.

"No can do," James shot back curtly as she popped out of bed, portable phone tucked between her ear and shoulder. "It's not enough, and I'll tell you why. We've got a strong case of negligence against your people, ERISA or no ERISA. Remember that Sanders' testimony about his call into Union Health's physician hotline is not likely to be controverted – at least not credibly. What I fully expect him to testify to first thing in the morning is that he speaks to a young man who has no formal medical training, who then, apparently, speaks to his floor manager, also equally untrained. You've got no record to show that your people bounced the problem off a medical expert. In fact, you've got no record of the phone conversation at all. And that's going to look very suspicious to a jury – especially since ninety-nine out of a hundred calls have a detailed write-up put into the computer."

"Well, I think you might be in for some surprises on that count," Willis interrupted.

"Oh, bullshit!" Ronnie retorted. "Don't try to bluff me at this late date, Sly. If your people try to change their stories, they're going to have to deal with the company's sworn answers to interrogatories and then own deposition testimony. And they're likely to screw it all up and contradict each other as well. Once that happens, whatever credibility they may have will be gone. So don't give me the surprise routine. I dealt with it a lot more when I was a prosecutor and our right to conduct criminal discovery from the defense was a heck of a lot more limited. I went into many a trial without a care about what the defense was going to do or say, and I still got more than my fair share of convictions." She smiled at the fact that she was heaping praise upon herself so effectively. *Two can play this game,* she thought. *And I can play it better!*

"Well, do you have a figure in mind?" Willis inquired caustically. Ronnie could detect faint whispers in the background. *Likely a Union Health representative with monetary authority,* she surmised. At least she hoped. Making her way into her study, she glanced at the last page of her notes from the afternoon mediation session.

"We thought the last offer we made through Judge Simonson was very generous. Four-point-three million."

"Come on, Ronnie," Willis whined. "There's no way my people are gonna pay four-point-three on this kind of case. The law's too tenuous. The whole basis for the claim could be wiped away at any time – by a court or by Congress."

"Wrong on that count too," she replied forcefully. "The trends I see in both the courts and the Congress lean toward expanding the rights of a victim of HMO abuse – not shrinking them. And God knows your insurance lobby is spending its millions night and day to buck the trend – all, I might add, without much apparent success. So I might concede your point that it could all be reversed in the wink of an eye, but I wouldn't put money on it."

"So is that your final figure?" Willis asked.

"Give me a second," she requested, as she rustled through some papers to create the impression she was working up a new set of figures. Then she hit the mute button on the receiver, set it down on the desk, and did a quick set of alternating stretches and contractions. It had all the promise of being an unusually long night. The illusion complete, she picked up the phone. "We can come down to three-point-seven-million," she announced.

"That's still way too much, Ronnie, but okay. Hold on a minute," Willis said, and suddenly she was hearing an easy-listening FM station. *He's still at his office,* she concluded. *Good. That probably means they've been there all evening. And they've probably had the corporate bigwigs in Chicago and wherever else they may be on the speaker phone for a major conference call.* Portable phone in hand, she scooted to the kitchen to get a Diet Coke out of the refrigerator. I'm going to need the caffeine.

"Ronnie, you're still too high," was the reply as the music abruptly ended. "But I do have some good news."

She winced. *Oh, no. Not the good-news line again.* She waited for him to continue.

"Union Health is willing to match the one million dollar cap on Sanders' medical malpractice policy. That'll give your clients a two million dollar settlement. That's a damn good deal here in Colorado and you know it."

"No, it's not," she shot back. "It's not a good deal at all. For one thing, the cap on what we can get out of Sanders is there only because the legislature thinks that doctors in this state need to be protected from exorbitant judgments. But there's no such special provision for insurance companies. And you know why?" she asked rhetorically. "Because society doesn't put the same value on them. And a jury is likely to think the same way."

She paused to collect her thoughts, then let go with another barrage. "No. Your client's not going to ride the coattails of Sanders' discount. You've done the figures on our economic damages. You know that two million doesn't even cover that element of damages. So your figure gives nothing for pain and suffering, loss of consortium and society, and so forth. Then on top of that, we've got a claim for punitive damages against your client that could effectively double it all. So no. You're not getting the benefit of Sanders' bargain."

"So you're rejecting a million dollar offer?" he inquired in disbelief.

"I think I made that pretty clear."

"You're willing to walk away from two million dollars?"

"Is there something about the word 'no' you don't compute?" she snapped.

Back in his office, Willis reeled from her verbal blow, then gathered his thoughts. "So where do we stand – money-wise?"

"Just a second." She pushed the mute button again and took a long swig of the soft drink. *How far can I push this?* she wondered. After a couple of minutes of letting Willis stew in silence, she came back on line. "Three-and-a-quarter," she abruptly declared.

"Three-point-two-five," he repeated as he jotted down the numbers. "Gimme a second." Barry Manilow returned for half a song. "They're willing to come up to one and a half," Willis countered when he came back on line.

"I'm ready to stop beating around the bush if you are," she offered. "If you want my bottom line figure, I'm ready to give it to you. But it's going to be a take-it-or-leave-it amount. No more dickering. It's late. We've got a brand-new case to try in the morning. And I've got a witness named Paul Sanders who promises to have some rather strong opinions about your company's policies. We've got more press in the courtroom than I've seen since the O.J. trial, and they're all going to get an earful from our enraged doctor friend. So if you're ready to get down to it, we can save your client a little bit on your bill."

"Go ahead," Willis replied with a touch of resignation in his voice.

"Bottom line is two-point-two-five million. Like I said, it's a take-it-or-leave-it figure."

"Back in a second," Willis replied. Carly Simon's lyrics were a welcome change. Feeling unusually optimistic, Ronnie waltzed in and out of the study and master bedroom, down the stairs to the more spacious living room, phone jammed snugly between shoulder and ear. Just as the tune ended, Willis came back on. "We might be willing to offer that figure if a big chunk of it can be paid out in a structured settlement."

"Not interested," Ronnie quickly replied. "Sanders already has a right under the statutes to force us to take most of his settlement money in some form of annuity. So we're not interested in having any more of it paid over time. And you're well aware that Mister Marchetti is financially solvent, with or without any award from this case. So there's nothing particularly attractive to him about trickling the money out over the next seventeen years for his child's benefit or setting aside a sum for her college education and letting the insurance company reap the benefit of the discount. No, it's a take-it-or-leave-it deal with a straight cash payout."

"Okay. Hold on," said Willis, and she was back to the radio station. Only this time, her nerves had gotten the best of her festive mood. Seated on the couch, she nibbled at her fingernails as the seconds ticked away. The familiar ballad in the background slipped right past her consciousness, burying itself deep somewhere into the recesses of her awareness.

"Ronnie." His voice startled her. "Okay. We've got a deal. Two and a quarter."

"Fine," James replied, resisting with all her professional might the urge to gurgle with glee. "You'll prepare the papers?"

"No problem. They'll be done tonight. You'll agree to the usual defense provisions – no admission of liability, complete confidentiality of settlement terms, and so forth?"

"Sure. Can you bring the papers by my office at seven-thirty?"

"I'll be there," he replied, and they signed off.

Still maintaining her semblance of professional control, Ronnie had one more call to make before turning in. Mark was home, nursing a scotch and water and relaxing in his leather recliner with the latest Patricia Cornwell mystery, when the phone rang. He was elated, of course, to hear his partner's abbreviated account of the fruit of her late-night negotiations. "How the Hell did you manage to push Willis up over two million?" he inquired in disbelief. "You had the authority from our client to settle with the HMO for as little as one million."

"I don't know," she replied. "I guess they were more afraid of Medrano and Sanders than I thought."

"Or maybe there's more out there than we know about their company's practices in cutting health costs," suggested Frey. "Maybe a few more little people who've slipped through the cracks and paid for it big time. But whatever . . . we can speculate endlessly. Good job, Ronnie. Better than good. Fantastic! I'll give Evan a call and let him know. You want me to try to reach the client, or are you going to call him?"

"If you wouldn't mind," she said with a heavy exhale, evidencing her exhaustion.

"I'll take care of it," Mark reassured her. "You get a good night's sleep. God knows, you deserve it."

With those words, she said goodnight and set the receiver on the end table. Slumping down deeper into the overstuffed sofa, with her legs up on the coffee table, she closed her eyes and watched in her mind's eye as she whirled around with a gorgeous but faceless partner to that last Carly Simon tune she had heard while on hold. When the distant, faint sound of the bedside alarm woke her the next morning, her spirit was still dancing to the same tune – and her body was still on the couch.

A Child's Blessing

Christmas was just less than two weeks away, but no one could have known from the weather. It was an unusually mild mid-December day. The twice-a-week stream of low pressure systems that brought the early snows of November had been forced to ride to the north by a week-long, persistent high pressure system which parked right over Colorado. Saturday promised to be as cloudless as the day before, and the air temperature warmed accordingly.

Dressed only in light winter clothes, Roman and his daughter drove over to the long term care facility for what had become their regular, lengthy weekend visit with Juliette. Though his wife had struggled valiantly during that fateful day in July to come out of the coma that had held her fast for months, she had never quite regained consciousness in medical terms. She was, the medical experts subsequently concurred, in a persistent vegetative state – that unique sort of physical limbo between somewhere between comatose and conscious.

Doctor Mayer had taken great care to explain the nature of her condition to Roman at the outset. "She's lost her cognitive neurological functions and awareness of the environment, so she doesn't have any of the higher cerebral powers. Of course, that means she's not suffering either. However, her basic brainstem functions, such as respiration and circulation, are relatively intact." Roman had acknowledged the physician's explanation tacitly. "Now, we don't want to get your hopes up unwarrantedly," Mayer had continued. "PVS can be very confusing to loved ones. At times, Juliette may appear somewhat normal. She will probably have regular sleep-wake cycles. She may open her eyes in response to external stimuli and look awake and alert, but she won't be able to speak or obey commands. She may occasionally grimace, cry, or laugh. She might also exhibit reflex movements like sucking, grabbing and startle responses. But those sorts of infrequent reactions do not necessarily indicate a return to normal waking consciousness."

"But there's a chance she might come out of this too, right?" Roman had inquired.

"A chance, yes," the doctor had responded. "Probably a greater chance that some measure of consciousness will resurface out of this persistent vegetative state than the odds we faced that she'd ever come out of the coma. And though the likelihood certainly isn't in her favor, she's surprised us all so far." He had gently stroked Juliette's forehead, his face beaming with an inner admiration for his star patient. "All we can do is continue the aggressive program we've had her on all these months and see what happens. And keep her comfortable and well nourished."

The familiar machines monitoring her life signs blinked and beeped in their customary manner of salutation as the two visitors entered the room. One of the team of nurses who attended to the long term care patients followed closely behind. Juliette lay motionless in her bed, her eyes open, staring vacuously. As Roman pulled over the chair, the nurse picked up the patient's chart and glanced over it. After noting various readings from the vital sign monitors, she hung it back on the hook and stepped around to turn down the volume as a courtesy to the guests. She smiled affably at Roman and his daughter. "You two have a nice visit. Just push the call button if you need anything."

Roman sat down beside the bed and put Juliet on his knee. He spoke softly to his wife. "Well, it's finally all over, Jules," he said. "They did a good job. You would have been proud of Ronnie. She's really turned out to be a heck of a lawyer." He went on to recount everything concerning the lawsuit that had occurred since he had last seen her the Sunday before the trial began – the jury selection, the opening statements, the testimony of the lead EMT on the search and rescue team, Doctor Crenshaw, the Pagosa pathologist, then Steinberg, Sally, and, finally, his own experience on the stand. His daughter watched him intently, as though she too was caught up in his infectious enthusiasm for the events of the past few days.

"Then this guy from San Francisco shows up out of the blue," Roman bubbled. "Seems that Sanders was being jerked around by the insurance companies too, and he was about as fed up with it as we were. So Mark rushed out to the house late Tuesday night and we signed this settlement agreement with Sanders. The next morning, we just blew old Willis right out of his shoes. Oh, you should have seen him, Jules. I've told you before how he gets a little redder in the face when he's flustered. I tell you, that morning he was as purple as an onion." Roman could not contain his laughter. Tears started rolling down his cheeks. Always one to share in the gaiety of the moment, Juliet giggled reactively, clapping her tiny hands out in front of her body.

But eventually, as her father's demeanor sobered with explanations of the financial terms of the settlements and his plans to invest the monies for their daughter's future, the toddler's attention waned. When she began to squirm on his lap, he repositioned her so she could reach her mother's left hand through the railing. "I guess they finally got the message," he added in conclusion. "I'm just sorry it took so much of my time and kept me away from you."

Juliet wriggled again on her father's knee, then extended her arms toward her mother. "Ma-ma."

"You wanna give your mommy a hug, sweetheart?" Roman asked as he slipped his hands around the little girl's waist, turned her on his knee, and rose from the chair. He lifted her over the bed rail and laid her down next to her mother's body. The child curled up against Juliette, her left arm across her neck.

As he reached back to grasp the chair and pulled it up under him, Roman caught a glimpse of the nurse walking back into the room. He leaned over the bed as he rose again from his chair and kissed Juliette and the baby. "I'll be right back honey," he said as he stepped away from the bed. Juliet snuggled up closer to her mother, putting her mouth up next to Juliette's left ear. Slowly her lips began to move, emitting soft babyish murmurs.

Roman turned and approached the nurse, who was arranging items on the stainless steel tray by the door. "Is Doctor Mayer in today?" he inquired, unaware of his daughter's goings-on.

"He was in the next room a minute ago," the nurse replied as she looked over her shoulder at him. "Do you need to see him?"

"Yes, please," said Roman. He stood a few feet from the doorway, his back to the bed. He could hear the sounds of faint voices in the next room over, then the subtle squeaks of crepe rubber on freshly mopped linoleum. Mayer turned the corner and came through the doorway.

"You needed to see me, Roman?" the physician asked, extending his arm in greeting.

"Yes, doctor," Roman replied as he received the doctor's hand. "Just wanted to let you know how everything came out in court." Mayer listened attentively as Roman again related the events of the past few days – this time in a more succinct format. "And we have you to thank in no small measure," Roman concluded.

"Not me, Roman," Mayer responded in modesty, jutting his chin in Juliette's direction. "I think your wife is the real hero in all of this. We've been nothing more than a good support team."

"You've been a lot more than that," Roman countered as he reached out to clasp the good doctor's shoulder.

"Well, thank you," the physician replied. "We always appreciate recognition. And it's especially nice to hear it from those we care so much about."

"So how are things with Juliette," Roman asked as he turned toward the bed. "I do need to get an update – see if anything's changed with Juliette. It's been a week since we last talked."

"Sure. Let's have a look here," Mayer said as he walked over toward his patient and plucked the dangling chart from its hook. Roman returned to his wife's bedside and reached down for his daughter. As he lifted her gently, Juliet's arm slid across her mother's jaw and under her chin. Instinctively the child pursed her lips and kissed Juliette's left cheek. Roman slung the petite body back up into his arms. The baby slid her arms around her father's neck, embracing it tenderly as she nuzzled under his right ear. Roman glanced over at Mayer, who was scanning the machinery. Juliet pulled her small head back and looked sagaciously at her father. Roman sensed her gaze and turned his eyes toward her.

The corners of the child's mouth were turned down, forming a slight pout. "Ma-ma go bye-bye," she said sullenly.

Roman peered at his daughter's face, puzzled by the meaning of her utterance. Her wide green eyes reflected his own image, as they had done in those few minutes after her wondrous birth when he held her tiny body in his arms for the first time. As his eyes darted from side to side, that unwelcome contingency he had repressed for those many months surfaced to his conscious mind. His heart raced in a burst of panic as he glanced over at Juliette. Her eyes were closed. As the lump in his throat swelled, he looked up at the doctor.

Mayer was sliding foot after foot of the printout tape from the bedside monitor through his fingers. Hurriedly he turned to his patient and leaned over her bed rail, fumbling to remove the stethoscope from around his neck. He placed the chest piece down under the neckline of Juliette's gown, swiftly sliding it up and down and from right to left. Withdrawing the instrument, Mayer spun back to scan the machinery. Roman stood silently, his eyes darting from his motionless wife to the kinetic frenzy of her physician. His eyes prayed for signs that would contradict his fears. Finally, the doctor dropped his hands to his side. His countenance alone was sufficient to deliver the sad tidings that Roman had dreaded to hear for more than fifteen months.

Shortly after lunch the following Thursday, Roman's brother and sister-in-law dropped by to accompany him to the funeral home. He had given specific instructions to the mortician for dressing his bride. Gazing into the casket, he could not help but remark how her beautiful face radiated a soft, peaceful light even in death. She was wearing the teal blue party dress that she had worn to their fifteenth year reunion. Her hands were positioned across her waist, left on top, with her wedding band and engagement ring prominent. On her right side, high up on the shoulder strap was clipped the rainbow pin she had kept in her jewelry box all those years, small chips in the colored enamel bands exposing the silver surface beneath. Around her neck was a thin gold chain, on which was strung Roman's senior class ring. After paying their respects, his brother and sister-in-law left Roman beside the coffin and stepped into the foyer, closing the doors behind them.

The funeral was held the following afternoon. A crowd of more than 200 people squeezed into the small neighborhood Episcopal church that the Abbott family had attended when they lived in Denver. Flowers of all imaginable varieties filled every available vacant space, their pleasing scents intermingling into an undefinable bouquet. Somber organ music resonated off the walls, the bass tones reverberating the stained glass windows.

After a moving eulogy by Juliette's sister and the rites of consolation performed by the pastor, those gathered filed by the open casket for a last glimpse of the deceased. As the assemblage gathered outside the church, the funeral director closed the cover of the casket and prepared it for transport. At the signal, Roman and the other five pallbearers approached as the wheeled bier was turned around. Each grasped a handle on the coffin, lifted at the director's cue, and slowly stagger-stepped their way through the nave and narthex and down the front steps of the church to the hearse at the curb. When the casket had been loaded and secured, Roman and the other pallbearers rejoined the members of Juliette's family in the narthex to accept words of condolence from the attendees. As the crowd dispersed to their cars in the parking lot, the funeral director and his assistant slid into the front seat of the long black wagon and drove off toward the crematory.

Many of those who attended the funeral made the short drive down the interstate to Castle Rock to extend their personal sympathies at the Marchetti home. A modest repast of sandwiches, cold vegetables, and dip was spread on the main dining table with punch and coffee to drink. Juliet spent most of the afternoon in her room, being entertained richly by first one grandmother, then the other. Exhausted, she ended up falling asleep right on the carpet sometime during the sixty seconds or so it took Grandmother Marchetti to refill her bottle with milk from the kitchen refrigerator.

By early evening, the last of the crowd gone, Roman left the cleanup duties to many of the family members and rode over to the crematorium with his brother. A thin black-garbed man was seated at a desk in the front office as the Marchettis entered. He rose, paid his respects, and handed Roman a small, plain, mahogany box. Neither brother spoke as they drove the sixteen miles back to Castle Rock. Roman solemnly cradled the box containing Juliette's urn in his lap.

When the last of the friends and family headed back to their homes after lunch Sunday, Roman put his daughter down for her early afternoon nap, gave a few parting instructions to Missus Hagan, grabbed his parka, and drove down the freeway to Colorado Springs. Exiting onto Highway 24, he continued on west to the entrance to the Pike's Peak climb, retracing the route he and Juliette had taken just a little more than five years before. Leisurely ascending to the summit late that December afternoon, he parked and waited patiently for the sun to set on the range to the west.

With the parking area deserted, he unfastened the latch and removed the brass urn from its box on the front seat. Then he popped open his door and slid out of the vehicle. Stepping away from the car, he spun around slowly and calculatedly, trying to fix the direction of the cool brisk easterly wind. He walked along the edge of the parking area, stopping now and then to gaze down the slope. His plan finally formulated, he climbed down to a secluded rocky precipice which jutted out from the western face of the summit. Carefully he unscrewed the cap of the urn.

He stood there stoically until the golden orb began to dip below the ragged black silhouette. As the sun sank lower and lower behind the ridge, the last brilliant rays of its light danced and flickered against the western sky like the fanned fingers of a heavenly hand. Murmuring an inward prayer, he cast his beloved's ashes into the steady breeze. The urn emptied of its contents, he stood there in sole silence, watching the cloud of whitish-gray whip around in the currents of wind, as if trying to hold on to its integrity, until the ashes became so widely dispersed he could no longer discern them.

A Happy Birthday

The day was one for celebration. The occasion – Juliet Abbot Marchetti's second birthday party. The guests – some one hundred family members, neighbors, and close acquaintances. The location – the Marchetti home in Castle Rock. A beautiful early autumn day – October 10, 1998. A scattering of puffy white cumulus clouds drifting in from over the high country to the west dotted a deep sapphire sky. The Indian summer morning had started off crisp, in the mid-thirties, but was expected to warm up quickly to the high-seventies under the rays of an abundance of bright sunshine. An occasional wisp of wind rustled the leaves of ever-changing colors, most of which were still tenaciously clinging to their stems of life.

According to the printed invitations, the festivities were scheduled to begin promptly at half past eleven. The large umbrella-shaded table in the spacious backyard was designated to be the center of activity. Gifts were to be piled high on the redwood picnic table, which Roman had moved onto the back patio and shoved into a corner against the brickwork. A thirty-by-forty-inch chocolate birthday cake from the small bakery four blocks away, tantalizingly topped with thick white frosting and a bounty of frilly pink trim, its life on center stage promising to be a short one, expectantly awaited its early demise on the kitchen counter. Three two-gallon tubs of ice cream – one, vanilla, another, strawberry, a third, rocky road – were waiting in the upright freezer in the garage for a similar fate to befall. As Roman completed the setup chores, Missus Hagan, the Monday-through-Friday live-in housekeeper, worked a day of overtime to bathe, dress, and preen the guest of honor.

The senior Marchetti and Abbott families were the first to arrive, both grandmothers being eager to add their finishing touches to the preparations. Tuna and chicken salad sandwiches still had to be made and cut. Chips had to be dumped into the largest bowls and dips spooned into smaller ones. Soft drinks had to be iced down and chilled in the large plastic coolers.

A few minutes before eleven-thirty, with Roman standing in position to receive them, the first non-family guests began to arrive – neighboring families with their younger children, many of whom went to the same daycare facility as Juliet. The Rifkins – Sally, Bill and their two offspring arrived next, followed by a host of lawyers, including Cindy Belatron, her husband, and youngest child, May Lynn Kwan and her husband, and the trio of Frey, Cooper, and James. Evan brought his wife; Mark brought the woman he had been seeing for the last four months; Ronnie came alone.

Roman was particularly delighted to greet Doctor Radhavishnu and two members of his staff and their families, who arrived just shortly before noon, apologizing "most profusely" for being late. "But, oh," he explained as he put his arm on Roman's shoulder, "the traffic was very bad – very bad indeed!" The fertility specialist had become a close friend who took a special interest in the development of one of his star "accomplishments," as he warmly referred to Juliet. Due in some measure, he was sure, to the publicity surrounding the trial and all those unconfirmed reports it had involved his clinic, he had more than doubled the number of assisted reproductive procedures he was performing each month.

As the crowd grew and the hoard of ready refreshments dwindled, Ronnie was quickly enlisted to restock the soft drinks and ice in the huge coolers so Mark could lug them out to the back porch. Finishing with the second empty container, she caught a glimpse of a belated and somewhat unlikely guest coming in the front door. Drying her hands on a nearby dish towel she strode over to greet Paul Sanders and his family.

"Doctor. Ronnie James," she said as she extended her hand, reminding him of her name.

"Of course, Miss James," replied the physician as they shook hands. "How could I forget?" No sooner had Sanders introduced his wife and youngest child than the three-year-old boy shot off to discover the source of the shrieks of glee coming from small voices in the backyard.

"My son has become close friends with little Juliet," the doctor explained as he watched his last-born disappear around a corner. "We moved down to Douglas County last February. Turns out the two of them now go to the same day-care center." Sander's wife caught a glimpse of an acquaintance, excused herself, and left the former adversaries in the comer of the front room.

"So how's your practice going?" Ronnie inquired.

"Quite well, over all," Sanders replied. "Busier than I want to be, actually. Had to hire on a colleague to take part of the workload, so things are finally just starting to settle into a groove."

"How'd your dispute with Union Health Management turn out?" James inquired. "We haven't spoken with Medrano since about three months after our case settled. Did he get that resolved for you?"

"Oh, yeah," Sanders assured the lawyer. "He did a terrific job of scaring the pants off of them. It all worked out to my satisfaction."

"Good," she commented. "Glad to hear that."

"And, of course," the doctor added, "you know that Union Medical Protective paid off on the other claim?"

"Yeah," Ronnie said in an understatement. "I remember a little something about those regular annuity checks crossing my desk over the last year or so. You still working with them – Union Health, I mean?"

"A bit," Sanders explained, "but their business has been tapering off lately. My choice, not theirs," he emphasized.

"Paul," came a cry of recognition from across the room as Roman hopped over to greet the doctor. "I saw Billy running around in the backyard and knew you'd be around here somewhere. Hope Ronnie isn't giving you the third degree," he said, pointing an accusing thumb at his attorney.

"No, we're getting along just fine," Sanders replied, then added wittily, "now."

"Well, it's good to have you here. We just started serving lunch so help yourself to some food. Most of it's out in the back." The doctor thanked him and went looking for his wife and son.

"He's a good man," Roman told Ronnie as Sanders moved out of earshot. "He just made a simple mistake."

"Daddy!" squealed a little voice as Grandma Marchetti brought Juliet up to her father. "Lookie," she added as she held out a small wrapped present.

"You have such a beautiful child," Ronnie said as she stroked the baby's golden brown locks. "She looks so much like her mother – more every day."

"Yeah, she does," Roman agreed as he took her in his arms. "I talk to her about her mother all the time. One of her favorite things to do is go through our old high school yearbooks. I show her all the pictures of her mom in those old annuals and read the inscriptions we wrote to each other. She likes them as much as her vast collection of Sesame Street books." When the child started to squirm in his arms, Roman bent over and set Juliet's feet on the ground. In a flash she was off to the backyard, trotting in that bouncy way toddlers do, holding the wrapped present well out in front of her.

After the crowd had devoured the vast array of sandwiches and chips, Ronnie approached Roman as he was working alone in the kitchen, putting the final touches on the birthday cake. "You been dating anyone since the last time we talked?" she abruptly inquired.

He gave her one of those looks that said, *It's none of your business, but you're such a close friend, I wouldn't dare to tell you that.* "No, I'm not," he replied instead. "There's just no time, what with raising the baby and running my company."

"Well," she said with an air of condescension, "don't ignore that part of your life."

"I appreciate your concern," he stated, "but I still need a little more time to heal. You don't replace a love like I had with Juliette in just a few dates."

"I know," said Ronnie in an empathizing tone, touching his shoulder affectionately.

Roman glanced down at the soft and delicate hand on his arm. "You trying to hit on me?" he asked in jest as they shared a laugh. She gave him a quick kiss on the cheek and turned to walk away.

"Just remember what I said," she instructed, glancing back toward the kitchen. As Roman looked up, he glimpsed a subtle look in her eyes. His expression telegraphed his sense of puzzlement over things left unspoken. Disconcerted by the awkwardness of the moment, Ronnie got a firm grip on her straying emotions and turned away.

Roman put two candles on the cake and slipped his hands and arms underneath the sturdy cardboard tray, slowly pulling it off the counter. With careful steps and audible warnings to those in his path, he made his way out to the main table in the backyard, the remainder of the crowd in tow. As the children framed the inside ring and their parents gathered on the outside, Grandma Abbott placed Juliet in her booster seat on the chair directly in front of the cake. Roman held up his hand for quiet.

"We're going to sing 'Happy Birthday' to Juliet," he announced, "but before we get started, I just wanted to thank everybody for coming. Now I want all of you to keep in mind that my daughter is only two years old and she doesn't have too much experience at this blowing-out-the-candles thing. So we're gonna need someone to be her official helper – someone with a lot of wind." He paused for dramatic effect. "Are there any lawyers in the house?" Juliet did not quite understand the joke or the roar of laughter from the adults that Roman's exercise of wit precipitated, but her delayed laugh was as loud as anyone else's.

Once the cake and ice cream had been cut and served, the parade of presents began, with each person or family who had brought a gift handing it to the birthday girl. Juliet giggled joyfully each time she opened another one, and her father carefully returned it to its gift box after holding up each dress, toy, or book for the crowd to see. But among them all, the gift from Grandmother Abbott stood out. As Juliet opened the slim, flat box, she saw a beautifully framed eight-by-ten picture of a two-year-old girl with long, wavy light brown locks, fastened on either side with small dark velvet bows. "Mommy!" Juliet squealed, recognizing the face from a small snapshot from the Abbott family album that her grandmother had shown her many times. Then the child looked up at her father, waving the picture like a trophy for him to see. "Mommy," she repeated.

"Yes, that's your mommy," Roman acknowledged as tears filled the corners of his eyes. Looking over at his mother-in-law, he mouthed the words "Thank you" and placed the framed picture back in its gift box.

When the last present on the picnic table had been delivered, opened, and displayed, Roman asked everyone to stay where they were as he threaded his way through the assemblage to the back garage door. With a clang and a bang, he rolled out a wheelbarrow full of wrapped boxes, set it down, and began calling off the names of every child in attendance. After he had handed out the last one, he turned to the crowd of adults. "That's why I insisted on RSVPs from all of you," he explained. "I just wanted all of the children to receive something today – something special."

As the clock wound its way toward four and the partying throng thinned down to a familiar few, Roman sat in the living room, talking to Frey and James. "You know," he said as the conversation rolled back to Sanders' appearance at the gathering, "the lawsuit was never about the money. That guy Willis had it all wrong."

Mark shook his head in wonderment as he recalled a scene from that not-too-distant event. "I'll never get over the look on Willis' face when you zinged him that afternoon. Pure inspiration."

"Yeah," agreed Roman, "and you know what?" The two attorneys waited for the answer. "It felt good. Really good!"

A peculiar smile of satisfaction formed on Roman's face. His eyes glowed with an inner peace. "But it was never about the money. I had my business, and Jules and I both had already saved up a good bit of money in the short time we had together. So the baby and I could have been financially comfortable with that." He hesitated as his expression changed to one of serious reflection. "I just wanted accountability from the persons responsible for what happened to her. That's all."

"We know," Ronnie reassured him with a gentle pat on the shoulder, "We know." But Roman was lost in his own mental wanderings, staring down at his lap.

"It doesn't matter whether Sanders was a good doctor or the best one around," Roman added. "The truth of the matter is, he made a simple mistake that day. The sad thing is, it was one that eventually cost us dearly. And I know the HMO was just trying to do a good job keeping down medical costs, but they screwed up too and it ended up costing Jules her life." His voice choked on the last words as he fought to regain his composure. Then a slight smile surfaced. He gazed out the front window as a late-afternoon gust brought down a cascade of golden aspen leaves.

"Six years ago, when Juliette was still living down in Texas, she came up to Colorado for a long vacation and I took some time off. Except for three or four hours at a class reunion a few weeks before, we really hadn't seen each other in sixteen years. We drove all over the state, camping out one night and hitting a hotel the next. But the night we got back to Denver, the Moody Blues were giving a concert at Red Rocks, so we stopped off there before driving back home."

His eyes glazed over with the sheen of fond reminiscence. "We were so much in love again by the end of that trip. And we stood there and listened to the songs, and it seemed like they were singing them just for us. I think about that night a lot – Jules standing in front of me, swaying with the music, my arms around her waist, her head against my shoulder. A couple of lines in one of their songs really hit me that night, and they've stuck with me ever since.

And if you wake up wondering in the darkness I'll be there

To close my arms around you and protect you with the truth.

He turned and looked at Mark. His eyes burned with the fire of a heartfelt conviction. "They just needed to own up to what they did wrong. That's all. You know, the truth."

He looked across at Ronnie. "And that's what I appreciate about Sanders. I know it seems a little odd, but I've gotten to know him quite well over these past few months and we've had some real heart-to-hearts."

He glanced back at Frey, then quickly again at James. "You might have wondered, but you probably didn't know – when he made that settlement offer to us during trial," Roman explained, holding up his thumb and forefinger, "he was that close to quitting his practice." The two lawyers both looked surprised – and maybe a tad incredulous. "No. I'm serious," Roman insisted. "He was! This whole thing with Jules had really shaken him. He even got to where he was passing on his patients to other OB/Gyns if they needed surgery. So I know what he's been through, and I can appreciate it on a personal level. And I know he's dealt with his part in this whole thing and faced it.

"But that HMO . . ." He paused, took a deep breath, and sighed. "I don't know. I guess the problem is, it's just a corporation. It's not really a living, breathing human being – something with feelings."

He laughed cynically at a passing thought. "I'd like to think that some of the people who run it would do the right thing – you know, the human thing. I know it sounds silly, but just one person – a real person – a vice-president or a manager or somebodies high up like that – who'd do what Sanders had the guts to do and accept responsibility for what their people did. I don't know – maybe even a letter would be enough."

He shook his head resignedly. "But they can't. I guess that's what happens when the corporation gets bigger than the people who give it life. And as long as that's the way it is, Juliette's blood will be on their hands."

Made in the USA
Monee, IL
04 November 2026

67391565R00184